The Rape of American Democracy

Other Books by James P. Rowles

Law and Agrarian Reform in Costa Rica [1]

El onflicto Honduras-El Salvador- de1969 y el orden jurídico international (The Honduras-El Salvador Conflict of 1969 and the International Legal Order) [2]

The Rape of American Democracy

Republican Actions and Democratic Failures, 2016-2021

What We Knew and When We Knew It

James P. Rowles

Trenchant Observer Press
San Francisco
2024

Copyright © 2024
By James P. Rowles
All Rights Reserved

Trenchant Observer Press
San Francisco

Mailing Address
P.O.Box 3271
Half Moon Bay, CA 94019

ISBN No. 979-8-9901590-3-7 (paperback)
ISBN No. 979-8-9901590-4-4 (hardback)
ISBN No. 979-8-9901590-5-1 (ebook)

Book design by Michael Grossman
Cover painting by Octavious Sage
Author Photo by Gerard Lum

Dedication

To

Molly Faraji, my companion

Russell R. Rowles, my father
Mildred Shotwell Rowles, my mother

Zaida Arguedas, my former wife

Gordon A. Craig,
John Henry Merryman, and
Abram Chayes,
my mentors

Edward M. Kovachy, Jr., my coach

And to the millions of people, including readers of this book, who long for and believe in a future governed by domestic and international law, and by reason and truth

Admonition

And yet, we are oppressed by one nightmarish idea: ***if a dictatorship in Hitler's style should ever rise in America, all hope would be lost for ages.*** [emphasis added] We in Germany could be freed from the outside. Once a dictatorship has been established, no liberation from within is possible. Should the Anglo-Saxon world be dictatorially conquered from within, as we were, there would no longer be an outside, nor a liberation. The freedom fought for and won by Western man over hundreds, thousands of years would be a thing of the past. The primitivity of despotism would reign again, but with all means of technology…

–Karl Jaspers, *The Question of German Guilt*[3]

Table of Contents

Part Four: 2019 – Year Three of the Trump Presidency..... 139

Part Six: 2020 – Year Four of the Trump Presidency (II): After the Election, the Conspiracy and the Coup Unfold 249

Part Seven: 2020-2021 – The End of the Trump Presidency: The Conspiracy and the Coup Accelerate 301

Preface

The years from 2016 to 2021 were years of momentous political turmoil in the United States, as first Donald Trump won the Republican primaries and the Republican nomination in 2016, and then in the November 2016 election won a narrow victory in the Electoral College to become the 45th President of the United States. Four tumultuous years followed during Trump's presidency.

In November 2020, Trump lost the presidential race to Joe Biden, the former vice president under President Barack Obama (2009-2017), but he did not leave the White House quietly. Instead, he maintained that he, Donald Trump, had won the election and that Biden had been "elected" through massive fraud. Trump, however, never produced any evidence of significant fraud. He brought some 60 cases in court alleging such fraud, but all were more or less summarily dismissed for lack of evidence.

Following the November 3, 2020 election, Trump proceeded with a plan to overthrow the election which culminated in the attack on the U.S. Capitol on January 6, 2021. The attack was unsuccessful. After the demonstrators were removed from the Capitol, Congress proceeded to certify the results of the vote in the Electoral College and the election of Joe Biden as the 46th President of the United States.

In July 2021, the House of Representatives formed a House Select Committee to investigate the January 6 attack on the United States Capitol. The Committee's investigation and public hearings elicited damning testimony and documentary evidence regarding Trump's involvement in the January 6 invasion of the Capitol, which turned out to be the culmination of a broad conspiracy to overthrow the election. The Final Report of the Select Committee sharply condemned Donald

Trump and his accomplices for their attempt to overthrow the election and the Constitution.

> *See* Final Report of the Select Committee to Investigate the January 6th Attack on the United States Capitol, House Report 117-663 (117th Congress, 2nd Session). December 22, 2022.[4] (The file takes a while to load.)

In the meantime, the House decided to impeach Trump for his attempt to overthrow the election. However, Senate Majority Leader Mitch McConnell (R-Kentucky) delayed the trial for so long that by the time it was held Trump had left office. He and other Republicans then voted against the conviction of Trump on the legally spurious ground that Trump was no longer in office.

During 2021, the Justice Department proceeded to prosecute the demonstrators who had invaded the Capitol on January 6. Attorney General Merrick Garland, however, steadfastly refused to investigate and prosecute Donald Trump for his coup attempt and other crimes. Significantly, Garland allowed the statute of limitations to run on the ten obstruction of justice felonies Robert Mueller had detailed with an outline of the evidence in his Report, which he submitted to Attorney General William Barr on March 22, 2019, and made public in a 448-page redacted version on April 18, 2019.

> *See* Special Counsel Robert S. Mueller, III, "Report on the Investigation into Russian Interference in the 2016 Presidential Election, Volume I of II," Department of Justice, Washington, D.C., March 2019.[5]

Throughout 2021, the Democrats appeared to enforce a strong taboo against even discussing the prosecution of Trump.

See, e.g., "Democrats Should Impeach Attorney General Merrick Garland–UPDATED December 24, 2021," *The Trenchant Observer*, December 24, 2021.[6]

While this book is of obvious relevance for voters deciding who to vote for in the November 5, 2024 elections, its importance and significance will extend far beyond these elections. Journalists, historians, researchers, and others who seek to understand the events which gave rise to Donald Trump and his authoritarian movement will benefit from examining in detail the major events and decisions described here. This point is developed further in the Introduction below.

During these tumultuous years in which the rule of law in the United States seemed to be at stake, we wrote frequent articles in *The Trenchant Observer: International Law, Government Decision-making, and International Security*, a blog in which we had been writing columns on international and at times domestic political developments since 2009.

This book consists of a careful selection of columns published in *The Trenchant Observer* during the years spanning 2016-2021.

Unfortunately, the website of *The Trenchant Observer* has been hacked, possibly by a state actor (Russian and Chinese spiders crawled the site over the years), and the website is no longer functioning. Consequently, the links to the *Trenchant Observer* columns cited in the text point to the pages on the *Way Back Machine* or *Internet Archive* on which the original articles can now be found.[7]

A note on the method employed in writing the original columns of *The Trenchant Observer* is in order. We continue to use this method in writing columns for the *Trenchant Observations* newsletter. Every day we review not only the *Washington Post*, the *New York Times*, the *Wall Street Journal*, and *The Atlantic* in the United States, but also leading newspapers and magazines in Europe including *Le Monde* (France), *El Pais* (Spain), *Die Welt* (Germany), *The Telegraph* (England), and *The Guardian* (England).

As we find news and opinion articles that throw light on important developments and seem exceptionally good, we list them with links in a draft version of a column on a subject that seems important, adding a link to the original article. In this book, these sources are sometimes listed in the "Background" section at the beginning of a chapter, are sometimes included in the main text, and are sometimes listed in the "Further Reading" section at the end of a chapter.

These references are more than footnotes listed as the authority for an assertion in the text, which is the customary function of a footnote in a book. Instead, they form an important part of the narrative in the corresponding chapter of the book.

In the ePub (eBook) or Kindle edition of the book these links are active, and by clicking on a link readers can go directly to the newspaper article or other source that is being cited. In the printed editions of the book, the URLs of the linked-to articles or sources are reproduced in the Notes section at the back of the book.

For the reader who prefers to read the printed version of the book, as we ourselves prefer to do, the ePub or Kindle version of the book may also be purchased at a sharply discounted price or as part of a bundle. Reading the printed version, one can follow along in the eBook version on a tablet or a smart phone and go directly to a source simply by clicking on the corresponding link in the eBook edition of the book.

This capability is merely an optional feature provided for the benefit of those who may want to read the printed edition while still having quick access to the original sources cited.

Given the breadth of reliable sources upon which the book is based, and the ease of accessing the original sources cited, the content and analyses in the present book cannot simply be dismissed as "fake news."

Introduction

Public Discourse in America

To understand how half or more of the electorate, particularly in battleground states, could be committed or leaning toward voting for Donald Trump on November 5, 2024, it is useful to consider certain changes in American society that have taken place over the last 50 or 75 years.

These changes, moreover, have taken place against the broader background of even deeper changes that occurred in Europe and the United States in the previous century, as described by José Ortega y Gasset in his prescient work. *The Revolt of the Masses.* (1930)[8] "The rebellion of the masses," he wrote, should not be understood as having "a meaning excessively or primarily political. "Public life," he wrote,

> is not solely political, but equally, and even primarily, intellectual, moral, economic, religious; it comprises all our collective habits, including our fashions both of dress and of amusement.

It is against this background that we must understand the following changes in American society over the last 50 or 75 years.

First, participation in civic organizations and civic life has plummeted during this period.

See Robert D., Putnam, *Bowling Alone: The Collapse and Revival of American Community,* rev. ed., 2000.[9]

Second, the public's ability to listen to and be guided by expert opinion has decreased sharply.

> *See* Tom Nichols, *The Death of Expertise: The Campaign Against Established Knowledge and Why It Matters,* 2nd ed., 2023.[10]

To be sure, anti-intellectualism and distrust of experts is not new in American political life.

> *See* Richard Hofstadter, *Anti-Intellectualism in American Life,* 1966.[11]

Third, civic education and knowledge of government, politics, and the world has greatly diminished.

> *See* Richard Haass, *An Introduction to the World,* 2023, pp. xv-xx.[12]

Fourth, the addiction to social media and the Internet among the young, and others, has had a detrimental impact on the ability of citizens to participate in reasoned debate.

> *See* Franklin Foer, *World Without Mind: The Existential Threat of Big Tech,* 2017.[13]

During the years covered by this book (2016-2021), the era in which Donald Trump dominated media coverage—in the 2016 presidential race, during the Trump Presidency (2017-2021), and in its immediate aftermath (2021)—and indeed in the subsequent years leading up to the November 2024 presidential election, it seemed that many Americans came to question the very concept of truth, as Donald Trump and his supporters dismissed any news article critical of Trump and his supporters as simply "fake news."

However, as Timothy Snyder has pointed out, democracy depends on truth.

See Timothy Snyder, *On Tyranny: Twenty Lessons from the Twentieth Century*, 2017.[14]

Snyder expresses the fundamental relationship between truth and freedom in stark terms, as follows,

Believe in Truth

To abandon facts is to abandon freedom. If anything is true, then no one can criticize power, because there is no basis on which to do so. If nothing is true, then all is spectacle. The biggest wallet pays for the most blinding lights.[15]

He observes further,[16]

As observers of totalitarianism such as Victor Klemperer[17] noticed, truth dies in four modes, all of which we have just witnessed.

The first mode is the open hostility to verifiable reality, which takes the form of presenting inventions and lies as if they were facts...

The second mode is shamanistic repetition...As Klemperer noted, the fascist style depends upon "endless repetition," designed to make the fictional plausible and the criminal desirable...

The next mode is magical thinking, or the open embrace of contradiction.... Accepting untruth of this radical kind requires a blatant abandonment of reason....

The final mode is misplaced faith.... Once truth had become oracular rather than factual (in Nazi Germany), evidence was irrelevant...

In the broader arc of history, we can see the impact of the shift from a culture of public discourse based on the written word to one based on entertainment and the values of television and the TV commercial. Neil Postman, in his classic book, *Amusing Ourselves to Death* (1985), describes this fundamental shift from an age of the printed word, which began with the invention of the printing press by Johannes Gutenberg around 1450, and what Postman calls the Age of Entertainment, which began with television in the 1950s and which now continues both on television and on the Internet.

> *See* Neil Postman, *Amusing Ourselves to Death: Public Discourse in the Age of Show Business*, 1985, 20th ed. 2006.[18]

In a world of political discourse dominated by the values of entertainment and television, one can begin to understand the impact of the social changes which have led to the present situation. These social changes have made phenomena like Donald Trump possible and opened the door to his election in 2016 and the threat of his potential reelection in 2024.

The implications for politics are grave. Writing in 1985, as if seeing through a crystal ball, Postman warns:

> When a population becomes distracted by trivia, when cultural life is redefined as a perpetual round of entertainments, when serious public conversation becomes a form of baby-talk, when, in short, a people become an audience and their public business a vaudeville act, then a nation finds itself at risk: culture-death is a clear possibility.[19]

Now, in August 2024, the United States faces one of the most fateful decisions in its history. Will the voters elect former President Donald Trump, a felon convicted of 34 counts of fraud by a Manhattan jury and who is awaiting trial on numerous other felony counts?[20] Will they elect a compulsive liar, someone found guilty of sexual assault by a jury in a civil proceeding in New York, and a political leader who has consistently demonstrated his sympathies for Vladimir Putin and Russia? Will citizens vote for Trump and for the Republican candidates for the House and the Senate, almost all of whom have prostrated themselves before Trump, who has remade the Republican Party in his image?

Or will they vote for the Democrats, and a return to a normal government, and legislators who are focused on solving the many problems which Americans face today?

Given the irrational factors that can affect mass opinion and how voters decide to cast their ballots, one cannot be sanguine about the outcome of the elections in November. In considering how to vote, voters would be well advised to consider the events between 2016 and 2021 described in this book.

The selection of Kamala Harris to be the Democratic candidate for president in 2024, and her subsequent choice of Minnesota Governor Tim Walz to be her running mate have given hope to Democrats who only weeks earlier were nearly despondent over the likely victory of Donald Trump as president and Republican candidates in the House and the Senate in November.

The challenge which Harris and Walz face remains formidable, however.

In any world where voters were guided by reason, Harris and Walz would trounce Donald Trump, J.D. Vance, and their MAGA supporters. Unfortunately, we don't live in such a world. The challenge Kamala Harris must now face is how to reach and persuade those Trump supporters and potential supporters who are not guided by reason, but rather by mass political emotions. Harris and Tim Walz, her vice-presidential candidate, must also build up a sufficient lead so that the election will not be thrown to Trump and the Republicans by some huge, unexpected event, as discussed further below.

This Book

These chronicles span the five years of political turmoil and trauma in the United States between 2016 and 2021. They are dispatches written at particular points in time, based on information that was publicly available. They tell the story of what we knew or could have known if we had been paying attention.

We were paying attention. Here we share our contemporary analysis of events as they unfolded and the fears and passions they unleashed.

Unlike most books on Donald Trump's last year in office and his attempted coup, this account addresses the responsibility not only of the Republicans but also of the Democrats over these five years for the political situation and the fascist threat that the country now faces. The book explores in some detail the key decision points where the Democrats might have acted more effectively to confront Trump and his growing authoritarian movement, including their failure to prosecute Trump in a timely manner.

The *Rape of American Democracy* connects the dots and addresses the fundamental question of what it all means for democracy in America today.

This book focuses not so much on the particular details of events, though these are covered, as it seeks to connect the dots and tries to answer the question of what is going on at a particular point in time in the context of what has gone before and been chronicled in earlier chapters in the book, and what it all means.

As John B. Mitchell, Professor Emeritus at Seattle University School of Law, explained to me a few years ago in response to my question of why people seemed so uninterested in talking about the specific events of the five years between 2016 and 2021,

> We don't want to remember. We are exhausted from the past four years (2017-2021). And we don't want to remember because it was all too painful. If we remember we will have to think, and if

we think we will understand. And if we understand what is really going on, we will have to act, and we cannot imagine acting when we don't know what to do and feel so exhausted.

This book, however, will not let you forget. Too much is at stake. This book will make you think.

It will help you remember exactly what happened when Trump appeared to obstruct justice in the ten specific cases detailed—with a summary of the evidence—in the Robert Mueller report. It will help you understand what Trump was doing when he appeared to be intimidating witnesses or retaliating against them for truthfully testifying in the House impeachment hearings.

This book will remind you of how Trump tried to interfere with electoral processes in key states after the election on November 3, 2020. It will help you remember how Trump tried to corrupt election officials, state legislators, and governors during the vote counts, the certification of voting results, and finally, the certification by the Congress of the election results on January 6, 2021.

Donald Trump and his co-conspirators sought to overthrow the election results and thereby the Constitution of the United States. At its essence, their actions constituted an attempted coup d'état. Ultimately, they failed. But they got frighteningly close.

Anchored in concrete facts from publicly available sources, the essays in this book will help you connect the dots, so you will be able to fully understand the broader picture of what was going on and how the Republicans and the Trump administration were readying the playing field for an attempt to hold on to power in the event Trump failed to win the November presidential election.

The usual approach in reporting on such events is to write from the perspective of the present moment when the results and outcomes of various ploys and actions have become known. This can lead to a rather dry, analytical and chronological, and at times misleading, accounting of events that took place.

The approach used in this book is different. Each essay was written at a specific point in time before the future course of events was known. Each essay draws on the information that was publicly available at that point in time. Each essay considers the strategy that Trump and his supporters appeared to be pursuing, analyzing the potential pressure points that lay in the future, and the nature of the actions Trump and his co-conspirators would need to take if they were to block the assumption of power by Joe Biden on January 20, 2021.

The essays in this book chronicle developments as they happened or were about to happen. Reading these articles, set off in separate chapters, the reader will acquire more of a sense of the history that was unfolding, including not only what Trump and his minions were doing and appeared to intend, but also the actions that were available to Democrats and other constitutionalists who sought to block Trump's machinations.

The result of this approach is not so much the painting of a picture of what happened, told in an analytical form from the perspective of the present moment, as it is a kind of moving picture of the process that was unfolding. Viewed in this manner, the reader can better appreciate the drama of the events as they occurred, and understand the extraordinary extent to which, day to day, American democracy seemed to be hanging in the balance.

The Rape of American Democracy will obviously be of great interest to journalists, politicians, and potential voters prior to the elections to be held on November 5, 2024. But its importance and lasting significance will extend far beyond the elections in November.

This book examines critical developments in the political situation that exists in the country in 2024 and which, regardless of who wins the presidential election and which party wins which houses of Congress, is likely to continue well into the future.

The story of Republican perfidy, of the Republican Party controlled by Donald Trump and his supporters, will not end in November 2024.

Moreover, there is considerable evidence to suggest that Trump will contest the election results if he loses in November,[21] and a repeat of the January 6 insurrection cannot be ruled out. Should he lose and try once again to overthrow the election, this book will provide a good road map of the strategies he might pursue and the hurdles he would have to overcome if he were to succeed.

This time, in implementing his strategy, he would have the benefit of having learned from all of the mistakes he and his accomplices made in 2020, and the chances of blocking the election of Kamala Harris would be augmented by the fact laws have been changed in ways that would favor such Republican efforts. In addition, election officials have been replaced in key battleground states with Trump supporters who will be more likely to do his bidding than the officials in 2020.

The political history of the United States will be indelibly altered by the events of the Trump era, and specifically by the events described here that contributed to the development of the present political situation in the United States.

Consequently, the book should be of enduring interest and usefulness for journalists, historians, and other academics, as well as ordinary citizens.

Part One

The 2016 Presidential Campaign

March 6, 2016

The Ugly Face of America: Donald Trump and His Supporters

"On some great and glorious day, the plain folks of the land will reach their heart's desire at last, and the White House will be adorned by a downright moron."
–H.L. Mencken[22]

Finally, a leading political figure in the United States, Governor Mitt Romney, the Republican candidate for the presidency in 2012, stood up and denounced Donald Trump, the leading Republican candidate in 2016, for the extreme positions he has taken and the deep character defects he has manifested in the race for the Republican nomination.

Trump supporters and others have responded, not by rebutting the points Romney has made, but by attacking Romney the man and the positions he holds or has held. Romney's criticism of Trump was powerful, if a bit late in the game. Still, it deserves a close reading.

The transcript of the speech can be found at https://www.nytimes.com/2016/03/04/us/politics/mitt-romney-speech.html (*New York Times*), and https://time.com/4246596/donald-trump-mitt-romney-utah-speech/ (*Time*).

Trump has received a great deal of "horse-race" coverage in the media, which at the same time has generally failed to investigate the significance and likely consequences of his proposals.

A key point to bear in mind is that Trump, in his changing formulations, is signaling to his supporters where his true sentiments lie, while then trimming back his statements so as to appear less extreme.

For example, his statement that he would use waterboarding and much worse (forms of torture) should be taken as such a signal. He backtracked afterwards and said he would have to follow domestic and international law, which prohibit waterboarding and other forms of torture. Then he said, on a following day, that he would act to change the law to allow waterboarding and other techniques. His followers got the point.

His long hesitation in repudiating the Ku Klux Klan served a similar signaling function. He signaled to his supporters what he really thought, and then walked back his statement so as to appear less extreme. They got the message.

The ugly face of America is to be seen in the millions of Trump supporters who either enthusiastically greet these signals that he is a racist and favors torture, or who are willing to look the other way and support him despite these statements and signals.

There is indeed an ugly face to America, which we have seen at Abu Ghraib, in the violence in the South during the Civil Rights Movement, and in the lynchings and other acts of violence carried out by the Ku Klux Klan in our history.

The shame of the Republican Party and many Republican officials, including other candidates in the Republican primary who remained silent for so long, is that they did not denounce Trump sooner. At least a few of them are trying to save some of the remnants of their honor by denouncing him now.

Trump is a demagogue, a crude and vulgar bully and misogynist, a racist, a xenophobe, an advocate of torture, a candidate who can quote

Benito Mussolini without a blush, and a loose cannon in foreign policy who should never have gotten this far.

He represents the ugly face of America, which unfortunately exists, and the threat that it represents.

Democrats and others in America would be making a great error if they were to assume Trump will not become the Republican nominee in the race for the presidency.

It would be an even graver mistake if they were to blithely assume he will simply help the Democrats in the November elections and could never become the President of the United States.

Bernie Sanders might beat him, but Hillary Clinton, with her baggage and both known and unknown liabilities and vulnerabilities, might not, particularly as foreign policy and America's place in the world move to center stage in the presidential race. Yet she remains the likely Democratic candidate.

FURTHER READING

Updated March 7, 2016

Foreign observers have also described Donald Trump as "The Ugly Face of America," even months before Romney's speech and when the present article was written.

See, Mohamed Chtatou, "Donald Trump: The Ugly Face of America," *Morocco World News*, December 23, 2015 (6:59 a.m.).[23]

See also, Dana Milbank, "Trump's Flirtation with Fascism," *Washington Post*, March 7, 2016 (6:21 p.m.).[24]

2

July 29, 2016

Trump Versus Clinton on Foreign Policy

We have written elsewhere, particularly in *The Trenchant* Observer (*see* the Preface), of Hillary Clinton's failures as secretary of state.

But to be fair to her, as has become increasingly clear, many of these failures are qualified, and ultimately reflect the fact that President Barack Obama had been micro-managing foreign policy since 2009.

Certainly, Clinton has a number of failures for which she alone is responsible.

Yet on substantive foreign policy, how do Clinton's experience, knowledge, abilities, and record compare to those of Donald Trump?

See Kim Ghattas, Trump v Clinton on Foreign Policy, BBC, May 8, 2016.[25]

First, as regards the comparison of her foreign policy record to that of Donald Trump, all we can say is that Donald Trump has no record.

Second, as to her experience in foreign policy, we can say that she has great experience, both as a Senator from New York and as secretary of state during Barack Obama's first term in office. She has dealt with Syria. She knows who Bashar al-Assad is, and what he has done over the years, particularly since the rebellion which began with civilian protests in 2011. In detail.

She may not have prevailed within the administration with her advice to Barack Obama, but she was in the arena. She was in the decision-making arena where U.S. foreign policy was formulated and executed.

Donald Trump has no experience in foreign policy. None. Zero. He has never been in the foreign policy arena.

Third, Clinton's knowledge of foreign policy issues and developments in foreign countries is vast. She is also familiar with foreign leaders, many of whom she has dealt with personally.

Donald Trump's interest in foreign policy, in contrast, seems to be of recent vintage. We will see, in the coming months, what he has learned from his advisors in prepping for the presidential campaign. Even that knowledge, however, is not likely to be as deep and as well digested as that of a person like Hillary Clinton, who has followed foreign policy at least since she was President Bill Clinton's First Lady in the White House beginning in January 1993, if not much earlier.

Fourth, Clinton's abilities are widely known, even if usually masked behind the campaign script and persona her campaign machine have created to win the presidency. She has been particularly careful not to criticize the foreign policy decisions of Barack Obama, in order to guarantee his support during the fall campaign.

It will be interesting to see whether her opponent and the press can prod her sufficiently so as to induce her to stake out her own positions on foreign policy issues—beyond boiler-plate platitudes— rather than hiding behind the coattails of Barack Obama as she has done to date.

Donald Trump, for his part, has great experience negotiating business deals in the private sector. Whether those skills and stratagems would serve him well in negotiating with foreign countries and leaders is a case he will have to make to the electorate.

On one score, that is, the ability to generate the support of allies and important alliances in pursuit of U.S. foreign policy objectives, the issues of character and loyalty are likely to be of key importance.

Will Foreign Policy Issues Be Central to the Campaign?

Hillary Clinton, eager not to criticize Barack Obama, has so far manifested a strong inclination to avoid serious discussion of foreign policy issues. Donald Trump has a huge opportunity to stress the foreign policy failures of Barack Obama and his administration (many of which are chronicled in the *Trenchant Observer* blog). Yet a strategy of strong criticism has its own risks, as it will lead him into territory where his knowledge and experience are thin, and where the likelihood of gaffes is high. Whether gaffes will make any difference in the political climate of 2016 remains an open question.

It will be up to the media, particularly the press, to push both candidates beyond the safety of platitudes into a real, serious, and sustained debate about the foreign policy of the United States, and the extremely grave international challenges the nation faces and will face in the next four to eight years.

3

August 16, 2016

Foreign Policy under Trump

2016 is a good year to be observing what people in the United States are saying about foreign policy.

There are new and dangerous currents in U.S. politics that may affect foreign policy. To try to understand where these dark, swirling waters may be taking us, we must admit the possibility of the Unthinkable, the Absurd, the kind of Unreason that swept all of the highly intelligent and educated men and women of Europe first into the vortex of World War I (1914-1918), and then into the maelstrom of Nazi Germany (1933-1945) and World War II (1939-1945) with all of its horrors and destruction.

No European, or American, could have imagined in 1914, 1933, or 1939 the horrors that were to come as Unreason gained the upper hand in the minds and actions of men

It is with a certain foreboding, therefore, similar perhaps to what some must have felt in Europe and America in the early 20th century as Unreason mounted the saddle and gained ascendency in the affairs of men, that one dares to think about a rational U.S. foreign policy in 2017.

In America, we now have as our Republican presidential candidate a Clown who will say anything, and a willing press corps that purports to take him seriously, no matter what buffoonery he espouses.

He says he would give Crimea to Putin.

Yet Hillary Clinton does not make any serious effort to explain to the American people why this is a disastrous idea.

This is a "teachable moment," but Hillary is so enmeshed in the grinding gears of her campaign machine and narrative, she doesn't even make the effort to go for Trump's jugular on this point.

Who is to say she has not adopted the wiser course? She's doing well in the polls.

Of course that could change. She may yet regret not going for Trump's jugular on Crimea.

Yet someone must make the argument and begin to educate the American people about foreign policy. For if they don't have leaders who can explain to them the basics of foreign policy, it is hard to see how a serious U.S. foreign policy can be formulated and executed beginning in 2017.

The Clown wants to give Crimea to Putin. Why not?

Russian aircraft using Iranian air bases bomb al-Assad's rebel opponents in Syria. Is that a problem? We are, after all, at Obama's direction "working through the Russians" in Syria, are we not?

The Clown campaigns for the presidency on a platform of torture. So?

Clinton cannot be bothered to give a detailed speech on how torture is wrong and violates our deepest values. To do so could cost her votes, she must think.

Expediency is the name of the game in 2016. Neither candidate is laying down bedrock principles which would govern his or her foreign policy in 2017.

In a way, it is a shame the Republicans nominated the Clown, thereby sparing Barack Obama and Hillary Clinton any serious criticism for the foreign policy fiascos of the Obama administration.

The bad news is almost too extensive to enumerate. A new Axis of Evil is taking root in the Middle East, with Russia, Iran, Hezbollah and Iraqi Shia militias working together to maintain Bashar al-Assad in power in

Syria. They are fighting against the Western-backed rebels seeking to overthrow al-Assad.

Meanwhile, Barack Obama is working with the Russians, testing them to see if they will do what they promise to do in Syria. He seems oblivious to their track record in Syria over the last five years. Or to simply not care.

He is winning "his war" in Syria—not to get the U.S. involved in efforts to force al-Assad to leave. *No matter what the consequences.*

In the South China Sea, China continues to build up its military capabilities in defiance of international law, as an international arbitral decision under the Law of the Sea Convention recently made clear.

In Europe, Putin plots and maneuvers to weaken NATO and the EU. The pacifists and appeasers among Europe's leaders are constantly looking for ways to ease the burden of sanctions on Russia, without addressing the causes that led to their imposition.

Meanwhile, Putin has put into play a massive yet nimble propaganda apparatus throughout Europe and in many other countries. The U.S. has hardly begun to respond, though the Voice of America and Radio Liberty continue to do an outstanding job with very limited resources. They are, however, no match for Putin's propaganda machine.

In Turkey, the key NATO member and great secular democracy founded by Atatürk, Tayipp Erdogan is proceeding to take down the last vestiges of the rule of law in the country. He has stripped his opponents from their positions in the media, the judiciary, and the military and the police, dismissing tens of thousands without due process of law. He has also recently launched a rapprochement with Russia.

Barack Obama has already checked out of the White House. No one is running U.S. foreign policy right now. Instead of attending to safeguarding the nation's foreign policy interests, he is looking for gimmicks such as a declaration on "no first use of nuclear weapons" to burnish his legacy or trying to fulfill his promise to close Guantanamo by expediting the departure of its inmates.

Things fall apart. The center does not hold.

Everywhere, it seems, the deepest values of our Western civilization are violated with impunity. Barbarism has replaced humanitarian law or the laws of war in Syria. In public discussions by leaders in the U.S. and elsewhere, we hear few defenses of the human values underlying such legal norms, which date to the U.S. Civil War.

A nation like Russia can invade a European nation and annex part of it, yet many leaders seem clueless as to the principles and issues at stake.

"Let Putin have the Crimea," Donald Trump cries out. "Let Hitler have the Sudetenland," Neville Chamberlain (Britain) and Édouard Daladier (France) cried out almost 80 years ago, as the great Unreason swept through Europe.

Everywhere, no one seems to be in control. Everywhere, national leaders seem clueless as to the fundamental principles of international politics upon which any international order, any international peace and security, might be founded.

Everywhere political leaders seem to have a very complicated relationship with the Truth.

Everywhere, the defenders of Western values seem to have lost faith in the two bedrock principles upon which international peace and security have been built since World War II: 1) nations are prohibited from invading other countries; and 2) the sanctity of the human person, the fundamental human rights of all human beings, must be protected from violation by governments.

Yet these pillars of civilization seem to be giving way.

This is the new Unreason. Like a tsunami it threatens to push aside everything in the way of its dark, swirling waters, which may take us far from where we want to be.

If indeed we survive.

4

September 10, 2016

What Trump Has
Learned from Putin

Donald Trump is now in a neck-and-neck race with Hillary Clinton for the presidency.

How is this possible, given the stream of blatant lies, distortions, and half-truths that continuously billow forth from his mouth, not to mention the unbroken stream of unforgivable insults and offenses that are his trademark?

First, the fact that he is even with Hillary Clinton tells us something important about the electorate and the way political opinion is formed in 2016. The old rules where character and truthfulness were critical factors in the choice of a president no longer seem to apply.

In part, this phenomenon is the result of the impact of "the infinite expansion of the present moment" with the advent of social media and electronic media that seem devoid of historical context, or even the context of what happened two weeks ago.

In part, it is the result of a failure of educational institutions in the project of civic education. There is no more important task than turning a potential barbarian into an educated citizen who can think about politics, morality, and political choices in an analytical manner and make decisions rationally.

In part, it may also be the product of the cowardice and lack of principles of many political leaders who have failed to oppose Trump, and to call him out for his lies, distortions, and unforgiveable insults and obscenities.

Taking advantage of this new political arena, Trump seems to have learned a great deal from Vladimir Putin. The latter's countless fabrications and distortions in the Russian media, and its echoes in the West, have provided a striking contemporary example of the effective use of lies and propaganda. Putin, the KGB man, has perfected these techniques and used them effectively in Crimea, Ukraine, Syria, in Russia, and elsewhere.

Trump appears to have enhanced his innate abilities as a B.S. master by learning from Putin. Is it any wonder that he so admires the Russian authoritarian leader?

The election of Trump in November would represent a major and portentous historical development. Yet it looms.

What would be the consequences of entrusting the nuclear codes to Donald Trump? No one knows. However, given his ignorance of international affairs and his personality, there is ample cause for grave concern.

Could he navigate his way through a Cuban Missile Crisis like John F. Kennedy did in 1962? Who could stop Trump from recognizing the Russian annexation of Crimea, or in effect destroying NATO?

The scenario of a Trump victory approaches.

5

September 13, 2016

Herd Journalists: Unwitting Tools of Trump?

Updated October 8, 2016

BACKGROUND

See,

1) Gunda Trepp, „Wahlkampf in Amerika Die Medien haben ihren Auftrag vergessen; Im amerikanischen Wahlkampf kommen viele Journalisten ihrer Sorgfaltspflicht nicht mehr nach. Sie setzen die erfahrene Clinton und den politischen Dilettanten Trump gleich. Doch diese Komplexitätsreduktion gibt es nicht nur in Amerika. Ein Gastbeitrag," *Frankfurter Allgemeine Zeitung*, October 8, 2016.[26]

2) Margaret Sullivan (Media Columnist), „It's Time for TV News to Stop Playing the Stooge for Donald Trump," *Washington Post*, September 16, 2016 (1:46 p.m.).[27]

Voters in the United States must make a momentous choice on November 8 when they choose a president. The issues that

15

face the nation and that must be decided by the next president are daunting.

For the last two days great media attention has been given to Hillary Clinton's comment at a fundraising event that half of Donald Trump's supporters come from "the basket of deplorables." She has since walked back the "half" word in the comment, but not the thrust of her remark.

Donald Trump is a master at throwing bait to the nation's herd journalists. Here, he launched an ad deploring Clinton's comment. This ad came from the same man who has made so many despicable comments himself, about John McCain, about the Muslim parents of a U.S. soldier killed in Iraq, about his intent to torture detainees in the future, and the list goes on.

He continues to repeat the assertion that he opposed the invasion of Iraq, when the evidence shows he did not. Last week on a nationally televised foreign policy forum, Matt Lauer, one of the highest-paid TV journalists in the U.S., allowed the false assertion to go unchallenged.

This is what the campaign coverage has been like in the U.S. this year.

The real story, however, is not about Trump or Clinton. Rather, it is about a lazy press corps and media that prefer to report the "he said, she said" story of the day, instead of digging into the issues—*every day, in every story*—that define the differences between the candidates.

Investigative journalism, where the journalists and their editors set the agenda, seems to be largely a thing of the past.

To be sure, some newspapers and new organizations do engage in investigative journalism from time to time. Yet such journalism is so unusual that it is usually newsworthy in itself, whereas an element of investigative journalism should be a part of *every* story.

Every story should be written from a "critical" point of view, and never merely repeat factual assertions that are untrue without citing the contrary evidence.

Among stories published recently was one about Trump donating $25,000 to a state prosecutor who was deciding whether or not to prosecute Trump and one of his enterprises. It was a great story, but one whose follow-up has been obscured by stories like the one on Clinton's comment about "the basket of deplorables."

Trump is allowed by the press to question the activities of the Clinton Foundation when Hillary was secretary of state, over and over, endlessly it seems.

Despite the fact that no malfeasance has ever been found, the press dutifully raises this dead horse every time Donald Trump mentions it, giving further life to a charge based solely on unfounded innuendo. Meanwhile, stories such as Trump's apparent attempt to improperly influence a prosecutor deciding on a matter affecting him directly are allowed to fall by the wayside.

Journalists know they are not serving the public interest when they run after Trump's bait, but they cannot resist the instinctive reaction of running with the herd.

Indeed, the worst "deplorables" in Trump's "basket of deplorables" are the herd journalists who are too lazy to write about substantive issues, or too afraid to not come up with the most recent statement by one of the candidates in the latest cycle of "he said, she said" excitement.

If ignorance of substantive issues and positions, or of questions of character and honesty, remains amidst the obscuring fog caused by this herd journalism, it is clear who the most consequential "deplorables" are.

They are the herd journalists themselves.

6

September 18, 2016

The Hidden Issue in the 2016 Election

How Will Voters Explain
Their Vote to Their Children?

How will Trump or Clinton voters explain how they voted in 2016 to their children and grandchildren?

That is a huge though hidden issue in the November 8, 2016 congressional and presidential elections.

"Dad, how could you vote for a man who disparaged the Muslim parents of a soldier who died for his country in Iraq?"

"Mom, how could you vote for a man who fueled racist emotions by claiming Barack Obama was not born in the United States for years, even after he produced his birth certificate?"

"How could you vote for a candidate who was so slow to disavow the support of the Ku Klux Klan, or who attacked a judge for being of Mexican descent after he ruled against him in a case?"

"Grandad, how could you vote for a candidate who lied all of the time? Didn't you know he was lying?"

"Grandma, how could you vote for a man of such low character to be president of the United States? Didn't you know what he said about other people? You knew, and you ignored all of that and its implications? How could you have done that?"

"Mom and Dad, you said you just had a feeling the candidate would make America strong again. Is that the way you want us to vote this year? Just on the basis of our feelings?"

"Mom and Dad, why weren't you thinking about your children and grandchildren when you voted?"

"Are these the kinds of people you want us to marry, or want us to become?"

"Dad, how could you vote for a candidate so ignorant of foreign policy and who was pro-Russian and praised Vladimir Putin because Putin praised him?"

"Didn't either one of you think of us and our future, and the nation and the kind of politics we would inherit as a result of your vote?"

"Come on, Grandad, explain to us your thinking in detail and what led you to vote the way you did. We're listening."

"Are you proud, now, of the way you voted and the consequences of your vote?"

"Looking at what has happened in our country, don't you feel any shame for having voted as you did?"

These questions suggest the real litmus test for voting one way or another in the 2016 presidential election should be: How will you feel, in a year or five or 20 years, explaining how and why you voted as you did to your 11-year-old or 20-year-old son or daughter, or grandson or granddaughter?"

7

October 7, 2016

Vice-Presidential Debate: Pence Pushes Kaine and Clinton on Syria

During the vice-presidential debate between Tim Kaine and Mike Pence, Pence revealed a powerful line of critique of Barack Obama's foreign policy towards Syria and Hillary Clinton's refusal, to date, to distance herself from it.

Donald Trump may well adopt this line of attack in the second presidential debate on October 9, 2016. Then again, he may disagree with Pence or not have the discipline to deliver the attack.

Excerpts from Mike Spence's and Tim Kaine's exchanges with the moderator, Elaine Quijano (from CBSN—the CBS streaming news channel), follow:

QUIJANO: I want to turn now to Syria. Two hundred fifty thousand people, 100,000 of them children, are under siege in Aleppo, Syria. Bunker buster bombs, cluster munitions, and incendiary weapons are being dropped on them by Russian and Syrian militaries. Does the U.S. have a responsibility to protect civilians and prevent mass casualties on this scale, Governor Pence?

PENCE: The United States of America needs to begin to exercise strong leadership to protect the vulnerable citizens and over 100,000 children in Aleppo. Hillary Clinton's top priority when she became secretary of state was the Russian reset. After the Russian reset, the Russians invaded Ukraine and took over Crimea.

And the small and bullying leader of Russia is now dictating terms to the United States to the point where all the United States of America—the greatest nation on Earth—just withdraws from talks about a cease-fire while Vladimir Putin puts a missile defense system in Syria while he marshals the forces and begins—look, we have got to begin to lean into this with strong, broad-shouldered American leadership.

It begins by rebuilding our military. And the Russians and the Chinese have been making enormous investments in the military. We have the smallest Navy since 1916. We have the lowest number of troops since the end of the Second World War. We've got to work with Congress, and Donald Trump will, to rebuild our military and project American strength in the world.

FURTHER READING

1) "Vice-Presidential Debate: Pence Pushes Kaine and Clinton on Military Action in Syria," *The Trenchant Observer*, October 7, 2016.[28]

2) "Syria: Russia's Military Assault on Western Civilization," *The Trenchant Observer*, September 26, 2016.[29]

8

October 28, 2016

Reopened Clinton E-mail Investigation

FBI Director Comey Should Consider Resigning

BACKGROUND

See Adam Goldman and Alan Rappeport, "Emails in Anthony Weiner Inquiry Jolt Hillary Clinton's Campaign," *New York Times*, October 28, 2016.

Whether merely bumbling and incompetent, or secretly moving to throw the election to the Republicans, FBI Director James B. Comey's letter to congressional leaders this morning, October 28, was such an obvious intervention in the U.S. presidential election—in violation of Justice Department guidelines to avoid public actions near an election—that he should consider resigning.

How an FBI director could announce that he was reopening the investigation into Hillary Clinton's e-mails, having previously decided there were no legal grounds to prosecute her, and not having reviewed the newly discovered e-mails in question, without understanding the scandalous impact his decision and communications would be likely to have on the election, defies understanding.

Given the gravity of the intervention in the electoral process, he should consider resigning or taking other drastic action that might reverse the harm he has done.

His actions appear to represent not only colossal errors in judgment, but also errors which directly undermine the integrity of the electoral process established by the Constitution for the election of the President of the United States.

Let us not forget that David Petraeus was forced to resign only days after the 2012 presidential election as the result of a call to his boss, Director of National Intelligence James R. Clapper, late on election day from someone at the FBI, who revealed that Petraeus had mishandled classified information—a fact that had emerged in an independent investigation. This occurred despite Petraeus being notified a month earlier by the FBI that it had concluded its investigation of him and found no grounds to proceed with the matter.

The United States is beginning to look like a Banana Republic, where "House of Cards" rules seem to be at play.

9

October 30, 2016

Donald Trump, Russian Stooge

Putin's Trojan Horse within Striking Distance of Victory

Donald Trump is within striking distance of winning the U.S. presidential election on November 8, 2016.

Polls have tightened.

The polls have varying degrees of methodological rigor, and all depend on models of who will vote. The range of results among them is far greater than the respective margins of error involved.

FBI Director James B. Comey intervened forcefully in the presidential election process on Friday, October 28, announcing he was reopening the investigation into Hillary Clinton's e-mails, casting a dark cloud of suspicion over her candidacy. The timing was such as to leave her no opportunity to rebut the insinuation that she was guilty of serious misconduct. The effect over the next eight days of this development is not known, and unknowable.

As occurred in the United Kingdom, the actual election results could vary widely from the polls' predictions. Overconfidence by Democrats resulting from the media chorus that Hillary Clinton is far ahead in the polls, and confusion over the meaning of the FBI reopening its investigation of Clinton's e-mails, could lead democratic voters to stay home, while pro-Trump voters could come out of the woodwork in large numbers to give him a narrow victory.

The momentum of the race may have been changed by FBI Director Comey's intervention, and the truth is no one really knows what will happen on November 8.

If voters were analytical and rational and held democratic values, it is hard to understand how the race could be as close as it is today.

Meanwhile, there is mounting evidence that, wittingly or unwittingly, Donald Trump is acting as a Russian stooge.

See,

1) Anne Applebaum, "Why Is Trump Suddenly Talking about World War III?" *Washington Post*, October 28, 2016.

> (W)e have a Republican presidential nominee who regularly repeats propaganda lines lifted directly from Russian state media. Donald Trump has declared that Hillary Clinton and Obama "founded ISIS," a statement that comes directly from Russia's Sputnik news agency. He spouted another debunked conspiracy theory — "the Google search engine is suppressing the bad news about Hillary Clinton" — soon after Sputnik resurrected it.
>
> Now Trump is repeating Kiselyov's threat, too. "You're going to end up in World War III over Syria if we listen to Hillary Clinton," he said this week. Just like Kiselyov, he has also noted that Russia has nukes and — perhaps if Clinton is elected — will use them: "Russia is a nuclear country, but a country where the nukes work as opposed to other countries that talk."

2) Matt Payton, "Donald Trump Uses 'Russian Propaganda' to Attack Hillary Clinton's Campaign," *The Independent*, October

12, 2016; "'The Republican Nominee for President Is Standing on a Stage Reciting the Manufactured Story as Truth,' Says Kurt Eichenwald."

A victory on November 8 for Donald Trump would be an immense coup for Vladimir Putin. It would signify a Russian triumph likely to undermine the solidarity of the European Union and the unity of NATO.

Trump has been friendly to Putin in his public pronouncements.

Until August, one of his principal advisors was Paul Manafort, a former advisor to Viktor Yanukovych, the former president of Ukraine who fled to Russia when his government collapsed in the face of street protests in February 2014.

Trump has refused to release his tax returns, which might well reveal his ties to Russian figures and organizations, if they exist.

If Trump is elected, the likely foreign policy consequences vis-a-vis Russia include the following:

1) a collapse of the coordinated EU and US economic sanctions imposed on Russia in response to its invasion and annexation of Crimea, and its infiltration and invasion of the Donetsk and Luhansk regions of Ukraine. The latter involved the overt movement of Russian military forces and equipment on an accelerated timetable beginning in August 2014;

2) an undermining of the stiff resolve and unity of NATO, which has been strengthening its defenses and deployments in countries bordering on Russia;

3) a short-circuiting of the stronger response to Russia Hillary Clinton promises to bring to the foreign policy of the U.S., in Aleppo and Syria and within NATO; and

4) a decreased likelihood that the U.S. would stand up to nuclear threats from Russia.

Donald Trump has provided no evidence he would be able to take firm action against the Russians in a nuclear showdown. The Russians have increasingly resorted to nuclear threats to achieve their objectives in foreign policy, from Ukraine to Syria.

In the 1932 elections in Germany, no one really imagined that Adolf Hitler might become chancellor.

In politics, unexpected things happen

10

November 5, 2016

Trump, Clinton, and the Risk of Nuclear War

BACKGROUND

See Sam Nunn, "Only Hillary Clinton Is Prepared for the Nuclear Threat; Donald Trump Is an Apprentice in the Nuclear World. Worse, He Has No Appetite for Learning," *Wall Street Journal*, October 24, 2016 (updated 1:09 p.m. ET).[30]

Many of us have heard and read all kinds of things about Donald Trump and Hillary Clinton and are sick of the stories about his character and alleged lies and actions, and about her character and alleged lies and corruption.

Yet one critical issue deserves our further attention before we vote. That issue is how our vote for president could affect our own individual chances of physical survival, our own physical existence, over the next four years.

In a word, the outcome of the election could affect not only our future, but whether we have a future.

While politicians and others seem to have forgotten the fact, we still live in a nuclear world in which both the United States and Russia possess thousands of nuclear weapons targeted at the cities and infrastructure of the other country. The time a president of the U.S. or Russia would have to decide whether to launch a retaliatory strike in response to a real *or perceived* incoming nuclear attack is probably less than 15-30 minutes.

The possibility of nuclear war triggered by accident, misunderstanding, or a false assessment of one's ability to out bluff the other side is far greater than we allow ourselves to contemplate.

Since the Cuban Missile Crisis in October 1962, when we came perilously close to a full nuclear exchange with the Soviet Union, Soviet, Russian, and American leaders have worked hard to decrease the risk of nuclear war. These efforts took the form of a series of arms control agreements in the ensuing 50 years and the adoption of a number of confidence-building measures on both sides.

However, such efforts have now ceased. No new agreements are being negotiated, while the continued viability of the INF agreement on intermediate-range nuclear forces in Europe is in question due to Russian violations of its basic provisions. Both sides appear to be developing new kinds of nuclear weapons.

Moreover, in the last few years Russia, under Vladimir Putin, has repeatedly resorted to nuclear threats to affect U.S. foreign policy actions in Ukraine, Syria, and within NATO. Russia recently conducted its largest civil defense exercise in decades.

Russian propaganda has put out the story in recent weeks that if Hillary Clinton becomes president it will lead to World War III. In essence, the argument is that if the U.S. strongly opposes Russia in Syria, it will lead to nuclear war. This amounts to an argument by Russia that if we do not vote for appeasement and Donald Trump, World War III will ensue.

The threat of nuclear war is real, but its source is not a potential failure to pursue appeasement with Russia.

See,

1) Michael Khodarkovsky, "Playing With Fear: Russia's War Card," *New York Times*, October 26, 2016.[31]

2) Anne Applebaum "Why Is Trump Suddenly Talking about World War III?" *Washington Post*, October 28, 2016:[32]

Back in March 2014, just after the Russian invasion of Crimea, Russia's most famous state television broadcaster presented the international situation in stark terms. 'Russia,' Dimitry Kiselyov told his millions of viewers, 'is the only country in the world that really can turn [the] USA into radioactive ash.' Against a backdrop of mushroom clouds and throbbing nuclear targets, he spoke ominously of how President Obama's hair was turning gray — 'I admit this can be a coincidence' — and the increasing desperation of a White House that truly feared that nuclear war might break out at any moment.

Now it's October 2016, and Kiselyov, who also heads Russia's state-owned news agency, is at it again. 'Impudent behavior toward Russia' has a 'nuclear dimension,' he warned ominously on Oct. 9. On the same program, he again featured photographs of Obama. Kiselyov said that there had been a 'radical change' in the U.S.-Russian relationship, and he added a threat: 'Moscow would react with nerves of steel' to any U.S. intervention in Syria — up to and including a nuclear response. 'If it should one day happen, every one of you should know where the nearest bomb shelter is. It's best to find out now,' another television channel has advised.

3) "Putin's Playing 'Chicken' in Syria and the Risk of Escalation to Nuclear War," *The Trenchant Observer*, October 8, 2015.[33]

Vladimir Putin knows that the weak foreign policy of Barack Obama will come to an end if Clinton is elected. Before we cave in to Putin's nuclear threats, let us bear in mind a few cold, hard facts.

Russia has invaded and annexed Crimea and invaded and still occupies the eastern Ukraine provinces of Donetsk and Luhansk, defying the cornerstone principle of the U.N. Charter and international law prohibiting the illegal use of force across international frontiers. Recently it has been committing war crimes and supporting the Syrian government in the commission of war crimes on a large scale in Syria, while operating in extremely close proximity to U.S. forces in and over the country.

Relations between Russia and the United States are probably at their lowest point since the end of the Cold War, if not the 1960s. Today, the possibility of nuclear war, accidental or resulting from an escalation over a non-nuclear event, is real—and substantial.

U.S. Elections: The Choice on November 8, 2016

Who, between the presidential candidates, has the knowledge and analytical skills, the ability to mobilize our allies, the steady temperament, and the absolute composure to see us through a nuclear crisis with Russia, or for that matter, with North Korea?

Our answer to that question may have a decisive impact on the likelihood of a nuclear war, and our own physical survival.

One might also ask, who has the vision and strategy to halt or reduce nuclear proliferation, as well as to control and reduce the risks of a nuclear confrontation with Russia or North Korea?

After stressing that there are no "checks and balances" on the president's authority to use nuclear weapons, Senator Nunn writes,

What about moral considerations? William Swing, a retired Episcopal bishop, recently offered, in a memo sent to about a dozen leaders, a powerful reminder of the importance of this year's presidential choice: "Whoever wins will have his or her hand on the weapons that could end life, as we know it, on this planet. We are not so much voting for a president as choosing a god. When you put your hand on the nuclear trigger and become the single agent of the Earth's destruction that is power beyond human imagining."

Is any human prepared or qualified to make this fateful decision for mankind? I think not. Yet this is the responsibility of the commander in chief. Temperament, composure and sound judgment are essential. So is understanding America's adversaries and allies and, most important, possessing the leadership qualities required to reduce the risk that such a terrible call will ever have to be made.

Contemplating Nuclear War and Our Own Deaths

We tend to avoid and even shun the thought of our own individual deaths, particularly in the near term. The thought is almost too terrifying to face directly.

Nonetheless, we must face the reality that who we choose to be president may have a significant impact on the likelihood of our and our families' physically surviving the next four years.

This may sound alarmist. Yet it is reality itself that is alarming.

Read closely the op-ed cited above by former Senator Sam Nunn, a long-time leader in the Senate on nuclear arms control agreements and related issues. Consider carefully each of the points he makes.

Then, look at the character of each of the candidates, and how each of them reacts under stress or direct challenge.

Which of them, Donald Trump or Hillary Clinton, has a record of steady nerves under intense criticism and confrontation? Which of them has the more stable and predictable personality? Which of them has experience in foreign policy and is more likely to gather highly qualified advisors around themself?

Above all, which of them is more likely to coordinate and follow expert advice in a crunch, even the ultimate crunch of a nuclear showdown or ambiguous signals that could possibly lead to accidental nuclear war?

11

November 11, 2016

The Full Catastrophe— Trump Is Elected

Donald Trump has won an electoral victory in the November 8, 2016 presidential elections, despite the fact that Hillary Clinton won a majority of the popular vote.

Amplifying Trump's power and removing most of the checks and balances on his actions, Republicans also won majorities in the Senate and in the House of Representatives.

Reality

The significance of events can sometimes be seen more clearly from abroad.

See,

German text

Carsten Luther (Meinung),"Der Ernstfall: Donald Trump war lange nur ein schlechter Scherz; Jetzt wird er Präsident; Die Welt muss sich fürchten vor dem, was diesem unberechenbaren Mann als Nächstes einfällt," *Die Zeit*, November 9, 2016 (9:30 a.m.).[34]

English text
Carsten Luther (Opinion), "The Calamity; For a Long Time, Donald Trump Was Just a Bad Joke; Now, He Has Been Elected President; The World Should Be Afraid of What This Unpredictable Man Will Come Up with Next," *Die Zeit*, November 9, 2016 (9:31 a.m.).[35]

Luther writes,

A totalitarian phony and deceitful dilettante has managed to get elected to the US presidency. Donald Trump is an epochal disaster that won't just change his vast country and its democracy for many years to come. The entire world will feel the effects of this aberration.

Many thought it was a joke when Trump announced his candidacy last year... Now, a racist sexual predator, a pathological liar and an excitable egomaniac holds power in the United States — a sickening outcome for all those who believe in democracy and human rights, or at least in the common sense of humanity at large and of Americans in particular. They only had one job, damn it! To prevent this man from becoming president.

Hopes

As Americans, we must hope—and pray—that president-elect Trump undergoes a metamorphosis, that faced with the grave responsibilities of his new office he becomes more disciplined, listens to his advisors more closely, and makes decisions after carefully considering the advantages and disadvantages of various options.

We can hope, but we must also admit that it is likely that at age 70 a number of his character traits are already baked into his personality.

On the other hand, Maureen Dowd of the *New York Times* has suggested that he may simply be skilled at playing different personas. Let us hope, then, if that is the case, that he adopts a new persona, one more consonant with being a dignified and respected—and ultimately successful—president of the United States, both at home and on the world stage.

See Maureen Dowd, "The End Is Nigh," *New York Times,* November 5, 2016.[36]

Illusions

In any event, we will need to guard against seriously entertaining any illusions that what we earnestly hope for will actually occur. That would be a big mistake.

Rather, we should hope for the best, and prepare for the worst. The worst would be that what we know and have seen of Donald Trump in the campaign and elsewhere plays itself out during his administration.

We should always bear in mind Ronald Reagan's admonition, originally offered in the context of arms control agreements but equally applicable here: "Trust but verify."

Given the fact that Donald Trump has ascended to the Oval Office by swimming into the White House through the sewers, we might hope that he would spend the next two months taking baths and showers to make sure he has left all of the residue behind him.

Reality and Cooperation

In terms of working with Donald Trump, Angela Merkel hit the right note, perhaps, in congratulating Trump on Wednesday, when she read the following statement:

Please accept my congratulations on your election as President of the United States of America.

You will assume office at a time in which our countries are jointly facing many different challenges.

Germany's ties with the United States of America are deeper than with any country outside of the European Union. Germany and America are bound by common values — democracy, freedom, as well as respect for the rule of law and the dignity of each and every person, regardless of their origin, skin color, creed, gender, sexual orientation, or political views. It is based on these values that I wish to offer close cooperation, both with me personally and between our countries' governments.

Partnership with the United States is and will remain a keystone of German foreign policy, especially so that we can tackle the great challenges of our time: striving for economic and social well-being, working to develop far-sighted climate policy, pursuing the fight against terrorism, poverty, hunger, and disease, as well as protecting peace and freedom in the world.

In the years ahead as president, I wish you a sure hand, every success, and God's blessing.

. . .

–Anthony Faiola. "Angela Merkel Congratulates Donald Trump — Kind of," *Washington Post*, November 9, 2016.[37]

In short, we should work with Trump in pursuit of common objectives and values, and work against Trump and seek to block any actions that would defeat our own objectives or undermine our deepest values.

As for our fellow citizens who voted for Trump, it was no secret Trump was a candidate who favored torture, who subtly or not so subtly welcomed the support of racists and xenophobes, who denigrated women, and who indicated he would be friendly to Vladimir Putin and Russia, and a candidate who cast doubt on the viability and future of NATO, the resolve of the West to resist Russian military aggression in Europe, and efforts by the U.S. and others to halt the commission of war crimes in Syria by Russia and the Bashar al-Assad government.

The important fact is that, knowing all of this, they were willing to vote for Trump, and did.

They will bear grave responsibility for what is likely to come.

Part Two

2017 – Year One
of the Trump Presidency

12

January 10, 2017

Trump's Appointments:

The U.S. Becomes a Banana Republic

Donald Trump has learned from Vladimir Putin that to carry the day you need only to overwhelm your adversaries with lies, distortions, and diversions that drive them to distraction, leaving them no opportunity for coherent, much less effective, opposition.

So, we have had five Senate confirmation hearings for cabinet officials on one day. The hearings were scheduled before some of the nominees had been cleared by the ethics office and, in some cases, before they had even submitted their paperwork. Trump has set the tone. He has never submitted his tax returns or other information sufficient to identify his conflicts of interest, which appear to be enormous.

Just like in a Banana Republic, he hired his 36-year-old son-in law, Jared Kushner, to be a top advisor, to help do his thinking in the White House, just like he did his thinking during the campaign.

With a few important exceptions (Defense Secretary Mattis, Secretary of State Tillerson) Trump made little pretense of finding the best qualified people in the country to fill cabinet positions. With some exceptions, he named people who were fellow billionaires or prominent retired military officials.

Generally, he seemed to favor individuals who were either billionaires or multi-millionaires, or who looked the part, as if they were contestants on one of his television shows. In one case, this led to an Indian-American governor, Nikki Haley, capable but with no foreign policy experience, being nominated to be ambassador to the United Nations.

As a former U.S. ambassador to the U.N. Economic and Social Council (ECOSOC), himself an African American and a wry observer of American attitudes told the author decades ago, the United Nations is where all the "funny-looking people" are. This attitude reflects the way many people thought 40 years ago.

In any event, Trump hasn't nominated any "funny-looking people" to other cabinet posts, except for Ben Carson, or many women, or indeed many individuals under the age of 60 or 65. There are generations of Americans who are not represented in his cabinet picks.

As for Carson, the full story may not be known as to why he remained in the primary race long after he had lost any serious support, further dividing the votes among Trump's rivals. He has no obvious qualifications to be secretary of housing and urban development, aside from his personal experience growing up poor and then becoming successful.

As in a Banana Republic, policy is made or not made in a dramatically haphazard way. Leading opponents of different departments and their programs have been named to head these same departments. One thing most, though not all, nominees have in common is that they hold extreme right-wing views, far from the mainstream of American politics.

The United States is in for a difficult slog, with a president of authoritarian tendencies and impetuous temperament, who will have in his undisciplined hands the power to destroy, and who has given every indication of his intent to use it.

He will have the power to destroy alliances and cooperative relationships with other countries or groups of countries, such as NATO and the European Union, or the current cooperative relationship with China leading the effort to slow global climate change.

He will have the power to enter war, to engage in abject appeasement of Vladimir Putin, and to make mistakes which could lead to nuclear war.

Psychologically, he shows little evidence of being a well-balanced person. This emotionally unstable person, our president, will have the power to destroy the world.

Before becoming president, Trump repeatedly violated the Logan Act, which makes it a felony for a private individual to interfere with the conduct of the foreign policy of the United States. Already by telegraphing his intent to do nothing to support the moderate Syrian rebels, he has emboldened Vladimir Putin to commit massive war crimes in one final push to eradicate the rebels in Aleppo.

Trump has uttered not a word of criticism of Putin or of Russia, not even of the Russian intervention in the 2016 presidential elections aimed at throwing the election to him.

Citizens are dumbfounded as the president-elect continues the same pattern of behavior which characterized his campaign and his earlier life. Supporters hold their breaths, in blind faith and clinging to blind ideology. Opponents are paralyzed by their own disbelief at what is happening and by the mantra of their democratic values, despite the accumulating evidence that disaster awaits us.

Trump may be smart, or clever, in an unprincipled way. But he has an authoritarian personality, is a compulsive liar, shows no respect for any individual, and to date has shown himself to be a man of low moral character.

The only question is how long it will take citizens who supported him to come to their senses, if they do, and to realize the catastrophe they have brought upon the country, and the world.

How long it may take for democrats and others to organize disciplined and determined resistance to Trump's assault on longstanding traditions, values, and even laws, sufficient as to halt or greatly slow the damage he will do, is a question upon whose answer the fate of the republic may depend.

Until such resistance by leading figures emerges, we can look forward to America becoming one of the biggest Banana Republics in history. Instead of directing rational and analytical arguments at Trump, citizens would do well to view again Woody Allen's classic 1971 film, "Bananas."

13

January 12, 2017

Russia as the Great White Power

BACKGROUND

See,

1) Alan Feuer and Andrew Higgins, "Extremists Turn to a Leader to Protect Western Values: Vladimir Putin," *New York Times*, December 3, 2016.[38]

2) Tom Hamburger, Rosalind S. Helderman and Michael Birnbaum, "Inside Trump's Financial Ties to Russia and His Unusual Flattery of Vladimir Putin," *Washington Post*, June 17, 2016.[39]

What has been puzzling during Donald Trump's campaign and post-election transition has been the billionaire's utter refusal to say anything negative about Vladimir Putin or Russia.

He has not hesitated to dismiss the collective judgment of U.S. intelligence agencies which have found that Russia intervened in the election and tried to throw it to Trump, but he won't criticize Russia or Putin.

The press has reported on Paul Manafort, Trump's former campaign director, and his ties to Viktor Yanukovych in Ukraine and others in Russia.

Michael Flynn, his national security advisor, has shown an affinity to Russia and Putin, sitting next to the latter at a conference, accepting speaker fees, and appearing on RT television, the state-owned propaganda operation. A warrior from Afghanistan, where he led intelligence for Stanley McChrystal's killing machine, he may see Russia as an indispensable ally in the twilight crusade against Islam.

Rex Tillerson, Trump's nominee to be secretary of state, has had a close relationship with Putin as head of Exxon Mobil for many years. Tillerson opposed the imposition of sanctions on Moscow after Russia invaded and annexed Crimea and invaded eastern Ukraine. His world view has been shaped by the foreign-policy interests of Exxon Mobil, not those of the United States.

Trump's senior strategic advisor, Steve Bannon, is an exemplar of the alt-right, or at least a fellow traveler, who has been very sympathetic to Putin's "defense of civilization" argument.

Trump's son, Donald Jr., has been quoted as saying at a conference in 2008 that Russians had heavy investments in Trump's business.

We can't understand the extent of that Russian influence because Trump won't release his taxes.

How are we to understand Trump's silence in the face of massive war crimes committed by Putin in bombing Aleppo and Syria, his soft-pedaling on Russia's presence in eastern Ukraine, and his dismissal of U.S. intelligence agencies' findings about Russian intervention in the election?

To put it bluntly, why has Trump been so cozy with Putin and the Russians, while they have been undertaking the greatest campaign of subversion of Western democracies in Europe since 1945-48, when the Soviets sought to expand their domination on the Continent?

In the midst of this assault on the political independence of Western countries and on both NATO and the European Union, an assault carried out by cyber-attacks, massive disinformation campaigns, and other tools of subversion, Trump has not only failed to speak to the threat, but also cozied up to its author, Vladimir Putin.

That is the same Vladimir Putin who is known as "the butcher of the Caucasus" (Grozny, Chechnya), the ruthless dictator of an authoritarian regime which has suppressed the press and other independent media, jailed opponents, and killed leading activists (such as Boris Nemtsov in February 2015).

Trump's diffidence, if not strong attraction, toward Putin and Russia is downright puzzling.

That is, it is puzzling until you remember that Donald Trump rose to political prominence with the racist "birther" movement and the support of the alt-right, including David Duke and the Ku Klux Klan.

Trump's white supremacist supporters look to Russia as the one great white power which might lead the struggle to defend and promote the white race.

Whether Trump shares their views or is merely willing to give them tacit encouragement in his pursuit of power, the race factor seems to go far in explaining Trump's coziness with Vladimir Putin and Russia.

To be sure, Trump's earlier ambition to get involved in Russia with his businesses, and his current financial ties to Russia and Russians, also appear to have helped in creating a sweet spot for Putin and a blind spot for Russia in his understanding of U.S. foreign policy and its objectives.

Today, he and his alt-right supporters share a deep affinity for Russia, if originally for different reasons. Those separate motivations seem to have fused in the 2016 presidential campaign. Now Trump may be extremely reluctant to antagonize his alt-right supporters. To do so could seriously jeopardize his prospects for reelection in 2020.

The sooner these grave considerations are recognized, the better the chances will be that Trump can be contained and prevented from giving up the crown jewels of the Republic to Putin and Russia. These include intelligence, operational details on military procedures and readiness, and other concessions against longstanding U. S. interests and policies, including strong support for U.S. and EU sanctions against Russia, and active support of NATO, the EU, and strong leaders in Europe such as Angela Merkel.

Russia, one must bear in mind, remains the greatest antagonist of America and its allies on the world stage today.

14

January 31, 2017

Is There a Russian Mole in the U.S. Government?

I t is worth musing about the potential significant connections between disparate events, particularly when considering the ominous direction in which President Donald Trump has taken the country since he became president ten days ago.

We've learned that when Steve Bannon and Donald Trump are creating a diversion for the press over there, we need to be looking over here, to see what they are actually doing that may greatly impact the government and the world.

See Dana Milbank, "Don't Get Distracted by Trump's 'Dead Cats'," *Washington Post*, January 25, 2017.[40]

For starters, there were a series of arrests of top intelligence officials in Moscow in the last few months. Earlier, U.S. intelligence officials had asserted high confidence in their judgment that Vladimir Putin was personally involved in Russian hacking of the November 8, 2016 presidential and congressional elections.

They also included in a two-page annex to their public report, on January 8, 2017, references to the so-called "Golden Showers" dossier compiled by a former British MI6 officer, Christopher Steele, on Trump and prostitutes in Moscow. The classified report on Russian intervention in the election and annex may have included references to evidence from human intelligence sources.

Now, a former KGB head, who may have been involved in fingering Putin for the Russian hack of the U.S. elections, has turned up dead in Moscow. He is also alleged to have been involved in the leak of information in the "Golden Showers" dossier, the contents of which were published by BuzzFeed.

While there was great skepticism about the "Golden Showers" dossier, given news organizations' inability to verify its allegations, the death of a former KGB head now suggests that the dossier is a legitimate subject of press inquiry and reporting.

See Grant Stern, "Ex-KGB Chief Thought Dead as Source of Trump Blackmail Dossier Leak," *Huffington Post*, January 29, 2017 (02:33 p.m. ET).[41]

There are various possibilities here.

One is that the Obama administration in its report on Russian interference in the election provided Russian intelligence agencies with the clues they needed to hunt down officials who had cooperated either with Steele or with U.S. officials.

A second is that someone in the U.S. government leaked information to the Russians that enabled them to conduct a "mole hunt" in Moscow, either as a result of receiving the classified report, or otherwise.

A third is that some of the information released by the Russians through their press is part of a disinformation campaign.

We need to get to the bottom of this matter.

See,

1) Scott Shane, David E. Sanger, and Andrew E. Kramer, "Russians Charged with Treason Worked in Office Linked to Election Hacking," *New York Times*, January 27, 2017:[42]

(O)ne current and one former United States official, speaking about the classified recruitments on condition of anonymity, confirmed that human sources in Russia did play a crucial role in proving who was responsible for the hacking.

The former official said the agencies were initially reluctant to disclose their certainty about the Russian role for fear of setting off a mole hunt in Moscow. ...

Mark Galeotti, a Russia expert at the Institute of International Relations in Prague, noted that the intelligence agencies' report on the election attack found with "high confidence" that Russia had carried out the election attack, which involved fake news stories and propaganda as well as the hacks and leaks.

"It was always pretty obvious that they had more than just the computer evidence," Mr. Galeotti said. "The arrests are a big deal."

The arrests, according to reports by the Russian newspaper Kommersant and Novaya Gazeta, among others, were made in early December and amounted to a purge of the cyberwing of the F.S.B., the main Russian intelligence and security agency.

2) Andrew E. Kramer, "Top Russian Cyber-crimes Agent Arrested on Charges of Treason," *New York Times*, January 25, 2017;[43] "If confirmed, the arrest would be one of the highest-profile detentions for treason within the F.S.B. since the breakup of the Soviet Union."

3) Tim Johnson, "Russians May Have Arrested a Source in U.S. Probe of Election Meddling," McClatchy DC, January 27, 2017 (7:26 p.m.).[44]

4) Russia Accuses Cybersecurity Experts of Treasonous Links to CIA; Rumours Swirl of Connection to Revelations about US Election Hacking, as State Media Says Sergei Mikhailov and Dmitry Dokuchayev 'betrayed their oath'," *The Guardian*, January 31, 2017 (18:19 EST).

5) Robert Mendick and Robert Verkaik, "Mystery Death of Ex-KGB Chief Linked to MI6 Spy's Dossier on Donald Trump," *The Telegraph*, January 27, 2017 (9:30 p.m.).[45]

6) Seth J. Hettena, "A Mole in the White House? We Now Have a Confirmation of Sorts That the Russian FSB Agents Arrested Last Month Were Working for the CIA," *Seth Hettena – Investigative Journalist* (blog), January 31, 2017.[46]

Is there a high-level Russian mole in the U.S. government who tipped off Russian officials regarding the identities of U.S. espionage agents in Moscow?

Trump's first ten days in office are reminiscent of the first days after Vladimir Lenin and the Bolsheviks took over the government in Russia in 1917.

The executive orders of the first week came so fast, and were so sweeping, that it has been hard for journalists to keep up by providing serious analyses and assessments of their impacts.

FBI Director James Comey, who (as mentioned earlier) seemed to help throw the election to Trump by announcing less than two weeks before the election that the FBI was reopening its e-mail investigation of Hillary Clinton, has had nothing to say about an FBI investigation that is apparently underway into contacts between the Trump campaign and Russian officials prior to the November 8 elections. We have heard nothing, not even in response to Democratic Minority Leader Harry Reid's letter to Comey on the subject last summer.

Meanwhile, top White House strategist Steve Bannon has played a key role in drafting and getting Trump to sign an executive order naming him to be a permanent member of the National Security Council (NSC), while downgrading the participation of the chairman of the joint chiefs of staff and the director of national intelligence to meetings where their input is needed—a matter presumably to be decided by Michael Flynn, the national security advisor.

If Trump and Bannon can pull this off, they will have succeeded in injecting the president's chief political advisor into deliberations which define the foreign policy and security interests of the United States, while enabling Flynn and Bannon to shut out the chairman of the JCS and the director of national intelligence from key deliberations.

This would enable Trump and Bannon to actually define what is the truth—without being contradicted in the NSC. In short, political control over national intelligence might be achieved.

As the flap over the executive order halting entry to the U.S. of refugees and nationals of seven Muslim countries grabs the headlines, we must wonder whether there is any connection between the arrests in Moscow and Steve Bannon's draft of Trump's executive order on the NSC.

Bannon and Flynn have both been reported to be drawn to Putin and Russia, if for different reasons, whereas President Trump has yet to make any strong criticisms of either Putin or Russia.

Will we ever know if there is a Russian mole in the highest levels of the American government? Will we ever know who that mole is? If there is a mole who tipped off the Russians, they are presumably guilty of treason.

Why do Trump and Bannon want to include Bannon on the NSC, while downgrading the participation of the top U.S. military and intelligence officials in its deliberations?

If they have something in mind with respect to Russia that they want to surprise the country with as a *fait accompli*, as they surprised the country in the last week with executive orders, what could that something be?

Could it be the lifting of sanctions against Russia, which were imposed after its invasions of Crimea and eastern Ukraine in 2014?

Could it be recognition of the Russian annexation of Crimea?

Could it be a reversal of U.S. support for NATO's strengthening of its defenses against Russia in the Baltics and Eastern Europe?

If Bannon and Trump are playing to their alt-right base, which is very fond of Russia as "a great white power," was the omission of any mention of the Jews in the Holocaust proclamation last Friday the powerful tweet of a dog whistle for that base?

If Putin has *kompromat* or compromising information on Trump, he may be using that as well as renewed hostilities in eastern Ukraine to pressure Trump to make one or more of the concessions listed above, or others.

FURTHER READING

1) "President Trump's Speech to Congress and His Proposed 37% Cut in the State Department's Budget," *The Trenchant Observer*, March 1, 2017.[47]

2) Anne Applebaum, "Why is Trump Suddenly Talking about World War III?" *Washington Post*, October 28, 2016.[48]

See the detailed Applebaum quote reproduced in Chapter 9, above.

3) Jonathan Freedland, "Don't Treat Donald Trump as if He's a Normal President. He's Not," *The Guardian*, December 14, 2017 (7:00 a.m.).[49]

15

February 7, 2017

Trump's Tsunami of Lies

BACKGROUND

See,

1) Lawrence Douglas, "Why Trump Wants to Disempower Institutions That Protect the Truth; The US President Is Attacking the Very Institutions That Are Meant to Expose Lies: Universities, the Media and the Judiciary; Democracy Is Impossible Without Them," *The Guardian*, February 7, 2017 (11:00 GMT).[50]

2) Joe Scarborough, "Trump's Dangerous Lie about Russia," *Washington Post*, February 7, 2017 (9:51 p.m.).[51]

Like Vladimir Putin, Donald Trump spews lies like a firehose. The biggest are massive lies meant as much to shape the landscape where truth itself can be recognized as to persuade the audience of their claims.

The big lies are so blatantly false that if we are distracted into "verifying" or refuting them, we may miss the avalanche of other lies that are hurled at the population in a continuous fashion, all the time.

More importantly, we may miss the bigger story, which is the president's assault upon the truth.

55

Every day there are new lies, deployed to weave the fabric of an alternative universe in which at the end of the day there appears to be no truth, or many truths comprised of "alternative facts," or a truth so smudged by alternative truths that no one can recognize it as the one authentic truth.

We need to see Trump's lies for what they are, assaults upon the very concept of truth itself, where any formulation or description of real facts can be dismissed by the Leader with the wave of a hand.

At first, we don't know what to think, and then the mass of swirling lies becomes so all-pervasive that the only way we can make sense of a frightening and utterly confusing reality, where truth has lost its moorings in real and observable facts, is to accept the narrative and version of reality which the leader puts forth, together with his propaganda apparatus, everywhere, incessantly.

Newspapers like the *Washington Post*, which are afraid to call a big lie a big lie, e.g., diffidently referring to Trump's blatant big lie about the murder rate being higher than it's ever been in 45 or 47 years as "a false statement," only play into the hands of the leader.

Such formulations reflect very fine rules of fairness, while the leader declares the sun is square, and then adamantly and repeatedly asserts that it is square, until people start to wonder, "Can the sun be considered, at least in some respects, or viewed from a certain angle, as square?"

We need to see Trump's lies for what they are, as misrepresentations of facts intended to deceive, and not merely as "false statements." The latter formulation could lead the reader to surmise it was simply an inadvertent false statement, or a careless one, when the statement is in fact "material" and would constitute perjury, a felony, if it were made in a court of law.

See Tom Jackman, "Trump Makes False Statement about U.S. Murder Rate to Sheriffs' Group," *Washington Post*, February 7, 2017 (1:25 p.m. EST).[52]

Trump, like Putin, Slobodan Milosevic of Serbia, and Soviet and German leaders before them, wears us down with his lies, which are too blatant and numerous to refute.

What we are left with is a tsunami of lies, whose tidal wave and swirling black waters sweep all before them, uprooting a building here or an independent press or judiciary there. All obstacles and objections are swept away in the tsunami's waters, which cannot be held back.

It happened under Milosevic in Serbia. It has happened under Putin in Russia, and it could be happening in America under Trump, now.

This great democracy, America, with its proud 240-year trajectory, deserves a president who respects the truth, and who speaks the truth. Stop lying, Mr. Trump.

FURTHER READING

1) "The Level-of-analysis Problem in Assessing Trump's Assault on American Democracy," *The Trenchant Observer*, March 11, 2017.[53]

2) "Democrats Need to Sue Trump and Republican Apologists for Defamation," *The Trenchant Observer*, November 22, 2019.[54]

16

February 26, 2017

The Trump Paradox: "Making America Great Again"

Without the Values That Made America Great

The great paradox of President Donald Trump is that he promises to the American people that he will "Make America great again," but in practice appears to want to do so without honoring and defending the values that have made America great in the past.

The following are opinions based on analysis of indisputable facts.

President Trump wants to make America great again while attacking the most respected newspapers in the country (e.g., the *New York Times*, the *Washington Post*, and the *Wall Street Journal*) as "the enemy of the people." By libeling these and other newspapers and media outlets and leading an assault upon the press, he violates a central tenant of American democracy, freedom of the press, which is protected by the First Amendment.

Freedom of the press is central to any democracy and is the first target of all would-be dictators and authoritarians.

He wants to make America great again by attacking a "so-called judge" who is a U.S. District Court judge appointed pursuant to provisions in the Constitution.

He seeks to make America great again by cozying up to Vladimir Putin and Russia, who are conducting a full-fledged assault on American and European democratic traditions and institutions; who have rejected the United Nations Charter's prohibition of the illegal use of force across international frontiers by invading and annexing Crimea, and invading and occupying eastern Ukraine; and who have continuously violated the most fundamental provisions of international and humanitarian law ("the law of war") in Syria.

He seeks to make America great again by attacking the unanimous conclusions of 17 U.S. intelligence agencies that Russia intervened in the 2016 elections with the intent to favor his campaign, and the involvement of Vladimir Putin.

Above all, Donald Trump seeks to make America great again by conducting an all-out assault on the very concept of the truth itself.

By continually spouting major and minor lies, he appears to want to reshape the landscape of truth, so that he can dismiss any criticism, however factually based, by simply labeling it "fake news." All the while, he is constantly generating "fake news" of his own.

The Trump Paradox is glaring and screams forth from the heavens. President Trump wants to make America great again while violating the traditions and values which, over the course of some 240 years, have made America great, one of the greatest nations in history, emulated throughout the world.

This matters.

17

March 21, 2017

Trump Orders Tillerson to Skip NATO Summit, Travel to Moscow Instead

News that Rex Tillerson would skip an upcoming NATO foreign ministers meeting and travel instead to Moscow is the kind of news that produces a "What the f...?" reaction, almost too grotesque and unbelievable to be true.

But it is true.

To be sure, Vladimir Putin has been lying low, not engaging in any particularly egregious behavior (except in eastern Ukraine), but apparently, he and Donald Trump have concluded it is now safe to proceed with pro-Russian actions.

This is the second big pay-off to Putin since Trump became president on January 20, 2017. The first was an easing of U.S. sanctions against Russia to enable the Russian FSB (successor to the KGB) to resume collecting licensing fees for imported cell phones and other electronic equipment. Trump administration officials justified this as a mere "technical adjustment," but in fact it was a favor to the very agency that was involved in the intervention in the 2016 campaign and elections in the U.S., and also the agency alleged to have compromising information on Trump (*kompromat*) as per the Christopher Steele "golden showers" dossier.

See "'Technical Adjustment' on Russian Sanctions May Involve More Than Meets the Eye," *The Trenchant Observer*, February 2, 2017.[55]

Beyond the salacious details about Trump allegedly cavorting with Russian prostitutes (which Putin boasts are "the best in the world"), the Steele dossier alleges that Putin himself ordered the Russian intervention in the U.S. elections, and that there was active collusion and cooperation between the Trump campaign and individuals connected to Trump and Russian officials.

While news media have generally reported that the allegations in the Steele dossier cannot be corroborated, in point of fact a number of details in the dossier—though not the details of the "golden showers" episode— have been confirmed by intelligence officials speaking on background. Moreover, the dossier was a raw intelligence product. One would not expect that all of its details could be corroborated, given the nature of Steele's sources.

See,

Andy Towle, "Rachel Maddow: Details of Trump-Russia Dossier Keep Checking Out as Its Author Reemerges from Hiding," Towleroad, March 8, 2017 (8:15 a.m.).[56]

2) Rachel Maddow, "More Pieces of Donald Trump Russia Dossier," MSNBC, March 7, 2017, found on YouTube: https://www.youtube.com/watch?v=5exiuko3-nQ.

Reflect for a moment on the message Trump is sending to our NATO allies, Russia and other countries.

Consider also the message Trump is sending to voters in countries like France who will participate in elections such as the French presidential election, where Marine Le Pen of the far-right Front National, with Russian financial support, is running on a pro-Russian platform.

Days after meeting with Angela Merkel of Germany, now the embodiment of the liberal military and political order based on the United Nations Charter, and for many the current leader of the Free World, Trump is doubling down by snubbing NATO and giving Russia a great propaganda victory.

What Trump is doing is anathema to foreign policy experts who understand the importance of not bowing to a dictator who engineered an unprecedented attempt to throw the 2016 presidential election to Trump, and to also influence the congressional elections, and who has invaded and currently occupies part of Ukraine.

The greatest irony is that Trump's actions come at the same time FBI director James Comey has confirmed in congressional testimony that Trump and his campaign are the current subjects of a counter-espionage investigation into cooperation and collusion with Russian officials during the 2016 campaign.

As for Tillerson, we should recall how he strained credulity by testifying in his Senate confirmation hearings that he had not discussed Russia with Trump.

See John Nichols, "Rex Tillerson's Jaw-Dropping Testimony Just Completely Disqualified Him," *The Nation*, January 12, 2017.[57]

Perhaps the best that can be said for Tillerson is that he is either oblivious or indifferent to the symbolism and impact of his actions toward NATO and Russia. Otherwise, he looks like a willing tool of the Trojan horse candidate who has become the pro-Russian president of the United States.

18

March 27, 2017

SATIRE AND REALITY:
Trump Brings Genius
and His Brilliant
Wife to the White House

President Donald Trump is known for his intuitive, even instinctual, grasp of complex problems and their solutions. While it took him months to select a secretary of state and to fill other key cabinet positions, he was led by blinding instinctual insight to choose two of his most important and intimate advisors.

While others might have taken months or even years to find the most brilliant man on the planet and his brilliant wife, Trump—through his extraordinary power of intuition—found the genius and the genius' wife in almost no time at all.

He put the young man quickly to work, meeting with the Russian ambassador and even a high-level Russian banking official, all before Secretary of State Rex Tillerson was confirmed. Even after Tillerson was sworn in, there was little need for haste in filling out the upper echelons of the State Department, or the Pentagon, as the young genius had everything under control.

Trump came to rely heavily on the young genius, particularly after his national security advisor, Michael Flynn, was chased from office because he told a little lie to Vice President Michael Pence, who took the whole thing *very* seriously. *Unjust,* the president thought. For telling a little lie to Pence. Flynn had not lied to the young genius or to *him.*

The greatest thing about the young genius was his brilliant wife, who was not only beautiful and charming, but also seemed to have her finger on the pulse of the younger and more normal people who made up such a large percentage of the electorate.

The young genius was charged with solving the Arab-Israeli and Middle East problems, general tutelage in the area of foreign policy, and now—one of the president's most brilliant ideas—leading government reform by applying principles from private business to the government of the country.

The president, himself from the world of business, had been absolutely amazed to hear from his advisors that this new concept had never been tried before.

As for the wife of the young genius, the president was delighted to use her on any and every problem where he needed advice. The genius and his brilliant wife were particularly useful to the president in mediating between the various power centers which had grown up, almost like mushrooms, in the corridors of power leading to the Oval Office.

When outsiders called the president's attention to the fact that the young genius was his son-in-law, Jared Kushner, and his brilliant wife the president's daughter, Ivanka Trump, the president shrugged his shoulders and simply observed, "Sometimes genius and brilliance surprise you, and turn out to be closer than you would ever think."

19

April 13, 2017

Unanswered Questions about the Death of Russia's U.N. Ambassador

and the U.S. Role in Suppressing His Autopsy Results

Russia's deceased U.N. Ambassador, Vitaly Churkin, may well have been aware of the details of Russian intervention in the 2016 U.S. elections. The State Department intervened to prevent autopsy results from becoming public.

Among those on the list of Russian diplomats and other top officials who died suddenly in the last six months is Vitaly Churkin, Russia's U.N. Ambassador and head of the U.N. Mission in New York.

See

1) Somini Sengupta, "Vitaly Churkin, Russia's U.N. Ambassador, Dies at 64," *New York Times*, February 20, 2017.[58]

2) AP, "NYC Medical Examiner Says More Study Needed in Death of Russian Diplomat," *CBS News*, February 21, 2017 (2:30 p.m.):[59]

NEW YORK – The cause and manner of death of Russia's ambassador to the United Nations needs to be studied further, the city medical examiner said Tuesday, a day after the diplomat fell ill at his office at Russia's U.N. mission and died at a hospital.

Further study usually includes toxicology and other screenings, which can take weeks. The case was referred to the medical examiner's office by the hospital, spokeswoman Julie Bolcer said.

3) Somini Sengupta, "New York Examiner Won't Disclose Cause of Russian Envoy's Death," *New York Times*, March 10, 2017.[60]

4) Dr. Catherine Mullaly, "US Mission to the UN: Do Not Release Vitaly Churkin's Autopsy Report," *Pass Blue* Independent Coverage of the U.N., March 12, 2017:[61]

Four days after Russian Ambassador Vitaly Churkin's sudden death in New York City last month, the United States Mission to the United Nations wrote to the New York City Mayor's Office for International Affairs and requested a communications blackout on Churkin's autopsy findings and cause of death. The result of this request means that the public may never know the official reason for the ambassador's death.

…

The autopsy communication constraints were not the case for a second Russian national, Sergei Krivov, who died unexpectedly at age 63 at the Russian consulate on the Upper East Side in New York City on Nov. 8, 2016. The chief medical examiner's office released his cause of death, which was "hemorrhagic complications of aorto-bron-cho-esophageal fistula due to probable neoplasm." Krivov died of natural causes.

5) Dulcie Leimbach, "Vitaly Churkin, 64, Russia's Longtime Ambassador to the UN, Dies Suddenly," *Pass Blue* Independent Coverage of the U.N.," February 20, 2017.[62]

A little-noticed passage from the Christopher Steele dossier on Russian intervention in the 2016 U.S. elections and collusion between Russian officials and Trump associates, also known as the "Golden Showers" dossier, declares that "Russian diplomatic staff in key cities such as New York" were used to direct payments to U.S.-based actors involved in the intervention into the election and the information flows involved.

Excerpt from Christopher Steel dossier ("Golden Showers" dossier), at p. 8:

COMPANY INTELLIGENCE REPORT 2016/095

...

2. Inter alia, Source E, acknowledged that the Russian regime had been behind the recent leak of embarrassing e-mail messages, emanating from the Democratic National Committee (DNC), to the WikiLeaks platform.

The reason for using WikiLeaks was "plausible deniability" and the operation had been conducted with the full knowledge and support of TRUMP and senior members of his campaign team. In return the TRUMP team had agreed to sideline Russian intervention in Ukraine as a campaign issue and to raise defence commitments in the Baltics and Eastern Europe to deflect attention away from Ukraine, a priority for PUTIN who needed to cauterise the subject.

3. In the wider context campaign/Kremlin co-operation, Source claimed that the intelligence network being used against CLINTON comprised three elements. there were agents/facilitators within the Democratic Party structure itself; secondly Russian emigrant and associated offensive cyber operators based in the U.S.; and thirdly, state-sponsored cyber operatives working in Russia. All three elements had played an important role to date. On the mechanism for rewarding relevant assets based in the US, and effecting a two-way flow of intelligence and other useful information, **Source claimed that Russian diplomatic staff in key cities such as New York, Washington DC and Miami were using the emigrant pension distribution system as cover**. [emphasis added] The operation therefore depended on key people in the US Russian emigrant community for its success. Tens of thousands of dollars were involved.

For the full text of the Christopher Steele dossier, *see*: Ken Bensinger, Miriam Elder (BuzzFeed News World Editor), and Mark Schoofs, "These Reports Allege Trump Has Deep Ties to Russia; A Dossier, Compiled by a Person Who Has Claimed to Be a Former British Intelligence Official, Alleges Russia Has Compromising Information on Trump. The Allegations are Unverified, and the Report Contains Errors," BuzzFeed, January 10, 2017 (3:20 p.m.; updated at 6:09 p.m.).[63]

Vitaly Churkin was the head of the Russian diplomatic mission and consulate in New York City. He certainly should have known the details about payments and information flows related to the Russian intervention in the 2016 elections.

Could his knowledge have become inconvenient to Vladimir Putin?

Why did the State Department do the Kremlin's bidding by suppressing publication of the autopsy report? In doing so they used extremely dubious legal arguments such as the assertion that Churkin's diplomatic immunity continued after his death and applied to his corpse.

These facts bear closer examination, particularly in view of the State Department's firm directions to the NYC Medical Examiner's office to make no public comment on the circumstances of Churkin's death, and to not publish the autopsy report.

Tillerson had recently been confirmed.

How could this have occurred, with one of the largest counter-espionage investigations in history underway?

Was it sheer incompetence, or a favor to Putin?

In any event, the FBI and the congressional intelligence committees looking into possible collusion between the Russians and Trump's associates will want to subpoena the autopsy report, and also look carefully into what Churkin may have known about the Russian intervention.

20

April 19, 2017

Has Tillerson Shown His Cards?

Exxon Mobil Moves to Dismantle Russian Sanctions

Revised April 21, 2017

Two of the things Rex Tillerson said in his Senate confirmation hearings appear to have been either extremely misleading or simply untrue.

The first was his assertion that he had not discussed Russia with Trump during the selection process leading to his nomination. This statement more than strains credulity, since one of the reasons he was picked was reportedly his longstanding relationship with Vladimir Putin.

The second was his statement that he had not lobbied against the Russian sanctions imposed in response to Russia's invasion of Crimea and eastern Ukraine in 2014. The National Association of Manufacturers and the U.S. Chamber of Commerce placed full-page ads in the *New York Times*, the *Wall Street Journal* and other papers strenuously arguing against the imposition of sanctions. Exxon Mobil was involved.

See "American Big Business Votes for Appeasement with Russia; Interview with Prime Minister Taavi Roivas of Estonia," *The Trenchant Observer*, June 25, 2014.[64] (Reader must scroll down on linked-to page to find specific article.)

Now, less than two weeks after returning from lengthy conversations with Putin and foreign minister Sergey Lavrov in Moscow, there is renewed interest on the part of Exxon Mobil in its application for an "exception" to the Russian sanctions.

See

1) Jay Solomon and Bradley Olson, "Exxon Seeks U.S. Waiver to Resume Russia Oil Venture; Exxon Mobil Applied to Treasury for Exemption to Resume Venture with Rosneft Forged in 2012 by Rex Tillerson," *Wall Street Journal*, April 19, 2017 (updated 3:53 p.m. ET).[65]

2) Clifford Kraus, "Exxon Mobil Seeks U.S. Sanctions Waiver for Oil Project in Russia," *New York Times*, April 19, 2017.[66]

Let there be no doubt. Such an exception, if granted, would quickly lead to the collapse of Russian sanctions imposed not only by the U.S. but also by the EU. Which of the 28 members of the EU would not have its own "special case" meriting an exemption from the sanctions?

Now it may be that Exxon Mobil's renewed push for an exception is just a feint, aimed at measuring the real level of resistance in the Trump administration to the lifting of the sanctions. Whether in earnest or a feint, the move provides a stark illustration of how Exxon Mobil's foreign policy objectives differ from those of the U.S.

Exxon Mobil stands to lose significant business opportunities in Russia. The U.S. and the West stand to lose the integrity of the United Nations Charter and Article 2(4) which prohibits the threat or use of force across international frontiers.

Russia's violations of this prohibition, by invading Crimea and eastern Ukraine, is why the sanctions were put in place. To weaken or lift the sanctions while Russia occupies these Ukrainian territories with troops would directly undermine the political, military, and security order established in the U.N. Charter in 1945.

Would Exxon Mobil make such a move, continuing its push for approval of its application for an exception with the Trump administration, without some sense of how receptive Tillerson might be, and maybe even some sense of the extent to which Exxon Mobil's oil exploration agreements were discussed in Tillerson's meetings with the Russians in Moscow?

Tillerson has recused himself from playing any formal role in the State Department's decisions regarding Exxon Mobil's request for an exception to the sanctions. That does not prevent him from giving a wink and a nod to his old friends and colleagues at Exxon Mobil.

The Senate should call Tillerson to testify about what he discussed with Putin and Lavrov, and whether the topics included oil and gas exploration in Russia by Exxon Mobil and others, or an "exception" to the sanctions.

We have a right to know Tillerson's thinking about sanctions.

We have a right to know why he has not filled the top positions in the State Department, seven weeks after he was confirmed by the Senate.

Tillerson, like Trump, needs to be held accountable for his actions.

To date, by his inaction he has crippled the diplomacy of the State Department and the United States. We don't know why he hasn't filled these positions, or his sense of urgency and his timetable for doing so in the future.

To date, we don't know what was said in his talks with Putin and Lavrov in Moscow.

We need to know.

21

May 8, 2017

Trump's Support for Marine Le Pen Shames America

BACKGROUND

Donald Trump has offered a tacit endorsement of Marine Le Pen in the French presidential election, describing the far-right leader as the "strongest" candidate in the first-round vote this Sunday.

The US president told the Associated Press that although he was not "explicitly endorsing" the leader of the Front National, she was the "strongest on borders, and she's the strongest on what's been going on in France."

. . .

"Whoever is the toughest on radical Islamic terrorism, and whoever is the toughest at the borders, will do well in the election," he said.

–Ben Jacobs (Washington), "Donald Trump, Marine Le Pen Is 'Strongest Candidate' in French Election," *The Guardian*, April 21, 2017 (16:26 EDT), (updated April 25, 2017 at 02:31 EDT).[67]

Trump's subsequent clever use of words to deny he supports Le Pen follows his typical pattern of saying things that send a clear message to his supporters, and then walking them back to confuse and avoid responsibility for what he says.

His tweet was a clear tweet, like on a dog whistle, which his supporters and right-wing racists and extremists in France could not fail to understand. Explicitly, he did say, Le Pen was the "strongest on borders, and she's the strongest on what's been going on in France."

The shame is that the Front National has a history and appeals to candidates that include holocaust deniers (like Jean-Marie Le Pen—father of Marine Le Pen—for many years the leader of the Front National) and others who minimize France's responsibility for collaborating with the Germans under the Vichy regime and German occupation during World War II. See AFP, " France's Jean-Marie Le Pen Defends Vichy Leader in Memoir," AFP, February 20, 2018 (12:43).[68]

For a world without memory, which many of Trump's supporters seem to inhabit, these details of history are not important. They might agree with Jean-Marie Le Pen, Marine's father and founder and long-time leader of the Front National, who repeatedly has said that the holocaust was merely a "detail of history."

That the President of the United States, a nation that led the battle against fascism and the Vichy and Nazi regimes in Europe, might express support for the candidate of the extreme right-wing party in France that harbors holocaust-deniers, is one of the most shameful acts of a truly shameful government.

The most important thing, for those who are still thinking and remembering the lessons of history, is to not let their sense of outrage be dulled by repeated and scandalous violations of the norms of civilization and simple decency.

The standards the Trump administration must be judged by are the same standards all governments in all countries must be judged by: its support for and observance of international law including the defense of human rights, in all countries, at all times.

When those standards are violated, those who believe in international law, human rights, and the United Nations Charter must stand up and denounce the violations, and the silence of those who look the other way.

See Ted Piccone, "Tillerson Says Goodbye to Human Rights Diplomacy," *Brookings Briefs*, May 5, 2017.[69]

To not support human rights, to not speak out about gross violations when that is inconvenient in dealing with authoritarian leaders and regimes, is similar to what Marine Le Pen has done, by not denouncing French participation in the deportation of Jews to concentration camps during World War II.

To meet with authoritarian leaders like Rodrigo Duterte of the Philippines, Vladimir Putin of Russia, or Recep Tayyip Erdogan of Turkey, or at a minimum to do so without insisting strongly on the observance of fundamental human rights and raising their violation as a central issue, is to join the collaborationists of World War II, and the appeasers of the present.

Duterte has boasted of personally murdering drug suspects. He is reported to have run death squads when he was mayor of a provincial city. He has urged the extrajudicial execution of thousands of drug suspects since taking office in the Philippines in June.

Putin launched the Russian military invasions of Crimea and eastern Ukraine in 2014 and has supported and joined in the commission of war crimes in Syria.

Erdogan is responsible for dismantling the rule of law in Turkey, with repression of a free press and the arrests of tens of thousands of individuals, and dismissals from their posts of tens of thousands of judges, army, police and other officials without any due process.

Western civilization, which has now spread throughout the world, is too broad and deep to not one day look back on the Trump administration and the Front National as gross departures from a story of progress over the last thousand years.

After Greece and Rome, this story began in its current phase with the Magna Carta in 1215, was expressed in the Enlightenment and the French and American revolutions in the 18th century, and culminated in the military defeat of fascism and the creation of the United Nations in 1945.

Those who glibly speak of the old "liberal international order" now being passé, without knowing anything about history or what generations throughout the world have struggled for and achieved, to extend liberty and prevent war, should be honest and simply say they want to abolish the United Nations Charter, and replace it with... with what?

22

May 11, 2017

Flynn, Comey, and Russians in the Oval Office

BACKGROUND

See Michael Crowley, "Trump's Big Russia Reset; With Washington in an Uproar over James Comey's Firing amid His Russia Probe, the President and His Secretary of State Welcomed Foreign Minister Sergey Lavrov to Town," *Politico*, May 10, 2017 (updated 05:35 p.m. EDT).[70]

Russians in the Oval Office

Vladimir Putin was absolutely beaming yesterday from the hockey game where he was interviewed by an American TV reporter. His opinion about the dismissal of FBI Director Comey: It was all done in accordance with American law and procedures. The smirk on his face was hardly concealed.

His foreign minister, Sergey Lavrov, met with Secretary of State Rex Tillerson in the morning at the State Department, and then with President Trump and Russian ambassador Sergey Kislyak at the White House. This was the same Russian ambassador who met with Michael Flynn, Jared Kushner, and other Trump associates during the campaign and the transition. These meetings are part of the FBI and congressional investigations into whether there was collusion with the Russians during the Trump campaign and transition.

The Trump White House did not allow American press or photographers to attend the meeting and gave no real details about who attended and what was discussed. What we know, we know from the Russians and the pictures they posted online on the Tass news agency website.

In the pictures, Trump and his guests were smiling broadly. Earlier, at the State Department, responding to a reporter's shouted question, Lavrov had expressed his contempt for the American press by pretending he hadn't heard of Comey's dismissal, concluding his sarcastic answer with a disdainful jerk of his head as he entered through the doors to meet with Tillerson.

We don't know why everyone seemed so happy in the pictures. Was it because Trump had fresh assurances that *kompromat* would not be used against him by the Russians, or his and the Russians' belief that by decapitating the FBI and firing Comey the investigation could be stopped before it got to Trump and details of the collusion?

Or perhaps the Russians were simply happy to be in Washington in the beautiful spring weather. Perhaps they were also happy that neither Tillerson nor Trump put them on the spot publicly for their invasions of Crimea and eastern Ukraine in the spring and summer of 2014, or their complicity and active participation in the commission of horrendous war crimes and crimes against humanity in Syria, or their violations of fundamental human rights in Russia by, for example, assassinating Boris Nemtsov in February 2015, or attacking the most important opposition leader today, Alexei Navalny, in the last few months (with liquid and chemical attacks, the second of which may have cost him the sight in one eye).

They must have been happy with Tillerson's recent speech to State Department employees setting forth the policy that while Americans would be mindful of their values, they wouldn't let those values get in the way when dealing with important economic or security issues.

In fact, the groundwork has been laid for the lifting of U.S. Russian sanctions as soon as Trump and Tillerson feel they can get away with it at an acceptable cost. Viewed in this light, the recent renewed push by Exxon Mobil for an exception to the sanctions must be understood not as unfounded but as simply premature.

There was no joint press conference. Lavrov gave a press conference at the Russian embassy, where he was free to spin his lies, denying for example that there had been any Russian interference in the U.S. elections in November.

By providing pictures, the Russians have actually done a great favor for the patriotic candidates who in 2018 will oppose those Republicans who have given Trump cover with the Russians, by acting to help him slow or block the investigations into his collusion with them.

Testimony of Sally Yates

The second big development in the last ten days was the testimony of Sally Yates, the former acting attorney general who gave the White House specific information that the then director of national security, Michael Flynn, was compromised with the Russians. He was subject to blackmail by them, given the differing accounts he gave to Vice President Mike Pence and the FBI regarding his conversations with the Russian ambassador about the easing of sanctions. He may, in fact, have been compromised by a lot more than that.

After receiving the information that Flynn could be compromised by the Russians, Trump and his White House did absolutely nothing *for 18 days*, dismissing Flynn only after news of Yates' warnings appeared in the Washington Post.

For 18 days, Trump left in place a national security advisor who was subject to blackmail by the Russians. Read this sentence again and reflect on its implications.

Trump Fires FBI Director James Comey

The third development in recent days has been Trump's brutal firing of FBI Director James Comey on Tuesday, June 9, and the huge lie he put out about the reason being Comey's mishandling of Hillary Clinton's e-mail investigation. In an interview with Lester Holt of NBC on June 11, Trump admitted that he was going to fire Comey in any event, and that he was thinking that the Russia investigation had gone on for too long.

Key Witness Michael Flynn

After Comey's firing, it was learned that subpoenas have been issued to Michael Flynn to produce all papers and records related to his contacts and business dealings with the Russians.

Flynn has apparently committed acts which might constitute serious crimes. If prosecuted and convicted, he could spend many years in prison. His earlier efforts to gain immunity in exchange for his testimony before congressional committees failed.

Flynn's testimony could be explosive. It may be the key to blowing open the conspiracy involving collusion with the Russians, if there is one. If he talks, he could bring the whole Trump charade on Russia crashing down. Hopefully he is under very good security protection.

Russia's "Trump card" Is Working

Putin's "Trump card" is already paying off. While the focus in the U.S. media has been on whether there was collusion between the Trump campaign and the Russians when the latter intervened in the U.S. election, less attention has been paid to the reasons for Trump's pro-Russian positions and failure to criticize Putin or Russia.

The strongest hypothesis for this behavior is that Trump has been compromised by the Russians. This will remain the strongest hypothesis until an alternative, more persuasive explanation, is presented.

Contrary to earlier reports in the press, a number of elements of the Christopher Steele dossier have now been corroborated. Other facts in that dossier, by their very nature, may not be subject to confirmation by news or intelligence agencies without Steele's contacts. Some of his sources may now be dead.

It is hard to imagine a U.S. administration not compromised by the Russians where:

1. The president has steadfastly refused to criticize Putin or the Russians directly for more than a year.

2. The secretary of state and the president meet with the Russian foreign minister in the Oval Office and at the State Department for the first time since Russia invaded and annexed Crimea in February and March 2014, and invaded eastern Ukraine in the summer of 2014; they hold no news conference; and they make no public mention of the invasions or the fact they have been the main causes for bad relations between the two countries and the imposition of U.S. and EU sanctions.

3. At these meetings on May 10, the president and secretary of state make no public comment on the Russian intervention in the November 2016 U.S. elections, at the direction of Vladimir Putin, and allow the Russian foreign minister's assertion at his press conference at the Russian embassy that Russia was not involved in any such intervention to go unchallenged.

In making judgments about Russian influence in the Trump administration, we should not seek to apply a criminal law standard of "guilty beyond a reasonable doubt," but rather use common sense and look to the conclusions that "a preponderance of the evidence" point to.

Are there any more likely explanations for Trump's policies and actions toward Putin and Russia?

FURTHER READING

"Trump's Attitude of Appeasement toward Russia Makes Big Inroads among Republican Voters, *The Trenchant Observer,* June 28, 2017.[71]

23

May 24, 2017

Normalization of the Unforgivable—Trump and an America Already Half Lost

With Donald Trump, we have been witnessing the normalization of the unforgivable.

The rise of an authoritarian leader in the United States, who, through outrageous lies, thuggish behavior, and the assistance of a large-scale Russian intervention in the 2016 elections, became president, would be great material for a movie but in fact be unbelievable, unless, of course, it actually happened.

During his campaign in 2016, the transition, and now his four months in office, Donald Trump has erased the boundaries of the impermissible, the unthinkable, and the very concept of the truth itself.

Now, in 2017, we can for perhaps the first time in many decades understand what happened after 1932 with the rise of the National Socialist Party and its leader in Germany. Timothy Snyder in *On Tyranny: Twenty Lessons from the Twentieth Century* describes the gradual acceptance by ordinary and erstwhile upright and honorable men and women of behavior which in earlier years had been unthinkable.

What is astounding is how fast the standards of decency and democratic life have fallen victim to the mean-spirited and hate-filled ideology of Trump and his supporters, and the ever-growing number of yes-men and apologists who are found among Republicans in Congress and in the party as a whole.

Many critics of Trump lean over backwards to insist we try harder to understand the hardships and frustrations of his core supporters. Few are willing or courageous enough to pass judgment on these voters, who made a Faustian bargain to accept Trump's hate, his attack on the truth, and his attack on the institutions of our democracy, including an independent press, in exchange for what he seemed to offer.

He offered an endless profusion of illusory promises of jobs and making America great again, which persuaded his undereducated base. He also held out the promise of curbing immigration. Others, guided by their own ideology of primitive capitalism, followed and continue to support Trump out of cynical calculations that under Trump they will be able to redistribute wealth and welfare to the rich.

So, Faustian bargains, of two varieties, have given impetus to the authoritarian movement of Donald Trump.

At present, it seems that Trumpism has taken over the minds of upwards of 40 percent of those who vote. Snyder recounts how, during the rise of Nazism, individuals suddenly flipped to become Nazis, succumbing to the power of mass psychology. Eugène Ionesco, in his play *Rhinoceros*, depicted such metamorphoses by showing those who suddenly flipped as assuming the form of a rhinoceros.

In America today we can see many politicians who have now assumed the form of a rhinoceros. The unthinkable has become normal. They argue that the unacceptable must be understood. They lie. They lie big time. They twist themselves into pretzels defending untruths.

Critics reassure themselves that everything is under control, and that the democratic institutions of the country will contain the excesses of Trump and Trumpism.

While in the end they may be right, an honest observer would have to admit that the outcome is uncertain.

Trump and his supporters could win the struggle for the soul of the country.

To appreciate that possibility we need only look at what they have achieved so far.

For example, they have achieved the normalization and acceptance of monstrous lies, such as those contained in Trump's new budget proposal, or in the statements of those who defend the health care bill that recently passed the House.

They have rendered the democratic principles of conflict-of-interest and nepotism nearly meaningless.

They have turned American foreign policy on its head, jettisoning the defense of human rights while cozying up to authoritarian regimes. They have weakened NATO's mutual self-defense commitments, while supporting those who would undermine the European Union.

Trump has already destroyed much of the fabric of civic life, where discourse in a democratic society can only be conducted with a certain respect for facts and the truth.

The most frightening fact is that after all his lies have been revealed for what they are, Trump continues to enjoy strong support among 35-40 percent of the population.

This is what has happened to America, in the last two years.

See David Ignatius, "Get Ready for the 'Impeachment Election'," Washington Post, May 23, 2017.[72] Ignatius writes:

> "Under our Constitution, the House and Senate are prosecutor and jury, respectively, for serious presidential misconduct. But this legal process probably won't be triggered without a poisonously divisive election. If recent history teaches anything, it's unfortunately this harsh fact: In the battle for America's soul, Trump could win."

What lies ahead can only be viewed with extreme foreboding, so long as Trump and the rhinoceroses who support him retain their hold on power.

Each day they chip away a little more at our concepts of the truth, of decency, and of the bulwarks against authoritarian behaviors that exist in a democracy.

We are desensitized. The outrage is drained from our souls. We begin to make excuses for Trump and his rhinoceroses.

We begin to acquiesce.

24

June 17, 2017

By Obstructing Justice, Trump Threatens the Rule of Law in the U. S.

In testimony last week, fired FBI Director James Comey testified to the occurrence of facts which constitute a compelling case of obstruction of justice by the President of the United States. According to the *Washington Post*, Trump's attempts to influence the investigation of Michael Flynn included not only his entreaty to Comey to let the Flynn matter go, but also similar appeals to other top intelligence officials.

Since the Comey testimony, Trump has engaged in a vicious series of attacks on Robert Mueller and others working on the investigation into the Trump campaign's contacts with Russians—before and during the 2016 presidential campaign, during the transition, and since Trump assumed office on January 20, 2017.

In effect, Trump not only appears to have engaged in obstruction of justice in asking Comey to drop the Flynn investigation and then firing Comey when he didn't, but also to be engaged in an ongoing series of actions aimed at influencing the investigation. These actions include his vicious attacks on Mueller and his team, and his very obvious attempt to plant uncertainty in the minds of Mueller and others as to whether they will be fired.

Each day, Trump engages in new acts of apparent obstruction of justice.

The country is faced with an unprecedented situation in which it is possible if not likely that a criminal clique is in control of the government of the United States and is systematically attempting to dismantle the ongoing investigations into their crimes. In the case of Trump, these include his "high crimes and misdemeanors," in the words of the Constitution stating grounds for impeachment.

The situation is somewhat similar to that faced by Guatemala not too many years ago, when a lawyer involved with drug cartels was installed as attorney general of the nation. He immediately began releasing drug criminals from prison, it was a matter of some weeks before he was removed from office.

Here, we have a president against whom a strong *prima facie* case of obstruction of justice has been made in sworn congressional testimony by former FBI Director Comey, who until the last few days has been universally respected as a man with a record of great integrity. The obstruction of justice consists in allegedly directing efforts aimed at influencing if not ending investigations into Michael Flynn, and Trump's own potential criminal activities and impeachable offenses.

Politicians have been reluctant to state the obvious: Trump appears to be guilty of obstruction of justice, and to be engaged in continuing efforts to obstruct justice. He may fire Special Counsel Robert Mueller within days. The desperate logic of his situation and his reported emotional state suggest that he will.

Important legal questions arise. First, if Trump attempts to fire Mueller in order to obstruct justice, would his order be lawful and produce legal effects? In other words, would Trump's order to dismiss Mueller be legally effective if the order itself involved the commission of the felony of obstruction of justice? Could Mueller or others challenge the dismissal in the courts?

While these questions may appear unrealistic, they merit urgent and serious consideration. To use an extreme example to make a legal point, could the vice president lawfully assume the presidency through the act of murdering the president?

We all need to recognize that Trump and his coterie are engaged in a no-holds-barred struggle for power and appear unconstrained by the rule of law in that struggle.

It is time for those who believe in the rule of law and the Constitution to stop showing deference to the president, and to start speaking out in candor about what is occurring.

Today, Senator Dianne Feinstein (D-California) did just that. She stated:

I'm growing increasingly concerned that the president will attempt to fire not only Robert Mueller, the special counsel investigating possible obstruction of justice, but also Deputy Attorney General Rosenstein who appointed Mueller.

The message the president is sending through his tweets is that he believes the rule of law doesn't apply to him and that anyone who thinks otherwise will be fired. That's undemocratic on its face and a blatant violation of the president's oath of office.

First of all, the president has no authority to fire Robert Mueller. That authority clearly lies with the attorney general—or in this case, because the attorney general has recused himself, with the deputy attorney general. Rosenstein testified under oath this week that he would not fire Mueller without good cause and that none exists.

And second, if the president thinks he can fire Deputy Attorney General Rosenstein and replace him with someone who will shut down the investigation, he's in for a rude awakening. Even his staunchest supporters will balk at such a blatant effort to subvert the law.

It's becoming clear to me that the president has embarked on an effort to undermine anyone with the ability to bring any misdeeds to light, be that Congress, the media or the Justice Department. The Senate should not let that happen. We're a nation of laws that apply equally to everyone, a lesson the president would be wise to learn.

–Senator Dianne Feinstein (D-CA). Because Senator Feinstein is deceased, she no longer has an office. The interested researcher should contact the National Archives. See https://www.archives.gov."

Senator Feinstein deserves our highest praise for her "profile in courage," for standing out when others were content to criticize without speaking clearly and consequentially.

FURTHER READING

Timothy Snyder, *On Tyranny: Twenty Lessons from the Twentieth Century*, New York: Crown Publishing Group, 2017, Chapter 8 ("Stand Out").

25

July 22, 2017

Trump's Implementation of Putin's Goals

We need to focus on actions taken by the U.S. that amount to Trump's implementation of Putin's goals.

With the daily revelations about President Donald Trump and his and his associates' contacts with Russians and their potential conspiracy to intervene in the 2016 U.S. elections, it is easy to lose sight of how pro-Russian U.S. foreign policy under Trump has become, and the ways in which Trump is implementing policies which further Vladimir Putin's and Russia's goals.

There are several different items to consider.

1. In the news this week is Trump's temptation to return the Russian diplomatic compounds seized under the terms of the sanctions adopted by President Barack Obama in December 2016, in response to the major Russian intervention in the U.S. elections. Putin and Lavrov have even threatened the United States with retaliation if the properties are not returned. Michael Flynn, it will be recalled, urged the Russian ambassador not to retaliate against the U.S. sanctions, as Trump would review them once in office. Russia at that time did not retaliate.

It appears that Trump wants to return the properties with no quid pro quo, with the result that aside from expelling 35 Russian intelligence operatives in December as part of Obama's sanctions and adding a few individuals and companies to the sanctions list, the U.S. will not have imposed any real penalties on Russia for its actions. These actions constitute a blatant violation of the international law principle of non-intervention in the internal affairs of another state.

2. In eastern Ukraine, there are gathering signs that the United States might be willing to abandon its European allies and the Minsk II Protocol of February 12, 2015, in order to give Putin a settlement on terms Russia desires.

Rex Tillerson recently suggested that he might be looking for a settlement of the Ukraine issue outside the framework of the Minsk II Protocol.

The United States has appointed a special ambassador to deal with the issue at the request of Putin, in effect injecting the United States into a peace process that up until now has been run by France, Germany, Russia and Ukraine under what is known as "the Normandy format."

It is something of a first for a U.S. president to create a diplomatic position and fill it in response to a request from a Russian leader.

Further, the leader of the Donetsk People's Republic, Alexander Zakharchenko, has just set forth a proposal for the creation of a new state in eastern Ukraine, effectively seceding from Ukraine in violation of all of the commitments contained in the Minsk II Protocol. The timing of the proposal, by a Putin puppet totally dependent on Russia, is probably not an accident.

See

1) Andrew Osborn and Natalia Zinets, "Pro-Russian Rebel Leader in East Ukraine Unveils Plan for New State," *Reuters*, July 18, 2017 (5:35 a.m.).[73]

2) Adam Garrie, "DONETSK: Alexander Zakharchenko Declares New State of Malorossiya," *The Duran*, July 18, 2017.[74]

3) The United States has just announced that it has cut off assistance to the "moderate Syrian rebels," removing the last leverage the United States had to resist the will of Russia and the Bashar al-Assad government in Syria.

4) Secretary of State Rex Tillerson has announced that the State Department is closing down its office responsible for identifying and pursuing war criminals. Punishing war criminals is no longer a mission of the State Department, which will come as a great relief to Vladimir Putin and other Russians who have been directly responsible for the commission of war crimes and crimes against humanity in Syria, and who have been complicit in the commission of such crimes on a massive scale by the al-Assad government.

This action will limit the State Department's role in identifying individuals who might be subject to sanctions under the Magnitsky Act.[75]

5) Tillerson has enunciated a policy that makes it clear that the United States will no longer exert pressure on other states to observe and defend human rights. In effect, the U.S. is shutting down its "bully pulpit" on human rights.

Following Trump's visit to Saudi Arabia, during which he participated in a sword dance with the Saudis but failed to mention the country's terrible record on human rights, a Saudi-led coalition imposed a blockade on Qatar in clear violation of international law.

In his visit to Poland prior to the G-20 summit in Hamburg, Trump praised the government but made no criticisms of the country's troubling record on human rights. In the last few days, the Polish congress has adopted legislation that effectively does away with independence of the judiciary in that country.

Significantly, in his conversations with Putin at the G-20 in Hamburg, Trump does not appear to have raised any human rights concerns, despite the ongoing suppression of a free press and public demonstrations in Russia.

In a word, the greatest beacon for the promotion and defense of human rights in the world, the president and government of the United States, has been turned off. Its power has been cut off. The light has gone out.

6) Exxon Mobil attempted in February to float the idea of an exemption from sanctions for its oil and gas exploration deals in Russia. When its efforts were revealed in the press, the opposition was intense, and the Trump administration abandoned any plans to ease the sanctions immediately. It has now been made public that Exxon Mobil also violated the anti-Russian economic sanctions while Rex Tillerson was its CEO.

It seems evident that he and Trump would like to lift the 2014 economic sanctions imposed against Russia following its conquest and purported "annexation" of Crimea, and its invasion of the regions of Donetsk and Luhansk in the so-called Donbas region of eastern Ukraine. For now, the political opposition is too strong. The imminent adoption of legislation requiring congressional review before the lifting of any sanctions will pose additional hurdles.

7) The Trump administration did Putin and Russia a big favor in December when they eased sanctions on the import of cell phones and related technology by the FSB (the former KGB) into Russia. The modification was sold as a "technical fix." However, it was a technical fix which enabled the FSB to continue controlling the import of cell phones and presumably making whatever "technical

fixes" on the phones themselves necessary to make them acceptable to the FSB for use in the Russian Federation.

To this observer, it appears that Trump is anxious to please Vladimir Putin and is doing everything he can, within current political and legislative constraints, to further the Russian president's agenda.

26

August 26, 2017

Charlottesville: Trump the Authoritarian on Neo-Nazis

Donald Trump was notoriously slow in condemning the support of White supremacists and neo-Nazis during the 2016 presidential campaign. Now, in his statements following the neo-Nazi and alt-right demonstrations in Charlottesville, Virginia on August 11-12, 2017, where one of their adherents drove a car into a crowd killing a young woman and injuring many others, his instinctive support for these groups has been quite evident.

In his first statement, Trump spoke of the "fine people" who were among the alt-right and neo-Nazi demonstrators in Charlottesville, North Carolina. It took him two days to condemn them, in a speech which seemed written by his staff to appease the enormous wave of criticism that followed his first statement. Shortly thereafter, he defended his original statement and showed once again where his sympathies lay.

This and many other actions by Trump have revealed for all to see his innate authoritarian tendencies. His assault upon facts and the truth, and the press and other media which report facts to the public and analyze and interpret them in seeking connections and larger truths, is a striking aspect of this authoritarian bent. His omission of any reference to Jews in the White House's annual Holocaust memorial statement was remarkable, and no accident. In Charlottesville, neo-Nazis were filmed chanting anti-Semitic slogans such as "Jews will not replace us," and repeating other slogans literally translated from the Nazi lexicon, such as "Blood and Soil" ("Blut und Boden").

Trump's infamous lies, such as his claims Barack Obama was not born in the United States during the "birther" movement, revealed a long time ago his racist sympathies or at least his willingness to lend white supremacists tacit approval to gain their support.

We have been so accustomed to Trump's lies and his other violations of our democratic norms and institutions, such as his constant defamation of journalists and the press, his continuing efforts to obstruct justice—by firing FBI Director James Comey, attacking Robert Mueller and his team, or trying to intimidate and shape the testimony of witnesses in the Mueller investigation—that such behavior has become accepted as normal or "normalized."

We are worn down by the constant assault of lies. These actions become so "normalized" that they begin to be accepted with a shrug of the shoulder by not only his supporters but also many of his critics. We begin to acquiesce in such actions, thinking or saying, "Oh, that's Trump. That's just the way he is."

Yet we must recognize Trump's assault upon facts, upon the truth, upon the press, and his sympathies toward or willingness to use neo-Nazi and other neo-fascists to further his political goals as grave assaults upon and threats to American democracy and the rule of law.

Before the election, it may be recalled, Trump refused to answer the question of whether he would accept the results, laying down a line of argument that the results would not be fair. Even after winning, he has maintained that three to five million votes in his favor were repressed or not counted.

In *On Tyranny: Twenty Lessons from the Twentieth Century* (referenced earlier), Yale historian Timothy Snyder has written a book of stark warnings about the rise of authoritarianism, including the threat Trump represents in the United States. Now he has written an Op-ed in the *New York Times* which brings those 20 lessons directly to bear on Trump in the wake of his statements about Charlottesville.

See Timothy Snyder, "The Test of Nazism That Trump Failed," *New York Times*, August 18, 2017.[76]

27

September 7, 2017

The Christopher Steele Dossier on Trump's Collusion with Russia

The top news story about Donald Trump has been and remains the nature of his and his associates' ties to Russia, their collusion with Russia before and after the November 8, 2016 presidential election, and efforts by Trump to cover up the commission of these apparently criminal activities.

A key question throughout the campaign and since the election has been why Trump has so consistently refused to utter a word of criticism of Vladimir Putin or Russia.

Since the publication by BuzzFeed of the Christopher Steele dossier in January 2017 (widely known as the "Golden Showers" dossier), a clear and coherent narrative of Russian intervention in the U.S. elections and cooperation with Trump associates has been available. Perhaps due in part to the salacious details of the "Golden Showers" episode, which could not be verified (not surprising due to the nature of the sources), news media gave the Steele dossier a wide berth, routinely dismissing it as unconfirmed and not verified.

See

1) Ken Bensinger, Miriam Elder (BuzzFeed News World Editor), and Mark Schoofs, "These Reports Allege Trump Has Deep Ties to

Russia; A Dossier, Compiled by a Person Who Has Claimed to Be a Former British intelligence Official, Alleges Russia Has Compromising Information on Trump. The Allegations Are Unverified, and the Report Contains Errors," *BuzzFeed*, January 10, 2017 (3:20 p.m.; updated at 6:09 p.m.).[77]

2) The text of Christopher Steele's dossier on Trump and Russia can be found here: https://www.documentcloud.org/documents/3259984-Trump-Intelligence-Allegations.html.

3) "More on the 'Golden Showers' Dossier Prepared by Former MI6 Agent Christopher Steele: Sources," *The Trenchant Observer*, March 7, 2017.[78]

Some investigative reporters, nonetheless, continued to look into its allegations, which have over the last eight months been largely verified or confirmed by subsequent events.

Now, John Sipher, a former senior CIA official, has published an insightful article which connects the dots, tying together allegations contained in the Steele dossier with the findings of independent reporting and with subsequent events. The article is published in *Just Security*, a publication based at the Center for Human Rights and Global Justice at New York University School of Law. In an editorial note, the content of Sipher's article is summarized as follows:

In this special Just Security article, highly respected former member of the CIA's Senior Intelligence Service, John Sipher examines the Steele dossier using methods that an intelligence officer would to try to validate such information. Sipher concludes that the dossier's information on campaign collusion is generally credible when measured against standard Russian intelligence practices, events subsequent to Steele's reporting, and information that has become available in the nine months since Steele's final report. The dossier, in Sipher's view, is not without fault, including factual inaccuracies. Those errors, however, do not detract from an overarching framework that has proven to be ever more reliable as new revelations about potential Trump campaign collusion with the Kremlin and its affiliates has come to light in the nine months since Steele submitted his final report.

For the original article, *see* John Sipher, "A Second Look at the Steele Dossier—Knowing What We Know Now," *Just Security*, September 6, 2017 (8:01 a.m.).[79]

Whatever the story of the day generated by Donald Trump, we should always bear in mind that the big story, the overarching story, is the story of Putin's and Russia's intervention in the 2016 U.S. elections, collusion between Trump and his associates with Russia, and Trump's ongoing refusal to criticize Russia or Putin—or even to fully recognize the validity of the intelligence community's findings regarding Russian intervention in the American electoral process

While there has been vigorous criticism of the Steele dossier, focused on this or that detail or the indictment of Igor Danchenko, a principal source, for false statements to the FBI, the overall thrust of the allegations it contains, if not all the details, have been largely borne out.

FURTHER READING

"Steele Dossier," Wikipedia, November 2021.[80]

28

November 7, 2017

Jettisoning Human Rights, Trump Supports Coup d'État in Saudi Arabia

If anyone wondered what U.S. foreign policy would look like once it abandoned support for human rights and democracy as key components, they need now look no further than Saudi Arabia and the Philippines to see that policy in the flesh.

In the Kingdom of Saudi Arabia, Trump has followed his sword dance with support for the current coup d'état underway in that country.

Following Trump's visit to the kingdom in May, he and his son-in-law, Jared Kushner, have looked the other way or supported an illegal Saudi blockade and boycott of Qatar, hosted the minister of the interior and crown prince in June, and now in November have given the new crown prince, Mohamed bin Salman (MBS), a green light to seize all the levers of power in Saudi Arabia, and to arrest and seize the assets of some of the most powerful men in the country.

Like Xi Jinping in China, MBS holds out the hope that he may be a modernizer.

However, there are few grounds for hope that he will move the kingdom toward democratic government and the rule of law when he substitutes traditional decision-making by consensus within the royal family with arrests and property seizures in the middle of the night, without even so much as paying lip service to the rule of law.

FURTHER READING

1) "Human Rights in Saudi Arabia: Will Trump Look the Other Way?" *The Trenchant Observer*, May 19, 2017.[81]

2) Robin Wright, "The Saudi Royal Purge—with Trump's Consent," *New Yorker*, November 6, 2017.[82]

3) Spencer Ackerman, "Trump after Saudi Palace Coup: 'We've Put Our Man on Top,'" *Daily Beast*, January 7, 2018 (10:34 a.m. ET, updated 12:28 p.m. ET).[83]

Part Three

2018 – Year Two of the Trump Presidency

29

January 6, 2018

The Question of Individual Responsibility for the Actions of One's Nation

We Americans share a culture, a way of life, and a history built on our Constitution and a dedication to the rule of law.

Yet we also share responsibility for the actions of our government, of our president and political leaders, particularly those serving in the Senate and the House of Representatives whom we have elected. When they commit transgressions of our democratic political order or kill innocent civilians in violation of the laws of war (humanitarian law) in foreign conflicts, we also share responsibility for their and our government's actions.

Is this a radical proposition? I think not. Not if we reason carefully about what it means to live in a democracy or to give full life to that democracy through our own thoughts, beliefs, and actions.

What are we to make then of politicians who approve of, or look the other way, when gross violations of our democratic order are committed, by our politicians, our legislators, and those who support them?

Does an individual citizen in the United States, or any country for that matter, incur any moral or other responsibility when he looks the other way when an injustice is committed, and does nothing to stop it? If the answer is "No," in what sense can we be said to be a country that is governed by its citizens?

If we elect billionaires to run the country, and they then implement policies that sharply favor the rich and powerful, and all of that was likely or even evident before we cast our votes, are we absolved of moral responsibility for the outcome?

If we elect politicians who vote tax or health care laws that deny access to health care to millions of people, resulting in thousands of deaths, or take money from the poorest and give it to the very richest citizens in our country, are these actions the actions of the politicians alone, or are they also *our* actions? Are we *ourselves* taking money from the poor and denying millions access to health care?

A great deal turns on our answers to these questions.

Yet let us take the inquiry a bit further. If our politicians tell big lies to the population about what they are doing, or if the president, for example, tells monstrous lies on a constant basis, and we do not speak out, are we complicit in his lies? Do we thereby incur moral responsibility? When the consequences of such big lies lead to sharp curtailment in spending for social services for the poor, or disrupt our fundamental sense of right and wrong, our fundamental moral values, or our very belief in the concept of truth, are we individually responsible for the actions and events which may follow?

When the president dismisses serious news reporting, backed by solid sources, as "fake news," and we do nothing, are we not individually responsible for the erosion of a culture of truth and of expertise based on facts?

Are we then complicit in the assault on the truth, or the very concept of truth itself?

Without the concept and practice of telling the truth, of course, no government can be held accountable for its actions. A country can slide down the slippery slope that leads to authoritarianism and dictatorship, and the crimes a dictatorship might commit to maintain itself in power, to realize the misshapen ideals of a of government not based on the rule of law, not based on the concept of justice, and not even based on the concept of simple everyday fairness.

If that occurs, are individuals responsible in a moral sense? Are we responsible? Individually?

If America slides into dictatorship as Germany, one of the most educated and advanced industrial countries in the world at the time, did in the 1930s, will we then be responsible for the crimes our government may commit, as Germans after World War II were viewed by many as responsible, as guilty for the crimes of the Third Reich?

Germans in 1945 had to address *The Question of German Guilt*, the title of a book published in 1946 in German as *Die Schuldfrage* and in English translation in 1947.

Will Americans one day have to face *The Question of American Guilt for* the country's slide into despotism, into a form of government where truth no longer holds our allegiance, where expert opinion based on analysis of the facts, the scientific facts, is no longer valued, and where it is no longer possible to criticize the government, its leaders, or its actions?

Or have we always faced that question, and become what our answers did or did not provide as a path into the future, into freedom?

Amid the ruins of his country following World War II, the German philosopher Karl Jaspers, in *The Question of German Guilt* analyzed in rigorous detail the many evasions and excuses then commonly heard in Germany in response to charges of guilt for what had occurred. Near the end of the book, he also warned,

And yet, we are oppressed by one nightmarish idea: if a dictatorship in Hitler's style should ever rise, in America, all hope would
be lost for ages.

We in Germany could be freed from the outside. Once a dictatorship has been established, no liberation from within is possible. Should the Anglo-Saxon world be dictatorially conquered from within, as we were, there would no longer be an outside, nor a liberation.

The freedom fought for and won by Western man over hundreds, thousands of years would be a thing of the past. The primitivity of despotism would reign again, but with all means of technology…

…

The German fate could provide all others with experience. If only they would understand this experience! We are no inferior race. Everywhere people have similar qualities. Everywhere there are violent, criminal, vitally capable minorities apt to seize the reins if occasion offers, and to proceed with brutality.

–Karl Jaspers, *The Question of German Guilt* (E.B. Ashton transl.) 2000, New York: Fordam University Press, p. 93.

Jaspers' warning was unmistakably clear, and rings true 71 years later, today, as it did in 1946. The successful defense of democracy and the rule of law in the United States, or its failure, will have fateful consequences throughout the world, for centuries into the future.

Consequently, the moral responsibility of individual Americans to uphold the rule of law and the constitutional and democratic customs and forms of government we have built up over more than two centuries, is enormous. We must think beyond ourselves. We are called upon to remember the country's deepest values, its greatest leaders, and the inspiring examples of those who built our democracy and whose legacy we are called upon to defend.

Americans are called upon to begin thinking today, if they have not already begun this journey, of *The Question of American Guilt,* and how their own actions may contribute to or impede the slide toward authoritarianism and the denial of truth which has already begun.

FURTHER READING

"When and How Did America Lose Her Soul?" *The Trenchant Observer*, April 11, 2019.[84]

30

February 5, 2018

Investigations: Americans Are Lost in the Weeds

As news reporters and cable news commentators fill their columns and air time with endless details about the Nunes Memo,[85] or the Democratic Memo, in the context of the investigation of Trump's contacts with Russia by the House Permanent Select Committee on Intelligence, we should recognize that Joseph Goebbels himself, the Nazi propaganda minister, would be immensely proud of the Trump Team's execution of his basic propaganda techniques. Get everyone arguing about something irrelevant. Distract attention from what is really going on. Create controversy. Confuse the public. Debate any opponent's criticism endlessly, until ordinary citizens are confused.

How many voters, do you think, paid attention to the story that top Russian intelligence agency leaders came to Washington last week (before February 5) to meet with top U.S. intelligence officials (and who knows who else)? Or to the story that this occurred only days before Trump announced that he would not implement the sanctions against Russia and Russians that had been enacted into law by the Congress, by overwhelming veto-proof majorities?

Few, I suspect. Americans were lost in the weeds arguing over the Nunes Memo.

Just stop for a minute and think:

Whereas there is ample and endlessly redundant evidence in full public view of Donald Trump's efforts to tamper with witnesses and impede the Senate, House and Mueller investigations into his relationships with Russia and Russians, he has everyone down in the weeds discussing this or that detail of the release or contents of a memo which is basically irrelevant, devoid of content, and which regardless of its content would not carry the water he is reported in his deluded state to think it could.

One awaits further indictments of Trump's associates. Only by putting Trump's enablers and liars in jail will any progress be made toward forcing him from office.

One also awaits real oversight of the Trump administration. A good place to start would be the State Department, where a close examination of Trump's policies and actions towards Russia might be undertaken, while a very serious investigation into the consequences of Trump's and Rex Tillerson's abandonment of the human rights component of U.S. foreign policy might be highly useful. So far, the consequences in both areas have been disastrous.

In the domestic arena, there is high scrutiny of Trump's actions and policies, and strong forces which can push back against the most disastrous ones. Sadly, this is not true in the foreign policy arena, where congressional oversight is all the more necessary.

These are the stories Americans and American media should be following, if they can get their noses out of the weeds.

31

April 16, 2018

Roger Cohen "Stands Up" and Speaks the Truth about Trump

Donald Trump and Vladimir Putin know, like Hitler and Stalin and other dictators or would-be dictators before them, that "the big lie" must be repeated endlessly in order to produce its propagandistic effect and be believed by the broad masses of the population.

The big truth also needs to be repeated, not simply stated once to then be forgotten.

Timothy Snyder in *On Tyranny: Twenty Lessons from the Twentieth Century* stresses the importance of standing up, of taking a position, and of speaking out. Roger Cohen has just shown us how speaking the truth, without mincing words, can facilitate the clarity of vision that we all need now as Donald Trump and his supporters threaten American democracy.

See Roger Cohen, "Tethered to a Raging Buffoon Called Trump," *New York Times*, April 13, 2018.[86]

Cohen writes:

We are tethered to a buffoon. He rages and veers, spreading ugliness, like an oil slick smothering everything in its viscous mantle.

114

He's about to bomb Syria. He's not about to bomb Syria. His attention span is nonexistent. He attacks the foundations of our Republic: an independent judiciary, a free press, truth itself. His cabinet looks terrorized, the way Saddam Hussein's once did.

President Donald Trump is dangerous. The main things mitigating the danger are his incompetence and cowardice. We live in a time that teaches how outrage can turn to a shrug, how the unthinkable repeated over and over can induce moral numbness, how a madman's manic certainties can overwhelm reason. He is very busy; people resist; he opens another front; people shake their heads. It's hard to remember on Friday what happened on Monday. Trump's is the unbearable lightness of the charlatan.

Disorientation spreads. Trump's main war, beyond all the military bluster, is on truth. This reflects his instinct for the jugular: Once the distinction between truth and falsehood disappears, anything is possible.

32

May 23, 2018

An Authoritarian President Orders an Investigation of Those Investigating Him

Americans are used to thinking that "the struggle for the rule of law" refers to the struggles of other peoples in foreign lands for the rule of law in their respective countries. But the struggle for the rule of law in *any* country is a permanent struggle, one in which advances can be made and even consolidated, while the threat that the rule of law may be undermined, suffer defeats, and even be lost, always remains present.

The United States is no exception to this rule. Within the last week, one of the frontiers between the rule of law and tyranny was crossed, when the President of the United States ordered the Department of Justice to conduct a criminal investigation into those who are investigating him.

A president should never be allowed to order an investigation by the Justice Department *of any kind,* and least of all, an investigation into his opponents or those he perceives to be his opponents. The very idea of the president ordering an investigation of those investigating the potential crimes he and his associates may have committed is anathema to the very concepts of democracy and the rule of law.

The fact that Republicans in Congress have not cried out against this travesty is fresh evidence of how far the Republican Party and its representatives in Congress have gone down the slippery slope that leads to authoritarianism.

One characteristic of authoritarianism is the use of the state to harass and sanction individuals who stand in the way of the will of the authoritarian leader. We see this now in Turkey with Erdogan's persecution of his opponents, in the Philippines where President Rodrigo Duterte and his allies have just removed the president of the Supreme Court, and in Russia where opponents of Vladimir Putin are barred from running for office (e.g., Alexey Navalny) or even murdered with impunity (Boris Nemtsov, in 2015).

A leader who uses the apparatus of the state to harass or persecute his perceived opponents, or to block lawful processes aimed at holding government officials accountable under the law—even the leader himself or his associates—is someone who has himself already manifested his authoritarian nature, and who has already traveled far down the path leading to authoritarianism.

33

May 26, 2018

Obstruction of Justice by Trump on an Ongoing Basis

See,

18 USC Ch. 73: OBSTRUCTION OF JUSTICE[87] From Title 18—CRIMES AND CRIMINAL PROCEDURE
PART I—CRIMES

§1505. Obstruction of proceedings before departments, agencies, and committees

…

Whoever corruptly, or by threats or force, or by any threatening letter or communication influences, obstructs, or impedes or endeavors to influence, obstruct, or impede the due and proper administration of the law under which any pending proceeding is being had before any department or agency of the United States, or the due and proper exercise of the power of inquiry under which any inquiry or investigation is being had by either House, or any committee of either House or any joint committee of the Congress—

Shall be fined under this title, imprisoned not more than 5 years or, if the offense involves international or domestic terrorism (as defined in section 2331), imprisoned not more than 8 years, or both.

Donald Trump appears to engage in obstruction of justice, within the meaning of the statute quoted above, every day or almost every day, in full view of the public.

Trump may believe that his actions are above the law, and that he cannot be reached by the law given the Republican phalanx which guards him in Congress, but much remains to be seen. There could always be a sealed indictment, requiring him to stand trial after he leaves office—or even before.

Significantly, Republicans in Congress who join him in his apparent acts of obstruction of justice may themselves be guilty of conspiracy to commit obstruction of justice. Consequently, they, too, are potentially liable to criminal indictments which may be handed down after they leave office—or potentially even before.

This is a factor which each and every one of them should take into account as they act to further the apparent conspiracy to commit obstruction of justice in which the president seems to be engaged, every day or almost every day.

34

June 2, 2018

Lost in Details, Critics Fail to Counter Trump Propaganda

Trump's critics do not understand how propaganda works, and how they must counter it.

Following the unfolding drama of revelations about Trump's crimes and those of his associates, intellectuals and leading print and cable media chase after the latest "breaking news" revelation or discovery.

According to them, the greatest political scandal in the last century has been reduced to a crime drama, where those who are caught up in the daily drama rarely think outside the crime box and Robert Mueller's criminal investigation. In doing so, despite the unquestionable importance of the essence of their work, they are playing into Trump's hands.

The nation awaits the result of Mueller's criminal investigation, while the nation suffers the consequences of Trump's political offenses and attacks on the rule of law.

If Mueller is responsible for everything related to Donald Trump, then everyone else is absolved of their own individual responsibility. They are excused from their own obligations to hold Trump accountable for his political atrocities, and the duty to force him to bring them to a halt.

What is going on can be viewed as a conversation on two levels, in two different bands of communication.

On the top level, intellectuals and journalists follow the facts and use reason to analyze events. They build the necessary case for one day impeaching or indicting Trump, and indicting those who surround him. But because they are intellectuals, they largely fail to appreciate what is happening on the lower level, in the lower communication band or channel that Trump is using to such great effect.

To understand Trump's use of propaganda and lies, a good place to start is Chapter Six of Volume 1 of *Mein Kampf* by Adolf Hitler. Hitler was one of the first to succeed in using mass propaganda to shape the entire landscape of public opinion in his country, using it to rise to power and solidify his hold on it.

Propaganda, he argued, must ignore the arguments and criticisms of the intelligentsia. It should not be directed at them, but rather at "the broad masses."

It should be aimed at the lowest elements of the masses. It should not be complicated, and on any issue should not consist of more than three or four points, and never consider various aspects of an issue, which would only confuse the masses.

The masses cannot remember things. Endless repetition is effective. The truth should always be subservient to achieving the purpose of the propaganda.

Above all, the propaganda should not be aimed at intellectual persuasion, but rather at connecting with the emotions and emotional concerns of the masses.

This is the key to understanding Trump's blatant lies and propaganda.

For example, his proposal to build a wall between the U.S. and Mexico is in fact a symbol which represents, in emotional terms, his adamant opposition to immigration. The emotional concerns of the masses to which he appeals include a strong desire to limit immigration. These individuals do not like what the country has become, or threatens to become, with so many immigrants.

Every time Trump refers to "the wall," he rings the emotional bell of the masses who want to limit immigration. We are not operating in a realm of rational analysis and understanding here, but rather in the lower level or channel of communicating directly with the emotions of the masses.

Rational arguments about the wall, or DACA (Deferred Action for Childhood Arrivals) "dreamers," are sent and received on the higher level or communication channel of rational analysis. They are simply not heard, or are summarily dismissed by the masses, who are tuned into the stronger messages they are receiving on the lower level or emotional communication channel.

Democrats and other critics of Trump do not understand or act on these basic facts.

Democrats are not sending any messages on the lower or emotional channel of communication, other than appeals to lofty ideals and sentiments, which tend to be expressed or heard more clearly on the higher, analytical channel.

The Democrats, without abandoning their analytical criticisms and affirmations, must develop their own messages on the lower, emotional channel, if they are to win the congressional elections in November 2018.

35

July 4, 2018

Trump, the International Wrecking Ball

Sometimes it feels like all the stars have gone out of the sky. Our lodestars. Those stars, which however tiny in the distance, throw off rays of hope. Visions of other possible realities. Of the world as it could conceivably be.

One of those lodestars is **Truth**. Most civilized men and women would like to live in a world built on truth, **not lies**.

We have to mention **Truth** first, for without it nothing good is possible.

Over 70 years ago, after the second of two world wars in the 20th century, the nations of the world joined together in 1945 to form the United Nations and to state in its Charter principles of international law and goals that would lead to the elimination of large-scale war.

For those with no experience of war, either as soldiers or as interested family members, friends, or observers, the goal of ending war has receded. In the U.S., in the 17th year of the endless war in Afghanistan, citizens have become inured to the ongoing warfare its government is engaged in, in Afghanistan as well as other countries.

The lodestar of peace has become but a pale and distant semblance of what it once was.

The prohibition of the use of force across international frontiers, as occurred in Czechoslovakia in 1938 and 1939, and Poland in 1939, and at Pearl Harbor in 1941 has lost its salience in the popular consciousness.

Mr. Trump wants the Group of Seven to readmit Russia. "Something happened," he said, and they were kicked out in 2014.

Other lodestars used to be U.S. governments and presidents who favored policies aimed at promoting democracy and human rights in foreign countries. The U.S., it was assumed, would always be strong in these areas.

Now, we are faced with a situation in which the U.S. government has been seized by a group of authoritarians and would-be authoritarians who take delight in crashing their wrecking ball against most of the steps forward we have made since World War II.

Our president is a brilliant reality show host and producer, and with his mastery of the media, a brilliant national politician. But he is totally clueless when it comes to matters of policy substance. This is particularly true in the area of foreign affairs.

He does not appear to have heard of international law. "Something happened" in 2014 which led to Russia being kicked out of the Group of Seven. If you were to ask him, away from his advisors, what that "something" was, he probably couldn't tell you. Or even if he mentioned the Russian invasion of Crimea, he probably couldn't explain why that was important.

A lodestar Mr. Trump is not.

So here we are. Mr. Trump's wrecking ball is being aimed at the institutions and policies which generations of Americans, and allies, have held dear. He seems to take particular pleasure in tearing things down, without offering to build anything to take the place of what he has destroyed.

The most maddening aspect of all of this is that he appears to be impervious to facts, and reason. Climate change is but one example.

This is what the world faces. About the only hope is that somehow other democracies and those fighting for democracy around the world will stand up to Mr. Trump and fight hard for those values and institutions which, until a short time ago, we all held in common.

On the world stage, the torch of freedom has now passed from American hands. Other countries need to pick it up and lead the battle for international law, human rights, and a sane world based on international cooperation through multilateral organizations, and the battle for truth and science and law. Others might usefully remember that more than half of the United States still holds these values and shares many of their own reactions to Mr. Trump.

One thing is clear: Trump is real, and a real threat to the liberal and democratic values and institutions of the West and other countries which follow or aspire to follow a similar path.

America's democratic friends can provide no greater service than to stand up for the values in which they believe, which are still shared by large numbers and probably a majority of Americans.

FURTHER READING

Margaret Sullivan, "Restoring the Voice of America after a Trump 'Wrecking Ball' Won't Be Easy. But It's Worth Saving," *Washington Post*, December 13, 2020 (7:00 a.m. EST).[88]

36

July 16, 2018

SATIRE: Transcript of Conversation between Putin and Trump in Helsinki

We have received through a chain of secret channels a "transcript" of the secret conversations between Donald Trump and Vladimir Putin, which took place at the beginning of their summit meeting on July 16, 2018 in Helsinki, Finland.

The "transcript" is actually a description of what took place during those two hours when only the principals and two interpreters were present.

The document which follows was compiled by Israeli and Finnish intelligence sources, as augmented by intercepts and additional information from other intelligence agencies. Because of the sensitive nature of the subject matter, not all information could be confirmed. What follows, therefore, should be viewed as a raw intelligence product.

Israel enlisted Finnish intelligence officials to assist in placing cameras and audio recording equipment in the room in which the meeting between Putin and Trump took place. The equipment was installed only after the room had been swept for bugs and the meeting had begun.

Trump and Putin are seen in the video sitting in two chairs. Shortly after the meeting begins, Putin asks Trump if he would like a neck and shoulder massage, so the meeting can be conducted in a more relaxed manner. Putin moves to stand behind Trump and starts to massage his neck and shoulders. Then, at Putin's suggestion, both men remove their shirts. Trump says softly that this is the first time he has been touched like that in a very long time, as things with Melania have been somewhat strained because of the Stormy Daniels affair.

Putin moves into deep massage, and also offers Trump something to drink. Trump falls asleep. Then, from the sidelines a hospital bed and certain medical equipment are wheeled into the room, and Trump is put on the hospital bed. Men dressed as doctors appear near the bed.

Putin explains to the doctors that the microchip they had implanted in Trump's brain at the Ritz Carlton Hotel in Moscow in 2013 (at the Miss Universe pageant), when Trump fell asleep after the "Golden Showers" show on the bed Barack Obama had slept on, had begun to malfunction. In particular, despite several software updates that had been downloaded to the chip when Putin gave Trump brief head massages on the sidelines of various multilateral summit meetings, the "Crimea" and "sanctions" components of the chip had failed to operate properly. To be sure, the "North Korean military games" component had worked flawlessly in Singapore, where Trump canceled the annual joint South Korean and American military exercises. Still, the most important components—"Crimea" and "sanctions"—appeared not to be working properly, as they had not produced the desired effects.

Because the five-year-old microchip had also shown other signs of decay, leading to some erratic behavior by Trump, Putin and his team had decided to replace the chip with a new and more advanced version, whose software could be updated using imperceptible sonic waves. This obviated the necessity of Putin giving Trump quick head massages on the sidelines of multilateral summit meetings.

The chip was installed quickly, and Trump's head was sewn up so expertly with the assistance of modern medical technology that there was no scar and not even a trace of an incision.

Following the operation, the hospital bed and medical equipment were quickly removed from the room, along with the doctors. Trump was then brought back to consciousness. At that point Putin directed flashing lights into Trump's eyes, explaining that the lights would help Trump with his troubled sleep pattern in the early hours of the morning. Trump had been given medicine that made him feel very good, and he thanked Putin for the neck and shoulder massage. Both men put their shirts back on.

The interpreters were then summoned back into the room, following an extended break for morning tea and coffee, made possible they were told by Putin's desire to conduct a conversation directly with Trump in English, which after years of study he had recently become proficient in.

The two leaders proceeded to tick off the items on their lists, though Trump was prompted not to change his responses on Crimea or sanctions until he received further instructions.

Smiling broadly, both men left the room to meet their entourages and to continue the larger group discussions planned for the rest of the day.

The actual film and audio of the secret two-hour meeting have not become available. Their content came as a shock to Israeli intelligence and political leaders. The latter, however, expressed their deep appreciation to the intelligence services, which had at least made it possible for them to understand what they were dealing with.

37

October, 7, 2018

Opinion: Lying Republican Senators Confirm Lying Supreme Court Nominee

The statements which follow represent the opinions and impressions of the author, and do not necessarily involve statements of known and proven facts.

Unmoored from Truth, or even shame, the Republic, rudderless, founders on lies as it abandons its course toward the safe harbor of Truth.

Donald Trump's assault on the Truth and his constant lying have borne poisonous fruit. The lying Republican President has nominated lying Brett Kavanaugh to the Supreme Court. Lying Republican senators have manipulated the confirmation process to hide or ignore perjury and possibly other misdeeds. Then, ignoring the perjury and not having seriously examined the allegations of sexual misconduct, they voted to confirm Kavanaugh.

In doing so, senators have ignored obvious perjury by Kavanaugh in his testimony to the Senate Judiciary Committee, while manipulating a supplemental FBI investigation in order to avoid the revelation of any inconvenient facts. They have also misrepresented the facts relating to sexual assault accusations against Kavanaugh, and his perjury before the Committee on September 27, 2018.

One thing appears certain about Brett Kavanaugh. He appears to be a liar, a bald-faced liar. He seems to have lied in his testimony to the Senate Judiciary Committee last week about his high school and early college drinking, about the meaning of words in his high school yearbook like "boof" and "Ralph" and "alumnius," and quite possibly about whether he sexually assaulted Dr. Christine Blasey Ford in 1982, as she alleged in her compelling and highly credible testimony. It seems that, if necessary, he would have even lied had he been called to answer the charges of Debbie Ramirez and Julie Swetnick, which President Trump and the Republicans on the Judiciary Committee carefully and successfully maneuvered to avoid.

Senator Jeff Flake had the power in his hand to force a real FBI investigation of the sexual assault allegation, simply by withholding his vote to report Kavanaugh's nomination out of the Judiciary Committee. It was a power that for him was too great to hold on to or to use. Instead, he came up with a complicated formula that in the event allowed the wielders of power to shamelessly orchestrate a cover-up, a whitewash of an investigation by the FBI.

The real story of America's descent into the abyss is perhaps to be found in the story of why Flake was afraid to use the power in his hand. Why was he afraid, and of what?

Decent people harbored some (diminishing) hope that Senator Lisa Murkowski (R-Alaska) or Senator Susan Collins (R-Maine) might vote against Kavanaugh. One or more could have cast a negative vote, but the ambivalence they had shown up to then, in the face of apparent lies and outrageous behavior by their colleagues, did not auger well.

To her lasting credit, Murkowski did vote against Kavanaugh. To her lasting discredit, augmented by a misleading and deceitful speech on the floor of the Senate justifying her vote, Susan Collins voted in favor of Kavanaugh. After raising doubts and orchestrating a delay to allow a manipulated FBI investigation, Jeff Flake, true to character, voted for the lying president's lying nominee without raising any objections to the abuse of process inherent in the FBI investigation that he had caused to occur but not overseen.

While many hoped against hope, they were hard-pressed to conclude that there is not a decent human being among the Republicans in the Senate, and that the same may be true in the House. The last decent Republican may have been John McCain. Many fervently hoped that this was not true, that there might have been several men or women of decency left among the Republican members of the Senate, but this was merely a hope—against overwhelming prior evidence—that somehow some synapse might occur in a few Republican brains to save the Republic.

Saving the Republic was indeed what was truly at stake. We have a president who lies big time every day and has built his career on lies, large and small, and by attacking the truth when it is reported in the media, the so-called "fake news" published by "the enemy of the people."

The Orwellian overtones are not subtle. "The Truth is the enemy of the people."

And this lying, would-be authoritarian president has nominated a judge to the Supreme Court who has extreme views on the reach of the president's power and his immunity from law, and the ordinary mechanisms that seek to secure that every individual is equal and accountable before the law.

Why should we be surprised that a lying president would nominate an apparently lying candidate to be placed on the Supreme Court, and that his lying Republican henchmen would do everything in their power, unconstrained by norms and traditions of decency and fairness, to put the lying president's apparently lying Supreme Court nominee on the Court?

This battle is about raw power. Republicans seem willing to tell any lie, to ignore any perjury, to do anything necessary to secure their power through gaining control of the Supreme Court. Even if their actions constitute a major break with the rule of law.

Would they kill to keep their power? That is one of the few factors that distinguish Trump from Hitler and Stalin. Hopefully, that is a question the nation will never have to face. Nonetheless, one must consider seriously what might happen should Trump call his supporters into the streets.

So, it appears that for now we will have "the Kavanaugh Court," controlled by the swing vote of the apparently lying nominee of a lying president.

The Supreme Court may not regain its authority and reputation for 50 years.

Kavanaugh's apparent lies will not be forgotten.

Long a beacon to the world, the Supreme Court, which ultimately sets the course for the United States, may now be a beacon that has gone out or is going out. Certainly, it will not retain its authority or legitimacy so long as a known perjurer sits among its justices.

The Supreme Court of Brett Kavanaugh, Donald Trump, and Trump's Republican lackeys will for all time stand as a monument to Trump's assault upon the Truth, and the lesson he has sought to teach the nation that Truth does not matter, not even if it is violated by a Supreme Court nominee who commits perjury before the Senate Judiciary Committee in order to achieve confirmation.

Kavanaugh's confirmation is apparently the product of the commission of the crime of perjury. It is a crime in which the Republican members of the Senate Judiciary Committee are fully complicit, as are the Republican senators (and one Democrat) who voted on the floor for his confirmation.

38

October 15, 2018

Devil's Bargain:
The Khashoggi Charade

In the first days after Jamal Khashoggi's "disappearance" in the Saudi consulate in Istanbul on October 2, 2018, press accounts quoting Turkish officials and also American officials left little doubt about what had happened. Khashoggi, an occasional columnist for the *Washington Post* and a relatively mild critic of the Saudi Arabian government and its new de facto leader, Crown Prince Mohammed bin Salman (known as MBS), had, in fact, been gruesomely murdered and dismembered on the orders of the highest levels of the Saudi government.

Turkish authorities leaked to newspapers that they had audio and video recordings that left no doubt as to what had happened in the Saudi consulate.

Fifteen Saudi officials had flown into Istanbul's airport on private planes on the morning of October 2, proceeded directly to the Saudi consulate, and after several hours there and at the residence of the Consul General of Saudi Arabia in Istanbul, had checked out of their hotels and departed the Istanbul airport on chartered private jets that same day.

We are now witnessing an elaborate and coordinated charade designed to protect Saudi Arabia, Turkey, and the U.S.

First, the Turkish officials realized, somewhat belatedly perhaps, that to make their recordings public would reveal that Turkey was bugging the Saudi consulate, in open violation of the 1962 Vienna Convention on Consular Relations. So far, the recordings have not been released to the public. They are not likely to be, which doesn't mean their contents have not been shared—in a highly reliable way—with U.S. intelligence officials.

Second, the Saudis understood that the Turkish evidence directly implicated MBS, the de facto day-to-day ruler of Saudi Arabia. MBS, while showing a reformist image to the West, and particularly to Jared Kushner and Donald Trump, has at the same time manifested a dark and authoritarian streak in dealing with critics and potential opponents back home in Saudi Arabia. Thus, while he has authorized women to drive, he has at the same time arrested those who were advocating for this right. He apparently kidnapped the Prime Minister of Lebanon, Sa'ad Hariri, and released him only after massive diplomatic pressure from Western capitals.

He has launched a blockade against Qatar, in what appears to be open and flagrant violation of international law, and maintains that blockade in force. He detained many powerful members of the royal family and other powerful individuals in the Ritz Carlton Hotel in Riyadh, where he reportedly shook them down for billions—all without the slightest hint of due process.

Apparently, in order to protect MBS, the Saudi government and MBS have adamantly denied any role in the "disappearance" of Khashoggi. Moreover, they have threatened to retaliate strongly against any country that takes measures against the kingdom as a result of the Khashoggi affair.

Third, President Donald Trump has come under considerable pressure to punish Saudi Arabia for the medieval and gruesome murder which the Saudis apparently committed within their consulate in Istanbul. His responses have been evasive and even shocking. He has even suggested that "rogue" elements of the Saudi government may have been involved. He has indicated that a claimed $110 billion arms sale agreement with Saudi Arabia will not be rescinded and made absolutely horrific statements to the effect that the U.S. should not care about a murder that does not take place in the U.S.

This is the way the Saudis and the U.S. are hoping to manage the crisis, negotiating what they think will be accepted as a plausible version of the truth, without affecting the power or position of MBS—or Jared Kushner and Donald Trump. It is rather shocking to hear Trump sound off as a Saudi propaganda vehicle.

Their "negotiated truth" will be an "alternate fact" whose purpose is to obscure the real truth, which they don't even feign to pursue.

Turkey, for its part, receives massive investments and many tourists from Saudi Arabia, important interests to take into account, in addition to the desire not to reveal Turkish intelligence is bugging foreign diplomatic missions.

Trump has apparently also been misleading in another regard. He has said, repeatedly, that he's waiting for the U.S. to receive the results of investigations into Khashoggi's death. Almost certainly he has received intelligence briefings from his own officials regarding the "proof" that Turkish officials have of how Khashoggi was murdered and dismembered in Istanbul. They have themselves apparently obtained intercepts that show that Saudi Arabia planned to lure Khashoggi back to Saudi Arabia in order to detain him.

The Saudis have offered no public explanation of what the 15 Saudi officials were up to when they flew in on private jets, proceeded to the consulate and the consul's residence, and then checked out of their hotels and departed Istanbul on private jets, all on October 2, 2018.

The charade that is underway is the narrative that the U.S. doesn't yet know what happened to Khashoggi at the Saudi consulate in Istanbul, that Turkey doesn't admit anything about the surveillance of diplomatic missions in the country, and that if anything happened—which the Saudis and the U.S. don't know yet!—it was done by rogue elements of the Saudi regime, and MBS was in no way involved.

If you believe that, I have a bridge I would like to sell you in Brooklyn.

It all boils down to a question that Trump implicitly raised: "How much is one human life worth?"

This issue is explored in depth in a brilliant play entitled *The Visit* (*Der Besuch der alten Dame*) by the Swiss playwright, Friedrich Dürrenmatt. The play explores the question of whether citizens of a small town should accept the offer of $1 billion to be split half and half between the town and its inhabitants, from a wealthy former resident who was wronged in her youth. The only condition for the "gift" is that the young man who wronged her must be killed.

There is no more sacred human right than the right to life.

The lack of importance attached to this right by Trump is painfully in view. No more poignant abdication of moral leadership by the U.S. in the world could be imagined.

Some murders can have major political consequences, such as those of Vladimir Herzog in Brazil (1975), whose murder led to a showdown among military factions in which relatively moderate forces prevailed.

The murder of Archbishop Oscar Romero in El Salvador (1980) unmasked the true nature of the Salvadoran regime, leading to pressure in the U.S. to cut assistance and support for the military regime. Archbishop Romero was canonized in Rome this month.

The murder of Steve Biko in South Africa (1977) gave impetus to the divestment movement and the end of apartheid rule.

Similarly, Khashoggi's murder is likely to have very significant consequences. The rule by terror of the Saudi regime has finally been unmasked, in a way which will be impossible to cover up.

FURTHER READING

1) "Khashoggi Affair: A Prince Must Go—or Two," *The Trenchant Observer*, October 19, 2018;[89]

"Khashoggi Affair: Murder Most Foul!" *The Trenchant Observer*, October 24, 2018;[90]

2) "News Reports: CIA Concludes Saudi Crown Prince Ordered Khashoggi Assassination," *The Trenchant Observer*, November 18, 2018;[91]

3) "Khashoggi's Assassination, Human Rights, and International Law," *The Trenchant Observer*, November 19, 2018;[92]

4) "Jamal Khashoggi: The Value and Cost of One Human Life," *The Trenchant Observer*, November 21, 2018;[93]

5) "Khashoggi Assassination: To Really Sanction MBS, Minimize U.S. and Allied Dealings with Him," *The Trenchant Observer*, March 1, 2021.[94]

Part Four

2019 – Year Three
of the Trump Presidency

39

March 2, 2019

Impeach Trump, or Read the Impeachment Clause Out of the Constitution

Americans, if they are following the Trump saga at all, or drawing on sources other than Rush Limbaugh and Fox News, seem to be caught up in a TV crime drama, a series with daily episodes, where they themselves are called upon to put together the pieces or at least to follow a breathtaking crime drama where the principal suspect is the President of the United States. It is an engrossing drama.

What makes watching or even trying *not* to watch this drama particularly painful is that the evidence of the president's crimes, like that of his incompetence, and that of his corruption and malevolent intentions, lies in plain view. Not only is he a scoundrel, but he has attracted around him a slew of scoundrels, a sad group of public "servants" and advisors who seem hell bent on *not* protecting and promoting the welfare of ordinary people, but rather on dismantling the protections that have been put in place over many years to ensure that we have a "government...for the people."

In these circumstances we must ask, "Why has Donald Trump not yet been impeached?"

The Democrats appear lost in their own morass of political calculations. If the House impeached Trump, how would that affect their individual and party election prospects in 2020?

While Nancy Pelosi and other Democratic leaders may have been shrewd to avoid the issue of impeachment in the 2018 congressional elections, it does not follow that such a strategy is wise or promising going forward.

What is the argument, now, against holding hearings in the House on impeachment, like the Watergate hearings that were held in 1973-74?

The problem with the Democrats' current approach is that the kind of hearings they are scheduling now are likely to drag out—perhaps for a year or more—and then it will be too late for them to have an impact on the 2020 elections. Moreover, the current approach lacks a central goal and focus, which should be to put together the arguments and evidence to support the impeachment of Donald Trump for what is already publicly known and for further "high crimes and misdemeanors" that may be discovered in the impeachment investigations and hearings.

If the Democrats delay impeachment hearings for a year, the debate in the 2020 campaigns is likely to be about whether such hearings should be held at all. If they are started now, on the other hand, the debate is much more likely to be about the crimes and actions of Donald Trump.

To put the matter in sharp perspective, we must ask whether failure to impeach Donald Trump for the "high crimes and misdemeanors" that are already on the record and in full view would amount, for all intents and purposes, to reading the impeachment clause out of the Constitution.

Polls suggest that 40 percent or so of the electorate are not following or thinking seriously about, or are readily acquiescing in, the crimes and other morally depraved actions of President Trump.

By holding impeachment hearings, the Democrats in the House have an opportunity to educate the citizenry about the facts, explained in coherent narratives, of Trump's "high crimes and misdemeanors."

If they fail to initiate impeachment hearings, very soon, they may find that Trump's war on the truth will have succeeded in confusing voters to such an extent that he wins the election again.

Democrats should not delude themselves into believing that the rest of the country shares their views of the president. Trump is a brilliant reality show host and performer, and a brilliant communicator on the emotional level that drives citizens to vote one way or another. He is a cunning propagandist and has a charismatic personality.

Can a reality show host and charismatic performer be reelected? Consider this: There is considerable evidence to suggest that American politics, on the national level, have become very much like a reality show.

In 2020, if the American people are not forced to confront the specifics of his actions and behavior in impeachment hearings, and are not thereby educated as to the truth, Trump can win again.

40

March 3, 2019

What Is Going on in the World?

What is going on in the world? For two years Americans have been lost in an obsessive fixation on their lying president, the investigations into his crimes, and his brilliantly disruptive war on the truth, on reason, and on what Steve Bannon has called "the administrative state."

Many others in many countries have followed this obsession or succumbed to their own obsessions with authoritarian leaders and factions and the disruptive policies and actions unleashed by the latter.

In the United States, Trump's war on the truth, reason, and policies based on discernible facts has led to great confusion and a politics of spectacle, largely aided and abetted by the mass media. Even notable exceptions, like the *New York Times*, the *Washington Post*, and other media outlets have not remained unaffected by the fascination and obsession with Trump and his enablers.

In all of this constant turmoil, amid constant lies by the president and his enablers, it has become increasingly difficult for the average citizen to learn what is actually going on in the world, this world of some seven billion people who live outside the United States.

Compared to earlier times, there are hardly any foreign correspondents from the United States stationed out in the world.

News about Trump and his enablers and his critics seems to push important news about the world not only from the front pages, but from *all* pages.

The enormous pressures to report on events happening at this very moment have led to less investigative journalism, and even less journalism by reporters with an understanding of history and the context in which events take place.

An important determinant of what news gets covered is the array of subjects that readers (or viewers) are interested in, and unfortunately in the age of Trump they don't seem to be interested in what is going on outside the U.S., or even outside Washington, New York, national politics, or personalities in the sports and celebrity worlds.

We know things are happening, but the assaults of Trump and his enablers on American society and institutions have been too numerous and on too many fronts to keep track of.

This leads to a certain kind of resignation, a certain kind of feeling of impotence, and a further lack of interest in what is going on in the world. This decrease of interest on the part of readers and listeners leads to a further decline in reporting on what is going on abroad.

We are in a situation where CNN and MSNBC have hit upon a great money-making formula, piggybacking on the print news of the day with "panels" comprised of journalists and commentators who just sit around and talk about the (mostly Trump-related) news of the day. Panels are cheap. It is cheap to rely on print journalists rather than your own news organization, your own reporters, or even your own foreign correspondents.

Both on CNN and MSNBC there is an almost total absence of news about what is going on in the world. The only exception seems to be occasionally when such news may be tied to some Washington policy debate.

One striking aspect of this phenomenon is the near total absence of news about the country where some meeting of leaders is taking place. When Trump and Kim Jung Un met in Vietnam recently, for example, there was very little reporting on what is going on in Vietnam.

Perhaps we are merely entering a new period like the Dark Ages.

So, what *is* going on in the world?

What is going on with global warming? How are different countries responding to the challenge? What is the Trump administration doing? Why don't people care? Maybe if they could read a little more about what people in other countries are doing, they would care—and act—more.

What is going on in Africa? Who has heard of the recent formation under the auspices of the African Union of an African common market? This is probably one of the most momentous developments on the planet in the last few years. In America, who has heard of it?

What is going on in Europe beyond the Brexit spectacle? Has anyone heard of Emmanuel Macron's call for a refounding of the European project? What is going on in the Balkans?

Indeed, what is going on with Russia, and inside of Russia? Does anyone remember the Russian naval attack on Ukrainian warships in the Kerch Strait in December 2018, and its seizure of the three ships and 24 Ukrainian sailors? They remain under detention in Moscow. Have any significant sanctions been imposed on Russia for this act of aggression and continuation of its conflict with Ukraine? How is the 2015 Minsk II agreement being implemented, and who is at fault for the lack of progress?

What is going on in the South China Sea? Are the U.S. and other nations actively resisting Chinese militarization of the area and asserting rights of freedom of navigation protected by international law?

What is going on in the Philippines? How many people have been killed in Rodrigo Duterte's war on drugs and his campaign of extrajudicial executions? In other areas, what has happened to the rule of law?

What is going on in Mexico and Central America? To read the State Department's travel warnings on Mexico and the region, one can be forgiven for thinking the situation sounds like Afghanistan.

By the way, what is going on in Afghanistan? Do Trump's attempts to negotiate peace with the Taliban, over the heads of the government in Kabul, amount to anything other than an effort to withdraw from the country by selling out the people—particularly the women—and the elected democratic government which, however flawed, we have supported for over 15 years?

We could go on and on. The point is that, with few exceptions, the media in the United States are not covering these developments.

By failing to do so, they are failing to make efforts to educate the American people about the world they live in. The media, in the U.S. and elsewhere, need to redouble their efforts to educate the citizenry, with an unrelenting focus on the facts, the science, and the fact-based analyses of experts which offer the only true path toward successfully navigating our future.

The alternative is a world of government lies and distortions of the truth, where malevolent actors have free rein.

41

April 1, 2019

Satire—April Fool's: Trump Resigns!

In a stunning development, President Donald J. Trump resigned today. While accounts varied, White House sources, speaking on background because they were not authorized to talk about such a sensitive matter, said the president had resigned because since he took office his golf handicap had gone up more than ten points. Sources said the stress of the Mueller investigation and "the Russia collusion hoax" had affected the president's golf game, and in recent days he had shot over 90 on several occasions. Trump reportedly felt deep embarrassment, if not shame, particularly among his friends at the Mar-a-Lago Club in Palm Beach, Florida, where he greatly enjoys spending weekends and golfing in a relaxed atmosphere among friends.

According to some accounts, the Mueller Report and its apparent exoneration of Trump on the collusion charge had not led to an improvement in Trump's golf game. He is seemingly still worried about the New York Attorney General's investigations into his business affairs and the details contained in the Mueller Report about his alleged obstruction of justice.

According to yet another source familiar with the president's thinking, Trump reached the decision to resign while playing a video game designed by unofficial chief strategist Steve Bannon. Bannon had developed a highly complex algorithm taking into account a wide variety of political variables that assessed how well the Trump administration was doing in dismantling the administrative state, and which also predicted the odds, on a daily basis, of Trump being reelected in 2020 and the Republicans retaking the House of Representatives and maintaining control of the Senate.

According to this well-placed source, Bannon's algorithm translated these complex variables into video images which communicated the essence of the findings to the president in the kind of visual format he prefers.

Early Monday morning, according to this source, when the president was playing Bannon's video game, he saw the video image of himself, dressed in football gear, punting a football far down the field.

Upon seeing this video, according to the source, Trump immediately tweeted that he was resigning.

In a news briefing held later in the day, White House Press Secretary Sarah Huckabee Sanders rejected the account that the president had decided to resign when he saw Bannon's video of him punting. However, she did not dispute the account that the president had resigned because of his golf handicap.

42

June 13, 2019

The Democrats May Have Already Lost the 2020 Elections After the Mueller Report

President Trump's Job Approval Rating Favorable 50 percent, Unfavorable 47 percent, Rasmussen Daily Tracking Poll, June 13, 2019.[95]

On five of the last seven days Trump's job approval rating was 50 percent or higher. On June 12 it hit 51 percent with disapproval at 47 percent.

The Democrats have been lulled to sleep by the other polls, which, however, are based on a flawed methodology. Rasmussen is the only daily tracking poll, and one of very few polls based on a model of "likely voters" — not just "adults" or "registered voters." In the past, their polls have been shown to be highly accurate in predicting election results.

So, why are the Democrats losing the 2020 elections?

First, while they have persuaded that portion of the population which thinks, follows news, believes in facts and analyzes them, and who have not made a "Devil's Bargain" with Trump for lower taxes and an increase in their personal wealth, they have failed after two years to make significant inroads with the broad masses of the population who support Trump.

They need to stop preaching to themselves and focus on piercing the propaganda bubble of Trump supporters.

After publication of the Mueller Report and the clear evidence in it of Trump's obstruction of justice and abuse of power, and his cozy relationship with Vladimir Putin and Russia, 50 percent of "likely voters" approve of his job performance.

See Washington Post Staff, "The Mueller Report, annotated," *Washington Post*, Updated December 2, 2021 (11:04 p.m.).[96]

If what they have done for two years has not worked, one might think the Democrats would try something else. But no, they continue their dithering approach to starting an impeachment process with televised hearings, which conceivably could gain the public's attention.

Following Nancy Pelosi's firm determination to avoid impeachment proceedings, presumably in the belief that they might have a negative impact on the 2020 elections, Democrats come across as cowardly, afraid of Trump, and unwilling to risk their seats in a battle for American democracy and the rule of law.

Just think of how dilatory they have been in holding Attorney General William Barr and others in contempt of Congress. Pelosi is slow-walking everything on the erroneous assumption that the House has all the time in the world. It doesn't. By some time in the fall, media attention will shift to the horse-race coverage of who is leading in the Democratic primaries.

Pelosi will have won with her delaying tactics. Democrats will have, in effect, bet the farm on her judgment.

But what if, as the poll results suggest, she is wrong?

Leading Democratic contender Joe Biden has strongly attacked President Trump, and rightfully so. But he forgets that things that may seem self-evident to Democrats over age 40 may resonate little, if at all, with younger voters.

To win them over, he must—at a minimum—explain to them why NATO has been and remains important, and why Trump's trashing of World Trade Organization rules and international law with his tariffs has been both reckless and unlawful.

It is hard to see how the Democrats can halt Trump's assault on the Constitution and the rule of law. About their only hope to stop Trump in 2020 is to start an impeachment investigation and hearings in the House, right away, without further delay.

If they use impeachment hearings effectively to educate the American public as to the facts of Trump's "high crimes and misdemeanors," they may just have a chance of overcoming Trump's current momentum.

The choice for the Democrats is not between starting impeachment proceedings now and beating Trump in 2020, but rather between continuing their passivity, on the one hand, and seeing whether they can use impeachment proceedings now to educate the public in order to beat Trump (and other Republicans) in 2020.

Yet even if they initiate impeachment proceedings now, House Democrats will have to vigorously fight Trump in the courts in order to pierce his "executive privilege" and other defenses.

Vigorous legal action means *now, without delay*, e.g., right after he asserts executive privilege to block a witness. To date, Democratic House leaders have been lethargic in response to Trump's actions.

Watch the Rasmussen daily job approval poll. It is the one scoreboard where Democrats, and everyone else, should have their attention firmly fixed.

FURTHER READING

"The Democrats May Have Already Lost the 2020 Elections—Part II," *The Trenchant Observer*, July 17, 2019.[97]

43

September 18, 2019

Nancy Pelosi Is Inadvertently Helping Donald Trump

At times it seems that no person has done more to enable Donald Trump's undermining of the Constitution and the rule of law than U.S. House of Representatives Speaker Nancy Pelosi.

By her obstinate refusal to allow the Democratic majority in the House to vigorously exercise its presidential oversight responsibilities, she has acted to ensure that no House impeachment inquiry takes place to educate the American people in time to have an impact on the 2020 election.

By slow-walking House reactions to Trump's flagrant abuse of power in keeping Executive Branch officials from testifying before House Committees, she has enabled the president's defiance of the Constitution.

When Attorney General William Barr first defied a House subpoena to turn over the unredacted Mueller Report, the House should have immediately found him in contempt of Congress. The Democrats had the votes. But Pelosi came up with a delaying tactic, saying the House should hold off until it had a group of contempt citations to process all at once. That would be more efficient, it was argued. Time passed. Nothing happened. Barr was never held in contempt.

Seeing that there were no consequences for defying House subpoenas, Trump adopted a blanket policy of defying all House subpoenas, while

153

advancing totally spurious executive privilege and other legal justifications for not submitting to oversight proceedings.

As a result of Pelosi's blocking actions, the House Democrats failed utterly to educate the American people about Trump's crimes and misdemeanors, the only stratagem that might have helped puncture Trump's bubble of lies and distortions, which continue to envelop half of those who are likely voters in 2020.

The Rasmussen Daily Tracking Poll tells the story. On September 18, 2019,[98] 51 percent of likely voters approved of President Trump, whereas 49 percent disapproved.

The Democrats have wasted the summer and what was probably their last chance to educate the American people by setting forth the details of Trump's misdeeds as established in the Mueller Report and by other evidence, in televised hearings.

Pelosi appears to believe that Trump can be beaten by talking about bread-and-butter issues and ignoring his massive assault on the concept of Truth, the Constitution and the rule of law. She seems to think that the Democratic majority in the House can be preserved though this approach, thereby assuring her own personal hold on power.

She is wrong.

It may be too late for the Democrats in the House to reverse course, but they should try. A strategy based on fear of Trump and his supporters is bound to fail.

So long as the Democrats fail to reshape the playing field, as has been the case to date, their chances of defeating Trump and the Republicans in 2020 remain highly dubious.

Their pursuit of further evidence of Trump's high crimes and misdemeanors is like that of a detective who insists on investigating whether a murder suspect has committed another robbery, when the murder victim, the murder suspect, the gun, and video evidence of the suspect shooting it at the murder victim, backed by fingerprints and DNA evidence, are already lying on the evidence table.

Ironically, by her obstinate blocking of vigorous and effective action by the House, with a view to educating the American people, Nancy Pelosi turns out to be Trump's greatest enabler.

If he wins the 2020 election and the country moves further down the road to authoritarianism, as surely it will if he is reelected, she will bear a great part of the blame.

Many Democrats are absolutely disgusted with her leadership and the cowardice of the House Democrats. There are few, if any, examples of successful resistance to authoritarian leaders in other countries through acquiescence.

John F. Kennedy's Democratic Party of Profiles in Courage has become, under her leadership, the party of Profiles in Cowardice.

44

September 27, 2019

Should the Goal of Impeachment be Education or a Quick Trial?

Impeachment Inquiry Begins

BACKGROUND

See Mehdi Hasan, "Democrats, Please Don't Mess This Up. Impeach Trump for All His Crimes, Not Just for Ukraine," *The Intercept*, September 26, 2019 (10:35 a.m.).[99]

Nancy Pelosi announced on September 24, 2019 that the House was conducting an impeachment inquiry.

For once, the Democrats in the House seemed to have overcome their fear of Donald Trump, with the help of a "smoking gun" in the form of the whistleblower complaint, the Inspector General's report, and the transcript of Trump's July 25 telephone call with Ukrainian President Volodymyr Zelensky.

Now the Democrats, having experienced some of the power the House is invested with by the Constitution, are torn between their fear of Trump and losing their own election, on the one hand, and their desire to impeach him for all of the main impeachable offenses he has committed, on the other. These cover a broad range of subjects, including his contacts with and cooperation with the Russians and the obstruction of justice reported, with detailed evidence, in the Mueller Report, as well as other offenses such as his violation of the emoluments clause of the Constitution.

The choice appears to be between a swift impeachment inquiry into the Ukraine affair and vote on articles of impeachment, on the one hand, and a more methodical and time-consuming examination of the broader range of "high crimes and misdemeanors" the president has committed, on the other. The first looks easy, and the second more difficult.

It seems that the same fear of Trump which kept the Democrats from launching an impeachment inquiry, before the Ukraine affair made support for such an inquiry possible, is operating again. Should they pursue a narrow strategy aimed at a quick impeachment based on the Ukraine affair, or proceed now—finally—with a broader impeachment inquiry under that rubric?

Fear may lead representatives in districts where Trump is strong to want to avoid a broader inquiry, while going for a quick and clean victory on grounds which Republicans will find hard to defend against.

Some may favor such an approach based on a belief they can win the votes in the Senate to remove the president from office.

If the goal is simply to impeach the president and go for an early trial in the Senate, this narrow approach may seem appealing.

The risks, however, are great.

Republicans and Trump would undoubtedly seize on the fact that the offenses outlined in the Mueller Report and others were not deemed to be impeachable offenses by the House Democrats, as a vindication of Trump's narrative that he committed no wrongs.

Indeed, the Democrats could, however unwittingly, end up legitimizing Trump's other "high crimes and misdemeanors." With no educational impact on the electorate from the impeachment inquiry, the Democrats will have failed to puncture Trump's propaganda bubble, bolstered his argument that he has been the victim of a "witch hunt," and done little to reshape the playing field in a way which might help them win the 2020 elections.

Moreover, it is quite possible that with Democrats' eschewing the goal of educating the American people through the impeachment inquiry, Republicans in the Senate, while conceding the impropriety of Trump's actions relating to Ukraine, may simply vote against conviction on the grounds that the offenses are not serious enough to warrant removal from office.

If, on the other hand, the goal of educating the American people and electorate as to Trump's "high crimes and misdemeanors" is pursued in a more methodical manner, over a longer period of time, the impeachment inquiry could reshape the playing field for the 2020 elections.

See "The Impeachment Inquiry as a Tool for Educating the American People and Electorate," *The Trenchant Observer*, September 24, 2019.[100]

In this article, we wrote:

The immediate goal of the Impeachment Inquiry should be to educate the American people and electorate. Should the Democrats skip this step in a race to getting out articles of impeachment, they may lose the only opportunity they will have to break through the bubble of lies and distortions which engulf Trump supporters.

Here, the Democrats themselves need to understand that Trump's support is a product of mass propaganda, which has much more to do with the kind of mass psychology found in Germany in the 1930s than with their own highly refined arguments.

They need to smash Trump's bubble. Only then will those who might otherwise vote for Trump be able to hear their arguments.

The Impeachment Inquiry represents their best shot at piercing that bubble of propaganda, lies and distortions.

Ultimately, the issue boils down to whether the Democrats want to challenge Trump while pulling their punches because of their fear of him and the voters, or to mount an all-out challenge to Trump and his enablers, and their corruption and abuse of power, with a view to winning the 2020 elections. To achieve the latter, they will have to overcome their fears and take risks regarding their ability to get through to the voters with rational arguments.

If they choose to fully use the great powers which the Constitution grants the House and the Senate, they may be surprised at how powerful and effective they can be.

The biggest question for the Democrats, as for the Republicans, is whether they can overcome their fear of Trump.

FURTHER READING

See "The Scope of Impeachment: Elizabeth Drew Supports a Broad Inquiry," *The Trenchant Observer*, November 16, 2019.[101]

45

October 2, 2019

Emphasis on "Breaking News" and "New News" Shields Trump

As the news media dig deeper into the circumstances of the Ukrainian affair, in which the transcript of a July 25 telephone call between Donald Trump and President Volodymyr Zelensky shows that Trump asked the Ukrainian for a favor, two factors that favor Trump are coming fully into view.

First, the current nature of the news business produces a relentless quest for new "breaking news"—in more and more and more detail—even when the main facts of a development are firmly established.

In the Mueller inquiry, this was further complicated by what may be termed the "criminalization" of the impeachment process, where political judgments became subordinated to the details of proving guilt of a crime beyond a reasonable doubt.

This process has worked to Trump's advantage, as only new news gets media attention. In essence, only the newest "high crimes and misdemeanors" get high profile coverage in the media.

The older crimes or abuses tend to get forgotten in this political process dominated by the new news, the latest outrages. Consequently, high crimes and misdemeanors such as the ten instances of obstruction of justice detailed with overwhelming evidence in the Mueller Report tend to

160

be forgotten or viewed politically as not viable grounds for impeachment. Here, the political judgments of pundits and legislators looking to elections substitute for serious analysis of real "high crimes and misdemeanors."

A second factor amplifies the effects of the first, and also has the effect of helping Trump. That factor is that politicians, including Democrats critical of Trump, are basically seen on television or quoted in the newspapers primarily as they are reacting to the "breaking news" developments of new news.

In short, Democratic lawmakers become mere passive responders to new news developments.

The net result is that no one among the Democrats—with the possible exception of Joe Biden occasionally on the campaign trail—is summarizing and repeating the narrative of the principal crimes and abuses committed by the president over time.

If the Democrats understood the psychology of mass communications, they would be repeating that story every week, fitting new developments into an increasingly powerful overarching case against Trump.

This they do not do. They don't know how to get through to ordinary people, including those in Trump's corner who believe his lies and distortions.

Yet only if they build an overarching narrative, only if they tie new developments into such an overarching narrative and repeat that narrative as often as Trump mentions "the wall," will they have a chance to reshape the playing field in ways which might facilitate Trump's removal, whether through impeachment or the 2020 election.

46

October 14, 2019

Democrats Must Speak to Those Operating Outside a Rational Framework

President Trump Approval Rating, Rasmussen Daily Tracking Poll, October 14, 2019:[102]
Approve: 49 percent
Disapprove: 50 percent

In three years, the Democrats have not succeeded in breaking through to likely voters who support Donald Trump, as the Rasmussen Daily Tracking Poll reveals.

With all of the corruption and "high crimes and misdemeanors" committed by Trump in the public record, from the transcript of the conversation with Ukrainian President Volodymyr Zelensky to the ten examples of obstruction of justice set forth in the Mueller Report, citing cogent evidence, Trump's approval rating among "likely voters" has hardly changed.

Trump has succeeded with modern propaganda techniques in destroying belief in the concept of Truth among half the voting electorate, and in confusing issues so that the salience of his crimes is lost among the noise and distractions created by his endless lies and crimes and vulgarities—and, increasingly, his veiled or not so veiled threats of or calls for violence—to such an extent that his support remains largely intact.

Democrats have failed to dent Trump's support among a large portion of the voting public.

They should ask themselves why they have failed.

To date, there is little evidence that such self-examination has occurred or has borne fruit.

Trump has succeeded in creating a cult following, in much the same manner as did the leader of Germany in the 1930s and other authoritarian leaders who mastered the techniques of mass psychology and mass emotions.

The Democrats have argued to, and largely convinced, the half of the voting population that listens to and can understand logical or rational argument based on facts.

Trump's supporters include the 30-40 percent who aren't interested in and/or don't want to hear rational arguments which are critical of Trump. These and others could understand such arguments if they tried, and perhaps do from time to time, but even they are not interested because they are happy with his policies—the appointment of ideologically conservative judges, harsh anti-immigration policies, and large tax cuts for the wealthy—which benefit them directly, for example. Or perhaps they are simply content with the good economic news from a continuing expansion.

Trump's supporters are either happy to participate in the tribal politics of what has become a personal cult, or happy to look away from the crimes and outrages of the president in the belief they are getting policies they want, and the president's outrages will not in the end have an effect on them personally.

Civility, Truth, who cares? Political accountability be damned! Participating in the group actions of a cult can be fun.

Democrats are courting failure if they believe more evidence of crimes and wrongdoing will move enough Trump supporters to make possible his removal from office, whether through a Senate impeachment trial, or through the 2020 election.

The only way they can win is if they devise a strategy that will get through to the half of the electorate that currently supports Trump.

How can that be done?

Democrats need to think in terms of reaching that portion of the voting population that is not operating within a rational paradigm or framework.

They need to build a powerful narrative around themes and values that might resonate even with the broad masses of the population who are operating outside a rational framework. Such themes and values include the following:

Decency.

Betrayal.

Of the Constitution.

Of the rule of law.

Of the country and its national security interests.

Of those who have fought in Iraq, in Afghanistan, and even of those who have served in Syria.

Truth. Morality. Decency.

The Democrats need to craft simple, powerful messages, and then repeat them until every voter, even those operating outside the framework of reason and facts, gets the message.

In many respects, Trump supporters are like the Germans in the 1930s who looked the other way when atrocities were committed and who believed that none of that would affect them personally. Yet they were affected.

Trump supporters will likewise be affected.

Today, they need look no further than Syria and the betrayal of America's Kurdish allies, the surrender of the latter's territory to Bashar al-Assad, Vladimir Putin, and Iran, and the creation of conditions for the re-emergence of the Islamic State organization, Al Qaeda, and other terrorist groups.

Democrats need to examine why they have failed to persuade the non-rational voters who support Trump and deploy a narrative based on facts that might gain their attention and support.

They should avoid the trap of just focusing narrowly on Ukraine, which could be old news by the time it reaches the Senate, and easily dismissed by the Republicans as wrong but not sufficient cause for removal of the president.

There is also the matter of the historical record. If Trump were impeached only for Ukraine, would that mean that his other actions were okay?

Democrats need to boil down Trump's many crimes, lies, and vulgarities to a simple narrative, one that likely voters can understand. A simple yet powerful story of corruption and abuse of power. They need talented writers to help put it together.

Only in this manner will they have a chance to remove Trump.

They need to stop talking exclusively to themselves, to other Trump critics, and start addressing those who have not been listening, enthralled as they have been with the siren music of the Trump delusion.

47

November 10, 2019

Who Will Make the Case against Trump?

The House Democrats Have Failed

The House Democrats and other Trump critics have failed to make the case against President Donald J. Trump.

Two questions arise:

1. Why has this happened?

2. Who, if anyone, will make the case against Trump?

The answer to the first question has much to do with the daily news cycle and its focus on new developments. *See* Chapter 45, above.

The second question is difficult to answer.

Currently, the House Democrats are focused on the Ukrainian affair, which involves Trump's withholding of military assistance for Ukraine while demanding Ukraine launch public investigations into Joe Biden's and his son's activities in Ukraine, and for a separate investigation aimed at supporting a conspiracy theory—long discredited by all reputable news sources—that it was Ukraine, not Russia, which was behind the intervention in the U.S. elections in 2016. U.S. intelligence agencies and Robert Mueller in his report found the intervention in the U.S. elections to have been directed by Russia and by Vladimir Putin himself.

Before the Mueller Report, Democrats excused their own inaction on the grounds that they were waiting for Robert Mueller to conclude his investigation and issue his report. After that report became public, instead of synthesizing and broadcasting its conclusions for the American public to digest, they placed their hopes in Mueller's one day of testimony to dazzle the American public. Dazzle, he did not. Instead, he referred to his report, which called on Congress to act on his evidence and conclusions.

This the Democrats did not do, allowing the mass media to repeatedly report that the Mueller Report had "fizzled." What in fact had fizzled was any determination on the part of the House Democrats to take on the conclusions and evidence in the Mueller Report in order to synthesize its findings and present them to the American people, in digestible form, as part of the case for impeachment of President Trump.

With the revelations about Trump's July 25 telephone conversation with President Volodymyr Zelensky of Ukraine, House Democrats debated whether to focus only on the Ukraine affair, or more broadly on the principal examples of Trump's alleged malfeasance in office, including matters detailed in the Mueller Report.

With a focus primarily on the Ukraine affair, but without definitively excluding other matters, House Democrats are now holding public hearings while moving quickly toward voting on articles of impeachment.

While final decisions have not been made on how broad these articles will be, the current focus remains on the Ukraine affair.

Still, the Ukraine affair probably represents one percent of the "high crimes and misdemeanors" Trump appears to have committed and to continue to be committing while in office.

Almost every day, it seems, he appears to engage in some form of obstruction of justice, whether witness tampering (e.g., by demanding that the identity of the whistleblower in the Ukraine affair be made public—despite the fact that their anonymity is protected by law), corruption, or some other abuse of power.

The apparent Trump conspiracy to commit crimes and intimidate witnesses and otherwise cover up those crimes seems to be sprawling and ongoing. The Justice Department and other government agencies appear to have been corrupted to serve Trump's personal ends, whether to avoid removal from office after impeachment or to win reelection in 2020, or to avoid prosecution after leaving office for crimes he appears to have committed.

The House Democrats delayed the impeachment inquiry for many months, losing valuable time. Yet if the impeachment process were viewed as an opportunity to educate the American people about the details of Trump's alleged malfeasance in office, it could serve an incredibly useful purpose, reintroducing facts and their analysis into the public discussion of his actions in office.

Whether they, or anyone else, makes the broader case based on all of the high crimes and misdemeanors Trump has allegedly committed, or a selection of the most salient examples, remains to be seen.

Who will make the case against Trump?

A brilliant synthesis of all the evidence that is out there is required, presented in readable form that can be digested by the American electorate. Whoever writes this synthesis should neither overestimate nor underestimate the intelligence of the American people when they become focused on matters of ultimate importance.

Nor should whoever writes this synthesis get caught up in the technicalities of the criminal law. Instead, they should focus on preparing a synthesis for what is essentially a political process. That does not mean that crimes, such as those described in the Mueller Report, should be overlooked.

Who, indeed, will make the case against Trump?

48

December 14, 2019

The Rule of Law in Retreat: The Two House Articles of Impeachment

With the adoption by the U.S. House Judiciary Committee of two narrowly focused articles of impeachment, centered on and limited to the Ukraine affair, we can observe in motion a major retreat by one of the world's leading democracies from dedication to Constitutional government and the rule of law.

House Democrats, timorous and afraid of taking on Trump head-on, have persuaded themselves that it is too risky to include in the articles of impeachment (roughly equivalent to a charging document or an indictment) matters beyond Trump's alleged abuse of power in the Ukraine affair and his obstruction of Congress in refusing to cooperate with the impeachment investigation.

The "abuse of power" charge is that Trump conditioned the delivery of military aid approved by Congress and a White House visit by Ukrainian president Volodymyr Zelensky on the latter's conducting and announcing investigations into Joe Biden and his son Hunter, and into a conspiracy theory involving a company called CrowdStrike.

According to this conspiracy theory, CrowdStrike had computer servers in Ukraine, which would prove that it had been Ukraine, not

Russia, which interfered in the November 2016 elections. By withholding the aid and withholding Zelensky's visit to the White House, the Democrats charge, Trump engaged in what was essentially extortion or bribery for his own personal benefit, to get dirt on a prominent rival for the presidency in 2020.

The "obstruction of Congress" count, contained in the second article of impeachment, is based on Trump's refusal to comply with subpoenas for documents and testimony from government officials relating to the Ukraine affair, even ordering them not to appear before Congress.

In so narrowly focusing the impeachment articles, omitting an article on "obstruction of justice" for the many cases detailed in the Mueller Report, the House Democrats have in effect conceded that the abuses of power and obstruction of justice Mueller described did not merit attention in their effort to remove Trump from office.

The omission of the obstruction of justice charge plays into Trump's narrative that the whole Mueller investigation was a "witch hunt" and a "hoax," and that he had done nothing wrong.

Even limiting their charges to the two articles, to remove Trump the Democrats need to secure the approval of two-thirds of the members of the Republican-controlled Senate.

Without having made a dent in Trump's propaganda bubble, they are extremely unlikely to achieve this result.

Barring a miracle, Trump will be acquitted in a Senate trial. He will then claim that he has been vindicated, with good prospects for riding this propaganda horse to victory in the November 2020 presidential election.

This is an extraordinarily sad development for advocates of Constitutional government and the rule of law.

The House Democrats' dramatic failure has had a major impact on perceptions, with Roger Cohen, a leading columnist for the *New York Times*, speaking of the likelihood of Trump winning the 2020 election.

FURTHER READING

"House Democrats, Stampeding Like Buffaloes, Are Heading toward a Cliff," *The Trenchant Observer*, November 15, 2019.[103]

Part Five

2020 – Year Four of the Trump Presidency (I):

Testing Elements of a Coup

49

January 19, 2020

Impeachment: The Republican Party on Trial

Among all the hype and Republican propaganda relating to the Senate trial of impeached President Donald J. Trump, it is useful to maintain a laser-like focus on the underlying question of just who is on trial here.

Of course, Trump is on trial for the high crimes and misdemeanors detailed in the two articles of impeachment approved by the House.

But let there be no doubt about it: Republican senators and the Republican Party itself are also on trial in the Senate.

We already know from the abundant details in the public record that Trump has been impeached for only a small percentage of the crimes he has committed in office.

The Senate "trial" is shaping up to be a massive battle between the facts and the truth, on the one hand, and the lies and diversions and irrelevancies of Republicans, in both the House and the Senate, on the other.

Those who have been interested in the facts and the truth will continue to support the Democrats and a judgment in the trial based on an impartial search for the truth. Those who have been willfully asleep, or who have directly sold their souls to Trump, are likely to continue to defend their leader, no matter what the facts and the evidence may show.

The Republicans will shout and wave their arms, trying to use every trick of mass propaganda to distract voters from the real evidence relating to the offenses for which Trump has been impeached. The Democrats will try to prove their case with facts.

Who knows who will win the propaganda war? Who knows if there are any Republican senators who will try to save their own Republican Party from the dustbin of history, and in doing so also act to save the Republic?

FURTHER READING

"Republicans' White-Knuckle Tactics in Limiting Governors' Powers Seal Image as Anti-Democratic Party," *The Trenchant Observer*, December 5, 2018.[104]

50

January 25, 2020

Trump as a World Historical Figure of Extraordinary Skill and Cunning

The Propaganda Bubble and the Cover-up

We have reached a point in the impeachment show that we predicted in the spring, when Nancy Pelosi was firmly resisting calls to launch a broad impeachment inquiry into the misdeeds of President Donald Trump.

The point at which we currently find ourselves is one at which few dents have been made in the wall of lies, distortions, and distractions that secure the Trump propaganda bubble, a bubble which enshrouds the consciousness of his cultish supporters, and increasing numbers of those he has corrupted. President Trump's job approval rating remains strong.

On January 24, the Rasmussen Daily Tracking Poll put Trump's approval at 49 percent, tied with his 49 percent disapproval rating.

The bubble must be defended against the truth at any cost, as demonstrated by the fact that Fox News quit showing the Senate proceedings on Thursday night, January 23, shielding its viewers from seeing Adam Schiff's powerful summation of the case against Trump.

Those he has corrupted double down, seeking validation through their own efforts to corrupt others, their own public lies and distortions, and their own active participation in a conspiracy to cover up the President's misdeeds. Others, who have made a devil's bargain to accept Trump in exchange for tax relief and strong stock market gains, will likely stick by their bargains.

Trump as a World Historical Figure of Extraordinary Skill and Cunning

As Bob Woodward has told us, Trump rules by Fear,[105] the title of his 2018 book on Trump and his administration.

Yet Trump is a master of other tools as well. He can apparently be quite charming, a quality he shares with some other notable demagogues.

Democrats should not underestimate him, or the threat he poses to American democracy.

Trump is a man of cunning media intelligence, the fruit of a lifetime of obsession and immersion. That he knows little else is disappointing, but after the 2016 campaign should not come as a surprise.

He is at the same time a master of the greatest Nazi, Soviet, and Russian propaganda techniques, and a highly skillful and engaging TV performer.

He is indeed a world historical figure, with incredible power to shape national values, the ability of Americans to appreciate the truth, and their capacity to adopt policies based on science and ascertainable facts. With his successful defiance of the Constitution and congressional oversight, he has acquired unprecedented power to affect the course of both domestic and world events.

Who could have predicted his enormous success in corrupting the political leaders of the Republican Party, and the consciousness and values of some 40-50 percent of the American electorate?

Since the spring, we have recommended using the impeachment process as a tool to chip away at Trump's propaganda wall and the propaganda bubble, which has reduced the conduct of affairs of state to a tribal clash. In that tribal clash, up to one half of the population does not appear to give a hoot about the truth or the core values which have been central to the American story in the past.

Well, here we are. The House Democrats ignored for too long our sage advice to use the impeachment process as an educational tool, to chip away with sledgehammers of truth at Trump's propaganda wall and to puncture the bubble of lies and distortions he has so masterfully created.

Now, with the House hearings and two narrow impeachment articles, they have begun. They have done an outstanding job within the narrow compass of their effort. But they have ceded control of the educational project to Mitch McConnell and the Senate Republicans, who seem determined to bring it to a swift end, to shut it down in time for the Super Bowl and the State of the Union Speech on February 4, 2020.

The Union is in terrible shape. To stress the travesty that is taking place in the Senate impeachment trial, Democrats should boycott that address.

A Grand Illusion?

Perhaps it was but a grand illusion, an unfounded hope that in the end truth and decency would triumph over corruption and the antithesis of those values which we liked to tell ourselves we hold dear.

That is the American Illusion, after all, that we are a moral people, blessed by American exceptionalism, a city on a shining hill, viewed by the rest of the world with envy and admiration.

But now, it looks like the Democrats are headed toward certain defeat in the impeachment trial of Donald Trump in the Senate.

Miracles are always possible. Yet moral courage, as Adam Schiff, the House impeachment manager, pointed out on January 23, is a rare thing. John F. Kennedy gave powerful examples of such courage in his

Pulitzer-Prize-winning book, *Profiles in Courage* (1956).[106] Now would be a good time for Republican senators to read that book.

We can only hope and pray that a sufficient number of them will vote to hear testimony from witnesses and subpoena critical documentary evidence which Trump has withheld up to now. As Adam Schiff said in closing his argument on January 24, "Give America a fair trial. She deserves that."

But hope is no substitute for resolute action to take on the challenges which reality poses.

51

January 30, 2020

Trump, the Impeachment Trial, and Hope

The House Managers have put on a good case in the Senate impeachment trial of Donald Trump. An eloquent case.

Unfortunately, the Republican party has been totally cowed and corrupted by our authoritarian leader, Donald Trump. Republicans control the Senate, with 53 votes. Tragically, not more than two or three appear ready to take a principled stand even on allowing witnesses and additional documentary evidence to be considered before they "acquit" Trump of the "high crimes and misdemeanors" for which he is charged.

Trump's defense lawyers have offered an endless stream of bad-faith arguments aimed at sowing confusion and throwing a lifeline to cynical senators who will vote to acquit Trump, ignoring the evidence that is in front of their eyes.

The arguments these senators will give to justify their votes for acquittal—against witnesses and documentary evidence—sound like Fox News talking points. Ignoring the clear evidence. Failing to rebut the factual evidence provided in sworn witness testimony and documents provided by the House.

The Republican Party has become, clearly and beyond the shadow of a doubt, a bad-faith party.

But where does that leave the rest of us, the half of the country which still believes in good faith, truth, and the rule of law?

Trump defenders and cultists speak and act as if it is all a big game, as if none of the lies and distortions of the leader make any difference.

Yet they do make a difference.

Trumpists lay the groundwork for a second term by the authoritarian leader, who will be beyond the reach of the law or the Constitution if the Republicans retain the Senate or gain the House and he is reelected in November.

How did America come to this point? How can it escape its current path of descent toward authoritarian government?

The answer is far from clear.

Democratic leaders should not abandon those who believe in the Constitution and the rule of law. After the sham trial and acquittal in the Senate, these believers in the rule of law need to have some reasoned grounds for hope, beyond the hopes of Democratic candidates to win their own individual elections.

They need to see defenders of the Constitution and the rule of law taking the fight to the leader and his apologists every day.

There are two things that the Democrats might do.

First, they can resume House impeachment hearings into the cases of obstruction of justice detailed in the Mueller Report and other "high crimes and misdemeanors." They should do so with a view toward piercing Trump's propaganda bubble, with a steady parade of witnesses and documentary evidence. Every day they should be wielding sledgehammers of truth to chip away at Trump's propaganda wall.

Second, in connection with continued impeachment hearings, they can assemble a comprehensive yet succinct and persuasive narrative that tells the story of the leader's actions to undermine the Constitution and the rule of law. This they should do in terms that even the half of the population that supports the leader can easily understand.

Can they succeed? Can America avoid an authoritarian government where the leader is above the law, and real congressional oversight is but a distant memory?

Who knows?

However uncertain the outcome, they—and we—must try. With every sinew of our being. Every day.

Amid the ruins of his country following World War II, the German philosopher Karl Jaspers, in *The Question of German Guilt* (1947)—originally published in German as *Die Schuldfrage* in 1946—analyzed in rigorous detail the many evasions and excuses then commonly heard in Germany in response to charges of guilt for what had occurred. Near the end of the book, he also warned:

And yet, we are oppressed by one nightmarish idea: if a dictatorship in Hitler's style should ever rise in America, all hope would be lost for ages. …

The German fate could provide all others with experience. If only they would understand this experience! We are no inferior race. Everywhere people have similar qualities. Everywhere there are violent, criminal, vitally capable minorities apt to seize the reins if occasion offers, and to proceed with brutality.

–Karl Jaspers, *The Question of German Guilt* (1947) (E.B. Ashton transl.), New York: Fordham University Press, 2001, p. 93.[107]

"Oh, don't be silly," a reader may say.

Yet if half the population has lost its belief in facts and truth, if the leader is above the law and can act without congressional oversight, if top government leaders have become subject to the leader's will, Jaspers' warning may not be so silly after all.

See Timothy Snyder, *On Tyranny: Twenty Lessons from the Twentieth Century*, New York: Crown Publishing Group, 2017.[108]

On Truth, Snyder wrote the following:

To abandon facts is to abandon freedom. If nothing is true, then no one can criticize power, because there is no basis on which to do so. If anything is true, the biggest wallet pays for the most blinding lights.

–Chapter 10: "Believe in Truth."

52

April 3, 2020

Lethal Incompetence: Masks

The eruption in demand for dwindling amounts of masks has resulted in a kind of global supply-chain bedlam. In the United States, the federal government has decided against commandeering American factories to create a new stream of masks. Instead, federal officials are competing against states, hospitals and medical suppliers for the same pool of masks, which come mostly from China.

–Jack Nicas, "It's Bedlam in the Mask Market, as Profiteers Out-Hustle Good Samaritans," *New York Times*, April 3, 2020.[109]

In the United State, three months after the administration of Donald Trump received intelligence and other information about the developing coronavirus epidemic, and over two months after its impact in the United States had become clear to informed scientists, the federal government has still failed to take the kind of emergency actions necessary to ensure that health workers have sufficient masks to protect themselves from infection while treating patients.

Two months after the threat was obviously clear to scientists, the U.S. government has not taken sufficient action to ensure that the public has access to surgical masks to help protect themselves, in conjunction with the social distancing and stay-at-home orders currently in place in over 30 states.

185

What is worse, the government has lied to the American people about the protection that might be offered by surgical masks to those members of the public who must go out in order to carry out essential tasks, such as buying groceries and going to pharmacies.

Aside from willful refusal to recognize and acknowledge the nature of the threat, based on science and the opinions of epidemiological experts, one of the greatest failures of the American administration has been its failure to marshal the enormous productive resources of the United States to produce the necessary equipment and personnel required to meet the threat.

The crippling failures included:

1) a failure to provide the many millions of tests required;

2) a failure to ensure the necessary supply of Personal Protective Equipment (PPE), including masks;

3) a failure to take effective action to produce a sufficient number of hospital beds, Intensive Care Units (ICUs), and ventilators; and

4) a failure to organize and deploy a sufficient number of medical personnel to staff the ICUs and operate the ventilators that may be needed to save hundreds of thousands, if not millions, of lives.

All of this lethally incompetent governmental response is epitomized by the decision not to order the production of masks in the U.S.

As Jack Nicas reports, "In the United States, the federal government has decided against commandeering American factories to create a new stream of masks." This decision is a poignant illustration of the lethal incompetence of this administration.

The second aspect of the present fiasco has been the continuing failure of the administration to tell the truth to the American people. Leaving aside the countless lies and misrepresentations that have come from the top of the administration, let us focus only on what they have said about masks.

First, they deliberately misled the American people by asserting that surgical masks are not needed by the general public because they offer no or little protection and, moreover, are not needed in view of the social-distancing and stay-at-home orders that are in place in a majority of states.

Their initially unstated rationale was that the masks were needed by medical personnel, and that this disinformation was necessary in order to manage the lack of capacity problem. In recent days, they have added a totally specious rationale for not recommending even the use of home-made masks—that such a recommendation could lead people to be overconfident about the efficacy of the masks and relax their compliance with social-distancing orders.

In other words, a duplicitous government has decided to lie to the American people in order to manage a lack of supply problem that is entirely of its own creation. The key point here is the belief by high government officials that the people are stupid (e.g., would relax compliance with social-distancing recommendations), or that they can be lied to (e.g., surgical masks are ineffective) in order to ensure that medical personnel get the masks.

The obvious contradiction between telling the public surgical masks are ineffective and emphasizing that they are needed by medical personnel for their own protection merely underlines the belief of officials that the American people are incredibly stupid, and that science can be ignored in order to manipulate them.

The net result has been a complete loss of governmental credibility, with the attendant confusion and disorganization one might expect. The coronavirus pandemic will not be effectively controlled by a lethally incompetent administration which has lost all credibility.

The administration must stop lying to the American people.

FURTHER READING

1) "Should Trump Be Impeached and Removed from Office NOW If It Would Save 100,000 Lives? 200,000?" *The Trenchant Observer*, July 15, 2020;[110]

2) "COVID-19 in the U.S.: How Can We Grasp the Significance of 200,000 Deaths?" *The Trenchant Observer*, September 12, 2020;[111]

3) "Trump's Failure to Protect the American People from the Coronavirus," *The Trenchant Observer*, October 12, 2020.[112]

53

May 14, 2020

Why Trump Is Likely to Win in November

As things are going now, President Donald J. Trump is likely to be reelected in the November 2020 presidential election.

It is important to understand why this is the case, if Democrats and others are to have any chance of increasing their prospects for victory in the election of the person who will be president until January 20, 2025.

Why is Trump likely to be reelected?

First, he is a political genius.

This is a fact that Democrats do not understand, and do not want to accept. Only a political genius could have achieved the support in the polls which Trump has maintained, given his record of crimes, abuses of power, and other malfeasance in office.

His malfeasance in office includes, most notably, his mishandling of the coronavirus epidemic, leading to the greatest economic catastrophe since the Great Depression and a death toll which now exceeds 80,000 people, and is likely to exceed 150,000-200,000 Americans by November 2020.

Trump has spent his entire life observing and trying to manipulate the media. He polished his sense of how the crowd responds emotionally to events during his 15 years (2004-2017) running *The Apprentice* on NBC. He has learned how to dominate each daily news cycle and continues to do so very effectively. With this power, he is able to distract public attention from reporting on his malevolent policies and misdeeds, and endlessly create new controversies that keep him in the spotlight while avoiding serious and sustained consideration of his lies and lawlessness.

Politically, he has sensed the deep emotional desire in the population to escape from the COVID-19 lockdown, physical-distancing, and mask restrictions. After much hesitation, inaction and dismissal of the seriousness of the pandemic, Trump reluctantly appeared to accept the advice of epidemiological experts and other scientists to urge lockdowns and other social restrictions—belatedly, and always with a wink and a nod to those who opposed such measures. In the end, however, he has finally and ultimately come down on the side of "opening up" the country, ignoring the warnings of his experts.

This appears to be politically astute. He will be able to campaign on the platform that he is and has always been the advocate of the working man (or woman) who wants to get back to work. In doing so, he will be appealing to a massive and deep emotional longing on the part of most people in the United States.

The fact that 200,000 people may die as a result of such an approach does not appear to be a matter of concern, either to the president or to the great masses of Americans from which he draws his supporters.

Second, Trump is likely to be reelected because of his successful use of mass political propaganda. He has led a largely successful war on the concept of Truth, at least among Republicans and other supporters.

Third, Trump has been conducting a successful and sophisticated social media operation, which operates effectively in spreading his propaganda. In comparison, Democrats and Biden are dead-in-the-water. There is a lack of decisiveness in Biden's campaign, which has not even been able to resolve its conflict with Michael Bloomberg's Snapfish company over who should be in charge of the campaign's social medial operations.

Fourth, Trump has been leading a successful process of *Gleichschaltung* (synchronization of views and positions) in taking total control of the Republican Party.

Fifth, he is the incumbent, and exercises all of the powers of the presidency.

Other factors pointing to a likely Trump victory include a lack of funding for the Democrats' social media operations, and the failure of the House Democrats to take on Trump directly through a broad impeachment inquiry.

Democrats appear clueless regarding the fact that Trump is beating them with his appeals to and manipulation of mass emotions. They don't understand how Trump's furtherance of a world of irrationality advances his objectives, whereas their own appeals to reason seem to have already reached the reachable and are now dismissed by broad masses of people who are tired of experts and reason.

54

June 2, 2020

Rehearsal for a Coup d'État?

Violence in American Cities and "the Chaos President"

BACKGROUND

See,

1) Ryan O'Connell, "Come November, a U.S. Coup d'État? Could Donald Trump Call Out the U.S. Army Again, after Losing the November Election?" *Salon*, June 12, 2020;[113]

2) Katie Shepherd, "'It Was Like Being Preyed Upon': Portland Protesters Say Federal Officers in Unmarked Vans Are Detaining Them," *Washington Post*, July 17, 2020 (6:58 a.m. EDT).[114]

Good historians and the best journalists with years of experience have an extraordinary skill: exceptional pattern recognition ability.

They are able to look at a wide and complex array of information and to discern what among the mass of reports and developments is truly significant, what is salient, what truly stands out. They are able to connect the dots. And by a process which involves intuition nurtured by years of experience as well as logic, they are able to see patterns.

In doing so, they are able to draw lessons from previous experiences which fit a given pattern, and even anticipate the range of possibilities for future developments. Their anticipations or intimations about the future are never simply true or false, but often provide critical checklists with which to monitor the direction in which events are flowing. In a similar manner, drawing on years of experience as an amateur historian, chronicler and analyst of political events in many countries, the author has noted a certain pattern of events in the United States which raises grave questions of national concern.

Looking at the impact of the coronavirus pandemic, the violence in major American cities since the killing of George Floyd by Minneapolis police on Monday, May 25, 2020, the pattern of President Donald J. Trump's lawless and authoritarian behavior over the last three and a half years and, more specifically, the manner in which he has fanned the flames of violence in America while evidencing darker motives, we are struck with the following question:

Are we witnessing a dress rehearsal for a coup d'état by Donald Trump and his allies?

Such a coup could be launched to prevent his having to turn over power to a successor as a result of the November 3, 2020 election, or even earlier as a result of impeachment by the House of Representatives and a vote to remove him from office by the Senate of the United States.

Why the House of Representatives is not pursuing a new impeachment inquiry given Trump's broad range of unconstitutional and lawless behavior, notwithstanding the wholly predictable failure of their first attempt based on two narrow grounds related to Ukraine, is beyond understanding. It could and should be the subject of separate articles by many people.

Could the violent riots and looting underway in many American cities provide an opportunity for, or be a rehearsal for, an unconstitutional takeover of the government by Trump and his supporters?

Consider These Facts

Before this possibility is dismissed as fanciful, the reader should consider the following facts:

1. There is clear evidence of coordination in launching the violent attacks attendant to demonstrations in major U.S. cities. Computers in Minnesota's state network of computers, and those of Minneapolis, for example, were subjected to large-scale denial of service attacks beginning on Thursday, May 28, if not earlier.

2. A significant percentage of those arrested in the Minneapolis area (20-45 percent according to reports) were from outside the city. Many arrived in cars and trucks filled with rocks and other materials. A number of them were wearing some kind of black uniform.

3. While the racial breakdown of arrestees has not generally been disclosed, there are reports that many of them were white right-wing extremists. Calls apparently went out on right-wing websites and social media for them to converge on areas where peaceful demonstrations were planned. On Sunday, President Trump made an appeal for his followers to converge on the White House Sunday evening: "MAGA NIGHT AT THE WHITE HOUSE," he tweeted.

4. The president and the attorney general have loudly proclaimed that the violence was caused by ANTIFA and other leftist groups, without offering a single shred of evidence to support their claims.

5. The president has himself fanned the flames of violence with incendiary statements, such as "When the looting starts, the shooting starts"; and statements that "vicious dogs" were ready to set upon demonstrators at the White House, and that the youngest, boldest, and most eager secret servicemen were being sent to the front lines.

6. The president has made no major public speech or statement condemning the George Floyd homicide, or seeking to calm the exalted spirits which exist in many disparate locations throughout the country.

For anyone who had studied Adolf Hitler's actions and trajectory, his seizure of power following the Reichstag fire on February 27, 1933 should not have come as a surprise.

Similarly, if Donald Trump were to use the coronavirus pandemic and riots in American cities as a pretext for sending in the U.S. military (which he has already threatened to do), no one who has studied his behavior should be surprised.

Race is an extraordinarily explosive issue in the United States. Trump has blown dog whistles or more to white right-wing racist extremists. He has threatened violence.

Race is an issue that is so fraught that, tapping into primordial fears and unconscious motives, it can be manipulated to move millions of people to violent and irrational behavior. Hitler, with his lies and propaganda, brilliantly used the Jews and the Communists as means to wreak his demonic will upon the world.

Trump has a similar brilliance at using massive lies and propaganda to achieve his political ends. With Hitler, he shares one overriding characteristic: an utter disregard for the truth.

Depending on how this dress rehearsal turns out, if that is what it is, Trump may in the future have both the means and the opportunity to launch a coup d'état in the United States.

This could happen if he loses the November election, claims fraud and refuses to turn over power, and sends millions of his supporters, many armed, into the streets. It could happen even earlier if he seeks to call off or postpone the November elections on the grounds that the COVID-19 risks are too great, given the advancing ravages of the pandemic.

The temptation for him to resort to such extremes may be growing, as his prospects for winning a fair election recede. Over 104,000 Americans have died from COVID-19 in the last three months. By November, the number could easily exceed 200,000, and probably will. Forty million

Americans are out of work. The real economy, notwithstanding a stock market buoyed by hopes and illusions, is in free-fall.

Has Russia Helped Fan the Flames of Violence?

One big question is out there: Has Russia helped fan the flames of violence by coordinating activities, including by carrying out denial of service attacks on Minnesota's government computers? If it wasn't Russia, who was it?

Ordinarily, the FBI and other intelligence agencies would be fully engaged in investigating these and related questions. It is highly dubious whether they are now in a position or have the will to do so under Attorney General William Barr and the Trump loyalists who now head the intelligence agencies.

Trump as the Chaos President

Worth recalling at this juncture is the fact that Steve Bannon, Trump's former (and perhaps current) close advisor, who is brilliant if in an evil way, has long been a great fan of Vladimir Lenin, who succeeded in bringing the Bolsheviks to power in Russia in 1917 amid incredible chaos.

President Trump is a chaos president. The current chaos serves his ends.

Could Trump attempt to launch a coup d'état in the United States? Absolutely.

Whether he could succeed is a question whose answer would be up to all of us, particularly those in the military, the National Guard, and in police forces around the country—and especially those who command them.

FURTHER READING

1) Missy Ryan, Paul Sonne and Josh Dawsey, "White House Intensifies Effort to Install Pentagon Personnel Seen as Loyal to Trump," *Washington Post*, June 25, 2020 (2:30 p.m. EST);[115]

2) Helene Cooper and Eric Schmitt, "Defense Secretary Faces White House Pressure on Aides and a Military Promotion; Senior Defense Department Personnel Who Are Perceived as White House Critics Are Resigning or Facing Reprisal," *New York Times*, June 25, 2020 (Updated 3:41 p.m. ET).[116]

55

June 6, 2020

Trump's Coup d'État:
A Framework of Inquiry

Elements of a Successful Coup D'état

To succeed, you have to control or "dominate":

1. Guns

    a. Military interference in military chain of command
        See Jon Bateman, "The Guardrails Are Off the U.S. Military; It's No Longer Guaranteed That the Pentagon Will Resist Unlawful Orders from the President; And the Rot is Deeper Than You Think," *Politico*, June 6, 2020 (7:00 a.m. EDT).[117]

        Jon Bateman is a fellow at the Carnegie Endowment for International Peace. He previously was special assistant to then-Chairman of the Joint Chiefs of Staff Gen. Joseph Dunford.

    b. Police
        1) Trump sends his "little green men" to police Lafayette Square and Washington, D.C.

c. Armed militia
    1) Michigan State House
    2) Armed men along march routes of demonstrators
    3) Armed men at demonstrations

2. Information

a. Attacks on press, lies, and propaganda

b. Assumptions
    1) The leader can control news and flow of information.
    2) Independent news media can be discredited or silenced.
    3) State propaganda (or Trump propaganda) will dominate the media and other news sources:
        aa. Fox News
        bb. One America News

c. Social media
    1) Why Twitter is such a big deal
    2) Russian help

3. Direct Control of Executive Branch

a. Assumption: Justice Department and Intelligence agencies can be subordinated to the leader's will, both defensively and offensively.
    E.g., Russian interference will not be reported.

b. Attack on Post Office
    1) Can be used to block voting by mail during coronavirus pandemic.

4. Neutralization or Control of Congress

a. Unconstitutional defiance of Congressional Oversight Authority

b. Political neutralization of impeachment power

c. Judicial review blocked or neutralized

5. Control or Neutralization of the Judiciary

a. Assumption: The Supreme Court and Federal Judiciary will not block Trump's federal government actions.

b. Assumption: Supreme Court will uphold president and Executive if challenged by state or local officials, or private parties.

6. Subservience or Neutralization of State and Local Leaders

a. Assumption: State and local leaders can be coerced (bludgeoned) into subservience or acquiescence.
    1) Use of budget
    2) Use of federal law, executive decrees, and Supreme Court

7. Big Business and Financial Sector Will Acquiesce, and Help

a. Assumption: Big business and Wall Street will go along.
    1) Benefits to companies
        aa) Benefits to companies (tax breaks, subsidies, bailouts, regulatory changes)
        bb) Benefits to key business decision-makers (e.g., key officers)

FURTHER READING

Elie Mystal,[118] "The Question Isn't Whether Trump Will Go Full Authoritarian—It's How We'll Respond; We Know That No One Is Coming to Save Us from Trump. So How Will We Save Ourselves?" *The Nation*, June 2, 2020.[119]

56

June 7, 2020

The Crowd in the Streets, and the Democrats' Failure to Lead

Race is an explosive issue, and there are crowds in the streets. Democratic leadership, of the crowd in the streets, is nowhere to be found.

It is as if an entire country just discovered that there is a long history of racism and racial oppression in the United States.

Everyone is smacking their forehead, expressing growing anger at one outrage after another.

A crowd, without leadership, becomes a mob, governed by the unpredictable passions that may sweep through its members at any particular moment. It is essentially irrational, and easily manipulated.

See Gustave Le Bon, *The Crowd* (1895).

There is no guiding, calculating intelligence directing the crowd, or at least this crowd, except potentially that of outsiders who understand mob psychology and seek to manipulate the crowd for their own purposes.

We may never know who instigated and coordinated the violence and the looting that occurred over the last ten days, but we can certainly say it

202

has served Trump's interests and it would come as no surprise if he and his followers turned out to be behind it.

With so many people so emotionally involved, indeed understandably so, there does not seem to be a guiding purpose or unifying plan of action to guide the crowd.

Martin Luther King, Jr. mobilized millions of Americans, black and white, to take part in massive demonstrations. But he had goals and used mass demonstrations to secure important objectives as part of a larger strategic plan or vision.

Today, in Minneapolis, the crowd demanded that the city disband the police department. A loud demand to "defund the police" is heard in many cities. This is the irrational behavior of a crowd. The idea, however appealing on an immediate emotional level, is utter nonsense.

Why would the Democrats, or even the demonstrators, want to turn every police officer in the country against Joe Biden and the Democratic Party?

You can see the political commercials the crowd is making for Donald Trump, of masses of people demanding that police departments be dismantled, so that looting and violence can again achieve free rein.

You can also see Trump setting up his campaign line that the country is threatened by mobs in the streets engaging in violence, arson, and looting.

Where are the Democratic leaders?

Are they afraid of the crowd?

Is there no one who can influence the crowd to not give ammunition to Donald Trump for his electoral campaign?

Has there been any Democratic leader who could urge the members of the crowd, strongly, to absolutely wear masks and to try to maintain physical distancing, as we are still in the middle of the coronavirus pandemic?

See Ross Douthat, "Why the Coronavirus Is Winning; A Virus Doesn't Care About Our Ideological Preconceptions," *New York Times*, June 6, 2020.[120]

Aren't there any Democratic leaders who can do more than cheer the outrage of the demonstrators and help steer them toward achieving concrete objectives?

Aren't there any Democratic leaders who can channel the energy and outrage of the crowd into specific voter registration and turn-out-the-vote programs that can help defeat Trump?

Will every demonstrator register to vote, and then vote in November? Where is the Democratic leader who will urge all the members of the crowd to make a solemn pledge to register to vote and to vote on November 3, 2020?

This is the least that we can ask of the Democrats and of the crowd.

We should also ask the House Democrats to begin an impeachment inquiry into the leader's abuses of power and violations of the law and the Constitution over the last three and a half years. They don't have to approve the articles of impeachment unless the votes show up in the Senate. That *could* happen. They just have to be ready.

The Democrats are not going to waltz to a victory over Trump and the Republicans in November.

They had better start fighting.

As part of that fight, they should seek to guide the crowd so that it does not engage in actions that feed into Trump's campaign narrative, while channeling the crowd's energies toward achieving real objectives in the brutal world of power politics.

At the end of the day, if Trump is reelected, all of the crowd's outrage and eloquent words will have no lasting impact. A reelected Trump would thwart them and their proposed reforms at every step of the way.

We all need to focus, soon, regardless of whether the demonstrations continue, on the 100-year catastrophe of the COVID-19 pandemic, and the battle to save our democracy at the polls on November 3 — or to remove Trump earlier through the impeachment process if that becomes possible.

The ultimate battle with Trump is over whether we want a government and a society ruled by Reason, or by Unreason. It is time for the Democrats to step up to the plate and fight, with all that they have, for a world of Reason.

FURTHER READING

1) "Demonstrators, Having Made Their Point, Now Play Into Trump's Campaign Narrative," *The Trenchant Observer*, June 2, 2020;[121]

2) "The Elephant in the Room: Russia's Role in the Demonstrations," *The Trenchant Observer*, June 10, 2020.[122]

57

June 19, 2020

Trump Uses Nazi Symbol to Seek Neo-Nazi Support

In reporting on events, we draw on factual evidence primarily, but try not to fall into the trap of thinking we have to prove every assertion as if we were in a court of law. To be sure, every effort must be made to avoid misrepresentation or simply making things up. Opinions should be supported by evidence. Assertions need to be sustained by a "preponderance of the evidence," but not by the criminal law standard of "proof beyond a reasonable doubt."

In essence, on some matters the test that makes sense is, "If it looks like a duck and quacks like a duck, it's probably a duck."

A current example is Donald Trump's recent use of a Nazi symbol that was used by the Nazis to identify political prisoners in concentration camps. This action should be called out for what it is: a blatant attempt to appeal to neo-Nazis and their sympathizers for support.

See Ali Beland, "Nazis Put This Symbol on Political Opponents' Arms. Now Trump Is Using It; The Upside Down Red Triangle Was Used in Hitler's Concentration Camps," *MotherJones*, June, 2020.[123]

There can be no excuses here. It was done by Donald Trump's campaign. That means it was done by Donald Trump.

The tragic state of our news media was revealed by the fact that most media stories focused on the fact that Facebook took down the ads using the symbol, rather than on the astounding and obscene fact that the President of the United States had used the symbol in appealing for neo-Nazi and white supremacist support.

With Trump appealing to fascists, fascism can't be far behind.

58

Seattle Protests: Democrats' Silence Gives "Law and Order" Advantage to Trump

The greatest charge against Donald Trump is that he has violated his oath to uphold the law and the Constitution. He has abused his power by violating the Constitution and the law so many times, in so many ways, that most of us have lost count, and have simply lost track of his transgressions.

Nonetheless, when Americans see scenes of a "liberated" zone in Seattle, while the police and other forces of order stand idly by, and Democratic officials essentially ignore their responsibilities to maintain law and order, what do voters think? What do they think about their Democratic elected officials' abject failure, in effect, to put down a rebellion?

When mobs pull down statues, and the debate is over whether the person to whom the statue was erected deserves to be so honored, instead of over the maintenance of law and order in a democratic society, what do voters think?

Democrats argue that Trump is the lawless president.

Yet how can Democrats make this argument in the 2020 elections, with any credibility, if they stand idly by when their own supporters break the law?

Why do they mindlessly cede the "law and order" issue to Trump and the Republicans? Surely their acquiescence in the lawless actions of mobs who "liberate" part of downtown Seattle or who tear down statues will figure prominently in Trump's and Republicans' election campaigns later this summer and fall.

Why are the Democrats so blind?

Why don't they seize the issue, and take a stand in favoring observance and enforcement of the law?

Why doesn't Joe Biden make a strong statement in this sense?

It would be easy for Democratic officials and candidates to take such a stand.

But they would have to lead, if only a little bit.

Otherwise, they may be seen both as hypocrites on the issue of Trump's lawlessness, and as dangerous politicians who would endanger public order out of fear of alienating voters who support such lawless actions.

Leaders explain the relations of things to their followers. In a democracy, with real elections, questions like the disposition of statues should be decided by elected officials or at the ballot box. A strong Democratic leader could explain this.

Americans are not living in Russia or the Soviet Union, where the tearing down of a statue of, e.g., Stalin, would have an entirely different meaning.

Do the members of the mob in Seattle really think they are launching a revolution? They should look at "the correlation of forces," think long and hard about what their actions mean, in a democratic society, and then go home. If they don't, Democratic officials in Seattle and the State of Washington should move—promptly—to remove them.

And if they want to win in November, Joe Biden and the Democrats should speak out loudly in favor of law observance and enforcement. Now.

The maintenance of public order is one of the pillars of a democratic state governed by law.

It is a bulwark of our democracy, and a first line of defense against neo-fascists and others who would undermine our constitutional order.

59

July 17, 2020

Trump's "Little Green Men" in Portland: Rehearsal for a Coup d'État?

The question of whether President Trump's deployment of federal forces in Washington, D.C. represents a testing of boundaries or a rehearsal of elements of a coup d'état is an important one. CNN has published an article about Trump's "little green men" running around Portland in unmarked vans and camouflage uniforms with no identifying information, picking up people off the street.

See Samantha Vinograd, "Trump's Use of Unidentified Security Forces Echoes Putin's 'Little Green Men,'" CNN, Opinion, June 7, 2020 (Updated 5:57 p.m. EDT, June 7, 2020).[124]

The account is reminiscent of the death squads in El Salvador in the 1980s, and the abductions carried out by the CIA in George W. Bush's first term, kidnappings which were euphemistically called "extraordinary renditions."

Op-ed articles today by Ruth Marcus in the *Washington Post* and Scott Martelle of the *Los Angeles Times* underline the significance of these events. Steve Vladeck analyzes, in detail, the legal issues involved and the legal authorities under which the forces may be operating, identifying critical legal questions which call out for answers. Roger Cohen writes of how things appear from a German perspective.

The use of unidentified forces in unmarked vans in Portland and earlier in Washington, D.C. is also reminiscent of the playbook Vladimir Putin used in Crimea and eastern Ukraine in 2014.

See,

1) Andrew Gawthorpe,"Trump Is Unleashing Authoritarianism on US Cities – Just in Time for the Election; Democratic-Run, Minority-Populated Cities Portrayed as Plagued by Anarchy Are a Much More Useful Political Foil for Trump Than Peaceful Metropolises," *The Guardian*, July 23, 2020 (12:47 BST);[125]

2) Ryan O'Connell, "Come November, a U.S. Coup d'État? Could Donald Trump Call Out the U.S. Army Again, After Losing the November Election?" *Salon*, June 12, 2020;[126]

3) Katie Shepherd, "'It Was Like Being Preyed Upon': Portland Protesters Say Federal Officers in Unmarked Vans Are Detaining Them," *Washington Post*, July 17, 2020 (6:58 a.m. EDT);[127]

4) Ruth Marcus, "What's Happening in Portland Shows Trump Is Ignoring the Constitution — and Attacking America," *Washington Post*, July 17, 2020 (1:19 p.m. EST);[128]

5) Scott Martelle,"Opinion: Federal Agents Deployed by Trump Spirit Away Protesters. What Country Is This?" *Los Angeles Times*, July 17, 2020 (11:47 a.m.);[129]

6) Steve Vladeck, "What the Heck Are Federal Law Enforcement Officers Doing in Portland?" *LAWFARE*, July 17, 2020, (4:17 p.m.);[130] and

7) Roger Cohen, "American Catastrophe through German Eyes; Trump Says He Wants to Protect Law-Abiding Citizens; In 1933, Hitler Issued His 'Decree of the Reich President for the Protection of People and State,'" *New York Times*, July 24, 2020.[131]

Cohen quotes a German friend, Michael Steinberg, as follows:

The American catastrophe seems to get worse every day, but the events in Portland have particularly alarmed me as a kind of strategic experiment for fascism. The playbook from the German fall of democracy in 1933 seems well in place, including rogue military factions, the destabilization of cities, etc.

60

July 27, 2020

Democrats' Timidity on Impeachment

Impeachment

All through 2019 the House Democrats dawdled and were afraid to use their most powerful weapon, impeachment, in confronting Trump and his unlawful and unconstitutional actions and policies.

House Democratic Leader Nancy Pelosi firmly resisted all efforts to launch a broad impeachment inquiry, even with Robert Mueller having laid out abundant evidence of obstruction of justice in his report. For two years the House Democrats had dodged their own responsibility to conduct an impeachment inquiry, arguing that they had to wait for Mueller to finish his investigation and to issue his report.

Their responsibility was to conduct a political impeachment inquiry, not a criminal inquiry, which was Mueller's brief. They fell into the trap of believing they had to prove every detail of any article of impeachment as if it were a criminal charge, getting all tangled up in trying to prove each element of a criminal offense.

Pelosi insisted on resisting an impeachment inquiry, that is, until the revelations in the Ukraine affair led her caucus to insist on launching an impeachment inquiry. But the House Democrats were cowards, afraid to push for a broad impeachment inquiry, in the deluded belief that "moderate" House members in swing districts would retain their seats if they only took Trump to task on the narrow issues in the Ukraine affair. They sought to repeat their 2018 strategy of slipping by Trump, focusing on local issues. But then Trump was not up for reelection in 2018.

Nancy Pelosi seized on this narrowly focused impeachment effort, which she helped to shape, and carried it forward though she and the House Leadership surely knew that they would lose a vote in the Senate to remove Trump from office. If they knew that, what was the point? It appears to have been to enable Nancy Pelosi and the House Leadership to retain firm control of their caucus.

The House Democrats have one enormous weapon they could have used, and might still use, to save the country from Trump's authoritarian abuses of power and—what is new—his incredible failures to defend the people of the United States against the depredations of the coronavirus and the accompanying devastation of the economy.

The Democratic Wager

The Democrats are betting on their prospects for winning the presidency in the November 3 election, and on retaining the House and possibly winning the Senate.

This bet depends on another bet: that free and fair elections can be held on November 3.

They are betting further that Trump will accept the election results and peacefully surrender power on January 20, 2021 if Joe Biden wins.

Congressional Democrats cannot conceive of a scenario in which Trump interferes with the elections or uses force to retain his hold on power.

Meanwhile, Trump and his collaborators have been putting into place, gradually but steadily, the elements necessary for a coup d'état and the seizure of power by the use of force, should that become necessary to retain their hold on power.

Destruction of the Concept of Truth, and Mismanagement of the COVID-19 Pandemic

Trump and his allies have succeeded in destroying, for upwards of 40 percent of the population, the belief in the very concept of Truth.

In every realm, but particularly in the area of public health, Trump has dismissed the concept of expertise, and has resolutely refused to follow the science and his epidemiological and medical experts regarding management of the COVID-19 pandemic. His policies will have contributed to the deaths of 200,000 Americans by November, and up to 300,000 by January 20, 2021.

Trump has corruptly subordinated the defense of the population against a terrible pandemic to his own private objectives, i.e., winning his campaign for reelection. He was impeached though not convicted in the Republican-controlled Senate—despite the evidence—for subordinating U.S. foreign policy in Ukraine to his personal political objectives. No less than in the Ukraine, his subordination of his duty to protect the health of the people of the United States to his personal political objectives should be viewed by the House and the Senate as an impeachable offense.

While the president may change his approach and strategy to managing the COVID-19 pandemic in order to increase his prospects for reelection, his failures and misguided actions to date are probably already responsible for tens of thousands of unnecessary deaths.

Nothing he does or says now can erase that record, or those deaths.

61

August 20, 2020

Raw Power: Only a Threat of Immediate Impeachment Can Constrain Trump

Democrats live in a world where rational analysis, legal and consti-tutional norms and procedures, and pure decency determine—or *should* determine—the outcome of political struggles.

Yet all the insightful and beautiful words and inspiring videos seen and heard at this week's Democratic national convention will not stop Donald Trump and his Republican collaborators from trying to steal the November elections or illegally seizing power between now and January 20, 2021. If this sounds like fantasy, please reflect on what they have already done.

Trump has already telegraphed his intentions and tried out a number of the elements such a seizure of power would entail.

The Democrats are lost talking to themselves in a world of Reason.

Trump is operating in a world of Raw Power and Unreason.

Trump and his collaborators engage on a daily basis in the Nazi propa-ganda technique known as "the Big Lie."

He has sent federal armed forces into Portland in a preview of what he could do in a raw struggle for power. Those federal forces, each and every one of them, dutifully obeyed what seem to have been unconstitutional orders.

Trump has demonstrated how the federal courts cannot be counted on to halt unconstitutional actions in a timely manner. Having learned from his mentor, Roy Cohn, Trump has perfected the art of delay and tying legal cases up in the courts through endless appeals. He now has a servile attorney general and Justice Department to aid him and do his bidding.

At the Pentagon, he has appointed political loyalists to key positions. They can be counted on to try to block any military actions that might be taken to thwart an attempt by Trump and his Republican collaborators to take over the government by force.

He has a massive propaganda operation, led by Fox News but also backed up by One America News, and other right-wing news outlets and social media, which he uses daily to push out lies and misinformation. He also has the backing of Vladimir Putin and Russian intelligence agencies.

In the world of Raw Power, Trump seems to hold all the cards.

Except one. The Power of Impeachment.

Democrats have been afraid to use this power fully against Trump.

Their impeachment of Trump on two narrow grounds related to Ukraine failed in the Senate to secure a conviction and the removal of Trump from office. Quite predictably, in the Senate Trump was protected by his Republican collaborators, who willingly ignored the facts in violating their constitutional oaths of office. The House Democrats either understood this would happen or naively assumed that Reason and the facts would carry the day.

They didn't. Democrats need to learn from this experience.

Democrats shied away from efforts to impeach Trump for the broad range of his high crimes and misdemeanors, including the clear pattern of obstruction of justice laid out in the Mueller Report.

As Trump's abuses of power have multiplied and grown in significance since his Senate acquittal in January 2020, we have heard nothing of preparations by House Democrats to use the threat of a new and second impeachment to constrain his actions.

This is the only tool in the world of Raw Power that the Democrats have.

They need to wake up from their illusions of normality, of constitutional government and the rule of law, and to prepare to use this tool. They should have teams of Democratic Representatives and lawyers putting together draft articles of impeachment. Today.

These articles of impeachment, updated as necessary, can then be immediately approved and sent to the Senate if Trump interferes with the election or resists a peaceful transfer of power on January 20, 2021. Either of these developments could potentially produce the 20 Republican votes needed for his removal from office.

To keep Trump in line in the world of Raw Power, the House Democrats must credibly use the Threat of Impeachment.

The Threat of Impeachment is the only tool the Democrats have to constrain Trump. They must use the tool. That means they must begin immediately to develop the threat and communicate it credibly to Trump.

The Threat of Impeachment can be used as a weapon of deterrence.

But if the train leaves the tracks, they will have to use it—with 20 Republican senators—to remove him from office.

FURTHER READING

1) Morgan Chalfant, "Trump Says He Would Put Down Riots on Election Night 'Very Quickly'," *The Hill*, September 11, 2020 (11:57 a.m. EDT);[132]

2) "Why Aren't House Democrats Preparing Articles of Impeachment for Trump?" *The Trenchant Observer*, August 10, 2020.[133]

62

September 4, 2020

Trump Appears to Consider Use of Force to Retain Power

Updated September 15, 2020

The American people have been pummeled by Donald Trump's outrages and lethal incompetence for almost four years. Now it is obvious that he will tell any lie, violate any law, and commit any outrage in order to stay in power beyond January 20, 2021.

The American people are worn down, beaten down. Many are discouraged, and some are bordering on hopelessness.

Will they find the energy and the hope necessary to act effectively to remove Trump?

Trump's strategy appears to be to suppress the vote, create massive confusion around the electoral process, and to rely on Russian interference in the elections in order to cling to power.

In the period around the elections and the tabulation of their results, we can count on the mobilization of white armed "militias" to suppress voting, and to create disturbances as they have in Portland and other cities. There is also a strong possibility that Trump may deploy federal agents and National Guard units to the cities where disturbances occur.

See,

1) Morgan Chalfant, "Trump Says He Would Put Down Riots on Election Night 'Very Quickly'," *The Hill*, September 11, 2020 (11:57 a.m. EDT);[134]

2) Timothy Johnson, "Roger Stone Calls for Trump to Seize Total Power If He Loses the Election; Stone Also Said Federal Authorities Should Seize All Nevada Ballots, Federal Agents and GOP State Officials Should 'Physically' Block Voting, That Trump Should Nationalize Police Forces, and That Trump Should Order Widespread Arrests," *Media Matters*, September 11, 2020 (2:11 p.m. EDT);[135]

3) Yasmeen Abutaleb, Lena H. Sun, Josh Dawsey and Rosalind S. Helderman, "Top Trump Health Appointee Michael Caputo Warns of Armed Insurrection After Election," *Washington Post*, September 14, 2020 at 8:20 p.m. EDT.[136]

The Post authors report:

(Caputo) also predicted that Trump would win the election but that Biden, the Democratic presidential nominee,[137] would refuse to concede. "And when Donald Trump refuses to stand down at the inauguration, the shooting will begin," he warned in the video. "The drills that you've seen are nothing. If you carry guns, buy ammunition, ladies and gentlemen, because it's going to be hard to get."

The interesting thing to note about the Stone and Caputo quotes is that these ideas seem to be in the air at the White House. Stone, a convicted felon pardoned by Trump who was in the middle of the Russian connection, is an extremely close confidant of Trump. (Caputo also has a Russian connection.)

Moreover, Trump is notorious for projecting his own thoughts onto others. Consequently, it is fair to say that Trump is probably thinking about transition scenarios where armed force is brought to bear.

In short, he appears willing to go to any length to ensure that if he loses the election the Republicans under his leadership will successfully seize and hold on to power.

Many of our most respected leaders and op-ed columnists have been issuing similar warnings.

That could never happen in America, many will say. Many in Germany in 1932 said the same thing, despite Adolf Hitler's attempted coup in Bavaria in 1923.

Why could that never happen in America?

Trump has been practicing many of the moves that would be necessary for a seizure of power in circumstances such as those suggested above.

Who would defend the Constitution and the Republic?

Would the Republicans, who have quietly accepted every constitutional outrage Trump has committed, act to defend the rule of law?

This is not likely. They have become complicit in Trump's crimes and abuses of power. If they themselves have not joined the Cult of Trump, they have at least become willing collaborators.

So, are these views just the overwrought impressions of an American participant in and observer of political developments in the U.S.? To answer that question, we should listen to the opinions of some of the sharpest foreign observers of the American political scene.

See, e.g.,

1) Jonathan Freedland, "The Danger Is Now Clear: Trump Is Destroying Democracy in Broad Daylight; More and More,

the President Voices Contempt for the Voting Process; Imagine What He'd Do If Re-elected," *The Guardian*, September 4, 2020 (16:57 BST);[138]

2) Lluís Bassets, "Un bolchevique en la Casa Blanca; Los reiterados abusos de poder de Trump revelan un uso de las instituciones como si fueran su propiedad privada, con la exclusión absoluta de la idea de una alternancia," *El País*, September 3, 2020 (00:30).[139]

63

September 8, 2020

What Does Trump Have to Do with International Law, Politics, and Security?

You cannot make plans for additions to your house while there is a bulldozer outside, with its engines revving, actively engaged in tearing it down.

As noted in the Preface, our main focus in *The Trenchant Observer* blog has been, since its beginning in 2009, international law, politics, and security. That is also the subject of this chapter, particularly in relation to Trump's presidency and his possible reelection.

What is the relationship, then, between this subject and the 2020 November 3 elections in the United States, Donald Trump, impeachment, and the presidential campaign between Trump and Joe Biden?

The answer is that Donald Trump, who is probably the most brilliant demagogue and authoritarian leader since Adolf Hitler, has operated as a malevolent wrecking ball aimed at tearing down the entire system of international law and institutions created since the founding of the United Nations in 1945.

He and his cult followers and collaborators have controlled the government of the most powerful and influential country in the world since January 2017 and have done great harm.

You cannot talk about the maintenance of international peace and security, in the words of the U.N. Charter, without talking about Trump and the unique threat he poses to upholding the entire system.

You cannot talk about international law, politics, and security without talking about Trump in the same way you could not talk about these subjects in the 1930s without talking about Germany, the Nazis, and Adolf Hitler.

As long as Trump is president, there cannot be any progress toward strengthening international law and institutions.

You cannot make plans for additions to your house while there is a bulldozer outside, with its engines revving, actively engaged in tearing down your house.

The first and essential step, no matter what your plans for future additions to your house may be, is to stop the bulldozer and the man operating it, and remove them both from the scene in a manner which gives assurance that they will not return.

So, naturally, we turn our attention to the actions of the bulldozer and the forces which may determine whether it and its operator will be stopped and effectively removed.

While you would prefer to deal with architectural plans for future additions to your house, you are compelled to think of politics and the actions that will be necessary to get the sheriff to come to your property and remove both the bulldozer and its operator.

Can there be any serious question that Trump has been tearing down the edifice of international law and institutions, and that if he is reelected, he will continue to use the bulldozer to tear down the house?

The answers to this question could comprise a book. Let us only address a few dimensions of international law, politics, and security.

First, Trump has acted to destroy the system of International Trade created in Havana in 1947, originally known as the General Agreement on Tariffs and Trade (GATT). The system is now known as the World Trade Organization.

Trump has repeatedly violated its most basic provisions by imposing punitive tariffs on China and other countries on the spurious legal ground that they are justified by the "national security" exception contained in the GATT rules.

To shield the U.S. from legal judgment by the WTO's highest dispute resolution body, Trump has refused to nominate the members it requires to constitute a quorum in order to function and consider a case and reach a decision.

This is equivalent to avoiding condemnation by a court by burning the courthouse down.

Second, in the realm of international peace and security, Trump has never criticized Vladimir Putin for invading Ukraine, annexing Crimea, and occupying two provinces in eastern Ukraine, whose occupation continues today.

He has never criticized Putin for interfering in the 2016 U.S. elections, or Russia's ongoing intervention in the 2020 elections. Such interventions represent flagrant violations of the international law principle prohibiting intervention in the internal affairs of any state.

International law and institutions are, among other things, instruments that can be used by the nations of the world to solve current and future problems.

Trump has withdrawn the U.S. from the 2015 Paris agreement on climate change. It is the only country in the world to have done so.

Trump firmly opposes multilateral efforts to deal with climate change. As long as he is driving the bulldozer wrecking the house, we cannot expect any decisive action using international law and institutions to address these issues. They are of existential importance for the future existence of humans on the planet.

Trump has withdrawn from the Intermediate Nuclear Forces (INF) arms control treaty with Russia and entered into a new nuclear arms race with Russia—which eventually will be joined by other countries such as China.

It currently appears likely that the U.S. will not renew the START Treaty with Russia, which has imposed a decrease in and limits on the number of nuclear weapons on each side.

Under Trump, nuclear proliferation by North Korea has not been halted.

Trump has withdrawn the U.S. from the six-nation treaty limiting Iran's nuclear capabilities, which has led to a slow break-out by Iran from the treaty's limitations. If Trump is reelected, we may see a much faster break-out by Iran from the treaty's constraints. He has proposed no alternative for reining in Iran's presumed nuclear ambitions.

Third, in the field of biological defense, the coronavirus pandemic has underlined the urgent need for ever-closer cooperation and coordination among the nations of the world to counter biological threats, including viruses. Trump's response has been to withdraw from and attack the World Health Organization (WHO), instead of leading efforts to correct its shortcomings and strengthen its capabilities.

It is evident that Chinese cooperation is urgently required in efforts to control dangerous experimentation with biological agents, and to control the spread of the coronavirus and others which may appear in the future. Such collaboration might be best achieved through the WHO.

Bashing China has not been particularly fruitful. Apparently feeling he had nothing to lose, Xi Jinping has crushed the autonomy of Hong Kong, in blatant violation of the treaty by which the United Kingdom returned sovereignty over the territory to the People's Republic of China, with the ex-colony's independence to be guaranteed for 50 years.

Trump did not object vociferously to this Chinese violation of international law.

The list could go on.

The most fundamental problem with Trump is that he does not believe in the usefulness of multilateral diplomacy, or in the utility of international law and institutions. The same can be said of law in general, at least if it might constrain his freedom of action.

The important point is that the man operating the bulldozer tearing down the house must be stopped.

That is why we write about Donald Trump, his actions, and the forces that will determine whether and when he is removed from office.

FURTHER READING

1) "International Law after Trump," *The Trenchant Observer*, January 10, 2019;[140]

2) "Trump Steers Dangerous Course in Venezuela," *The Trenchant Observer*, January 25, 2019;[141]

3) "Stupid and Incompetent Foreign Policy Towards Venezuela – 'Intervention to Protect Nationals'," *The Trenchant Observer*, January 26, 2019.[142]

64

September 19, 2020

The Michael Reinoehl Assassination

The press and the media failed for over six weeks to seriously cover the Michael Reinoehl assassination on September 3, 2020, in which President Donald Trump and Attorney General William Barr were involved, and then failed to launch follow-up investigative reporting.

The facts of this incident are very complicated. The press covered this piece and that, but never really engaged in investigative journalism that connected all the dots or went further than contemporary news reports.

Interested readers are invited to read through the titles of the following news articles. (In the ePub or eBook edition, readers may click on the link and go directly to the article and read it themselves.)

See,

1) Trump Tweet at 8:40 p.m. EDT on September 3, 2020: "Why aren't the Portland Police ARRESTING the cold-blooded killer of Aaron "Jay" Danielson. Do your job, and do it fast. Everybody knows who this thug is. No wonder Portland is going to hell! @TheJusticeDept @FBI";

2) CBS/AP, "Suspect in Killing of Right-Wing Protester Fatally Shot During Arrest, CBSnews.com Updated on: September 4,

2020 (8:09 p.m.)[143] First published on September 4, 2020 / 1:49 a.m. (includes Trump's tweet with time of 8:40 p.m.);

3) Tom McCarthy, "Suspect in Portland Killing of Far-Right Protester 'Shot Dead' by US Marshals; Federal and Local Officers Were Trying to Arrest Michael Forest Reinoehl, 48, on an Arrest Warrant, Says Sheriff's Office," *The Guardian*, September 4, 2020 (16:44 EDT);[144]

4) Hallie Golden, Mike Baker and Adam Goldman, "Suspect in Fatal Portland Shooting Is Killed by Officers During Arrest; Law Enforcement Agents Killed Michael Forest Reinoehl While Trying to Arrest Him, Four Officials Said. He Was Being Investigated in the Fatal Shooting of a Supporter of a Far-Right Group," *New York Times*, September 3, 2020 (updated April 12, 2021).[145]

Golden, Baker, and Goldman reported:

> The Pacific Northwest Violent Offender Task Force that attempted to arrest Mr. Reinoehl included members of the U.S. Marshals Service, the Lakewood Police Department, the Pierce County Sheriff's Department and the Washington State Department of Corrections.

5) Neil MacFarquhar, Mike Baker and Adam Goldman, "In His Last Hours, Portland Murder Suspect Said He Feared Arrest; Law Enforcement Agents Killed Michael Forest Reinoehl While Trying to Arrest Him for the Shooting Death of a Supporter of a Far-Right Group," *New York Times*, September 4, 2020.[146] No time is stated for the dispatch. (The date of this article is a little suspicious. The author was following these events very closely and

did not see this article even when searching on the *New York Times* website. The fact that no date was given for the date of publication is also curious.)

MacFarquhar, Baker and Goldman report that dispatch calls showed the first shots were fired at 6:54 p.m. (an hour and 14 minutes after Trump's tweet);

6) William P. Barr, "Statement by Attorney General William P. Barr on the Tracking Down of Fugitive Michael Forest Reinoehl," September 4, 2020 (Office of the Attorney General, Press Release Number 20-883.)[147]

7) Jose Barrett and Alejandro Lazo, "New Details Emerge in Killing of Michael Reinoehl; Suspect in Portland, Ore., Shooting of Right-Wing Activist Had Drawn Handgun as Task Force Pursued Him, Law-Enforcement Officials Said," *Wall Street Journal*, Updated September 4, 2020 (8:14 p.m. ET);[148]

8) Jon Passantino, Bob Ortega and Majlie de Puy Kamp, "Suspect in Fatal Portland Shooting of Right-Wing Activist Killed During Attempted Arrest, US Marshals Say," CNN, September 4, 2020 (Updated 10:34 p.m. ET);[149]

9) Megan Specia, "What We Know about the Death of the Suspect in the Portland Shooting; The Suspect, Michael Forest Reinoehl, 48, Was Killed by Law Enforcement Agents Just Five Days after the Deadly Shooting of a Right-Wing Protester," *New York Times*, September 4, 2020.[150] No time is stated for the dispatch.

Megan Specia is a correspondent on the International Desk in London, covering the United Kingdom and Ireland. She has been with The Times since 2016;

10) Maxine Bernstein, "Witness Says Officers Never Gave Commands Before Firing at Michael Reinoehl Outside WA Apartment," *The Oregonian* (OregonLive), September 9, 2020 (4:43 p.m. updated 4:50 p.m.);[151]

11) Tim Elfrink, "Police Shot Portland Slaying Suspect without Warning or Trying to Arrest Him First, Witness Says," *Washington Post*, September 10, 2020 (4:14 a.m. EDT);[152]

12) Tatiana Cozzarelli, "Michael Reinoehl Was Executed By the Police; New Eye Witness Accounts Have Surfaced of the Police Gunning Down Michael Forest Reinoehl While He Was Unarmed," *Left Voice*, September 10, 2020. (quotes from Trump);[153]

13) Tim Dickenson, "The Feds Say They Tried to Arrest Portland Protest Murder Suspect Michael Reinoehl 'Peacefully'; A New Eyewitness Describes a Violent Ambush; The "Takedown" of Michael Reinoehl by a Federal Fugitive Task Force Resembled an Execution, According to a New Eyewitness," *Rolling Stone*, September 11, 2020 (1:16 p.m. ET);[154]

14) Aron Rupar, "'There Has to Be Retribution': Trump's Chilling Comments about Extrajudicial Killings, Briefly Explained; He's Not Waiting for the Facts to Come in," *Vox*, September 14, 2020 (5:10 p.m. EDT).[155] By A@atrupar;

15) Michelle Goldberg (Opinion), "Trump's Shredding of Civil Liberties Won't Stop with Antifa; An American Was Killed by Federal Agents and the President Called It 'Retribution.' We Are So Far Gone," *New York Times*, September 14, 2020;[156]

16) Rolf Boone, "Portland Shooting Suspect Michael Reinoehl Pointed Gun at Officers, Investigators Say," *The Oregonian*, September 17, 2020 (updated 6:47 p.m.);[157]

17) Aaron Mesh, "Sheriff Says Michael Reinoehl, Suspected in Portland Protest Killing, Was Armed When Officers Shot Him. The Sheriff's Office Said the Gun Reinoehl Was Carrying Was a .380 Caliber Handgun—the Same Caliber Weapon He Allegedly Used to Kill Aaron J. Danielson," *Willamette Week*, September 17, 2020 (7:18 p.m., Updated September 18 at 12:24 a.m.)[158]

Mesh reports the following:
> "While this firearm is the same caliber as the weapon used in the Portland homicide investigation, we will not know if this is the same weapon until ballistics testing can be conducted at the crime lab," the news release reads. The weapons will be sent to a busy Washington State Patrol Crime Lab, Brady acknowledged, which means results could take as long as 2-3 months, he said. Ballistics testing is done in Tacoma, he said.

18) Yaron Steinbuch "Accused Portland Shooter Michael Reinoehl Pointed Handgun at Officers, Cops Say," *New York Post*, September 18, 2020 (7:41 a.m./Updated);[159]

19) Evan Hill, Mike Baker, Derek Knowles and Stella Cooper, "'Straight to Gunshots': How a U.S. Task Force Killed an Antifa Activist; New Accounts from the Scene Raise Questions about Whether Michael Reinoehl, Suspected of Killing a Far-Right Trump Supporter, Pulled Out a Gun before Officers Fatally Shot Him," *New York Times*, October 13, 2020 (Updated October 15, 2020);[160]

20) "The Last Days of Trump's Fascist Campaign," *The Trenchant Observer*, October 28, 2020;[161]

21) "Killings of Aaron Danielson and Michael Reinoehl," Wikipedia.[162]

65

October 17, 2020

Where Can Trump Go to Escape the Law? Russia?

Where Can He Go?

The thought of losing the election is rumbling around in Donald Trump's mind.

If he loses, where indeed can he go to escape the reach of American Law and Justice?

See Colby Itkowitz, "Cat videos, 'Hamilton' and a Threat from Trump to Leave the Country," *Washington Post*, October 17, 2020.[163]

Itkowitz quotes Trump as follows:

"Could you imagine if I lose? My whole life, what am I going to do?" Trump said at a campaign rally in Georgia. "I'm not going to feel so good. Maybe I'll have to leave the country, I don't know."

Trump has good reason to think about leaving the country if he loses the election.

Where can he go? What factors should determine his choice?

First, he needs to pick a country that doesn't have an extradition treaty with the United States.

That rules out Canada, the U.K., the remaining 27 members of the European Union, and even countries like Turkey and Costa Rica.

Jair Bolsonaro would seem to offer a hospitable environment for Trump in Brazil. **Problem: Extradition Treaty.**

What about neighboring Bolivia? **Problem: Extradition Treaty.**

Moreover, Trump must also bear in mind that even a country without an extradition treaty with the U.S. can extradite him to the U.S. in accordance with its own internal law. **Problem: Extradition is possible without a Treaty**

A Trump Tower "Non-extradition Community" in a Non-extradition Country?

If Trump plans his escape carefully, he might actually make a lot of money by moving with a large group of his collaborators to a non-extradition country, where he could build a new Trump Tower for his friends and collaborators. After his own suite, the star attraction might be the William P. Barr Justice Suite.

Given the amount of money he and his collaborators are likely to bring with them, Trump might be able to negotiate a great deal with, e.g., Vladimir Putin or Kim Jong Un. If he chooses Russia, he can use his existing plans from 2016, though with Putin on the top floor Barr would be downgraded to the third most opulent suite.

Of course, fiscal considerations will need to be taken into account. He will need protection from his creditors.

Panama might be an ideal jurisdiction for secretly transferring and hiding money. **Problem: Extradition Treaty.**

Where to go to escape the law is not a novel question.

See, Offshore Citizen, "Non-extradition Countries – The Best Place to Run to." The list of countries and advantages of each are listed here: https://offshorecitizen.net/citizenship-by-investment/ non-extradition-countries/.

Trump can reach out for help from Offshore Citizen by sending in a form or calling them here: https://offshorecitizen.net/contact/.

The question of where Trump can go is a hot news story, more important even than Joe Biden's hypothetical decision on whether to pack the Supreme Court.

CNN, MSNBC, and even FOX should be all over this story until Trump chooses a country to escape to.

Timing will be critical. Trump would be well advised to resign, get his pardon from Mike Pence, and depart the country before January 20, 2021.

He wouldn't want to get arrested on the way to the airport.

See the full list of countries Trump may be considering as candidates for relocation, and the arguments, pros and cons:

1) "Where Can Trump Go to Escape the Law? The Bahamas?" *The Trenchant Observer*, October 20, 2020;[164]

2) "Where Can Trump Go to Escape the Law? China?" *The Trenchant Observer*, October 21, 2020;[165]

3) "Where Can Trump Go to Escape the Law? Will He Make It to the Airport?" *The Trenchant Observer*, December 12, 2020;[166]

4) "Where Can Trump Go to Escape the Law? The Bahamas? (Updated)," *The Trenchant Observer*, December 17, 2020;[167]

5) "Where Can Trump Go to Escape the Law? Israeli Settlements on the West Bank?" *The Trenchant Observer*, December 24, 2020.[168]

66

October 28, 2020

Trump's Support of Violence, and the Closing Days of the Campaign

Former President Barack Obama has been delivering at his rallies by far the best critiques of Donald Trump and his administration. So far, his is the best effort to put the case against Trump and his record in a relatively short, engaging, and cogent form.

How do you, after all, summarize the apparent crimes of a fascist political leader who has committed countless abuses over the last four years, and who is committing new abuses and telling "big lies" every day?

Plot to Kidnap Michigan Governor Gretchen Whitmer

The grimmest outrages include Trump's raising doubts about the conspiracy to kidnap and perhaps kill Michigan Governor Gretchen Whitmer, when the conspirators have already been arrested and jailed by the FBI and the Justice Department. "Maybe it's a problem, maybe not," Trump said.

This is one of the most shameful statements ever made by a president of the United States. Trump is, in effect, giving encouragement to apparent traitors plotting to overthrow the government.

Reinoehl Assassination

Another outrage is the unexplored role Trump played in the assassination of Michael Reinoehl on September 3, 2020, near Seattle. In a tweet, Trump egged on the Justice Department-led police operation to get Reinoehl, complaining about the fact that they were taking so much time. An hour or so after Trump's tweet, Reinoehl was assassinated by these federal and other police officials. Quickly thereafter, Attorney General Barr praised the successful operation.

See,

1) Aaron Rupar, "'There Has to Be Retribution': Trump's Chilling Comments about Extrajudicial Killings, Briefly Explained; He's Not Waiting for the Facts to Come In," VOX, September 14, 2020 (5:10 p.m. EDT);[169]

2) Trump Tweet at 8:40 p.m. EDT on September 3, 2020:

> Why aren't the Portland Police ARRESTING the cold blooded killer of Aaron "Jay" Danielson. Do your job, and do it fast. Everybody knows who this thug is. No wonder Portland is going to hell! @TheJusticeDept @FBI

3) Evan Hill, Mike Baker, Derek Knowles and Stella Cooper, "'Straight to Gunshots': How a U.S. Task Force Killed an Antifa Activist; New Accounts from the Scene Raise Questions about Whether Michael Reinoehl, Suspected of Killing a Far-Right Trump Supporter, Pulled Out a Gun before Officers Fatally Shot Him," *New York Times*, October 13, 2020 (Updated October 15, 2020).[170]

There is so much material here.

Trump's campaign, in its last days, boils down to a massive and unabashed campaign of huge lies. It is an attempt to envelop voters in a cloud of lies and propaganda, in order to obscure reality (e.g., the COVID-19 pandemic) from their view, so that they will vote on the basis of Trump's phantasmagorical version of what is going on in the world.

If Trump succeeds in stealing the election, or seizing power through an ongoing attempted coup d'état, his government will lack any legitimacy. He will have to be impeached and removed from power by the Senate, whether before or after the new Congress is convened on January 3, 2020.

FURTHER READING

1) Robert Kagan, "It's Up to the People to Foil Trump's Plot against Democracy," *Washington Post*, October 30, 2020 (8:00 a.m. EDT);[171]

2) "Civic Leaders Issue Joint Appeal to Protect the Rule of Law in the 2020 U.S. Elections," *World Justice Institute,* October 28, 2020;[172]

3) Elizabeth Dwoskin and Craig Timberg, "The Unseen Machine Pushing Trump's Social Media Megaphone into Overdrive, Researchers Say the Online Feedback Loop between Trump, High-Profile Influencers and Rank-and-File Followers Is More Dangerous Than Russian Disinformation," *Washington Post*, October 30, 2020 (6:00 a.m. EDT);[173]

4) Brian Stelter, *Hoax: Donald Trump, Fox News, and the Dangerous Distortion of Truth*, Atria/One Signal Publishers, 2020"

5) Jamelle Bouie, "Trump's Perverse Campaign Strategy; If the President's Allies Are Talking about the Moment 'Shooting Will Begin' and 'Martial Law,' It's Not by Accident," *New York Times*, September 15, 2020;[174]

6) "Trump Dominates the News, and Democrats Are Losing, *The Trenchant Observer*, September 17, 2020.[175]

67

October 31, 2020

"Trump Has Blocked Out the Sun"

See Michelle Goldberg, "Four Wasted Years Thinking about Donald Trump," *New York Times*, October 29, 2020.[176] Goldberg writes, presciently, "Trump has blocked out the sun. Only when he's gone will we see how much we've been missing."

Not long ago I wrote in my journal, "Today, Trump ate my consciousness." I suspect this has been the experience of many people, on far too many days.

It is as if Donald Trump, obsessively monitoring the media his entire life, stumbled upon a formula which enabled him to commandeer our attention, and our consciousness, for many hours each day.

Trump's ability to develop a cult following among some 35-40 percent of the population has morphed into *a mortal threat to all that we hold dear—Truth, Integrity, Decency, Character, Facts, Science, Law, Freedom, Democracy.*

Because we value democracy and the rule of law, our attention has been riveted on Trump. While some of the more naive among us may have found Trump amusing at first, we all now know that he represents a deadly threat.

In our quest to understand what we were seeing, right before our eyes, Timothy Snyder's little book, *On Tyranny: Twenty Lessons from the*

241

Twentieth Century (mentioned earlier), published in 2017, was immensely helpful. It provided needed historical perspective, and a guide to the path toward authoritarian rule on which Trump was driving us forward.

Guided by Snyder, we read other books and plays. Eugène Ionesco's *Rhinoceros* (mentioned briefly earlier) captured in graphic form what we were seeing every day with our own eyes. As individuals in Germany and elsewhere had "flipped" into becoming Nazis as a result of the pressures and influence of mass political psychology and propaganda, in Ionesco's play individuals in a small town who "flipped"—like the newly minted Nazis had done—assumed the outward form of a rhinoceros.

I saw the play in June 2019. And since Trump's campaign in 2016, I have watched a steady stream of Republican congressmen and senators and Trump officials reveal by their actions and words that they had "flipped," undergoing a metamorphosis that turned them into rhinoceroses following Donald Trump.

Trump's policies and daily outrages made increasing inroads into my consciousness after he took office in January 2017. But as I began to fully grasp how Trump's assault on the truth and the rule of law had gained control of the minds of nearly all Republicans, the parallels with the rise of fascism and Adolf Hitler became increasingly evident. Many years earlier I had studied twentieth century European history and German history in particular. Now those lessons about the rise of fascism began to reverberate ever more loudly in my head.

After "the adults in the room" departed, leaving Trump alone with his sycophants in the White House, and particularly after a craven Senate Republican majority acquitted Trump in January 2020 on impeachment charges relating to Ukraine—when the factual evidence was overwhelmingly against him—Trump increasingly dropped any pretense of adhering to democratic norms and the rule of law.

So we have come to a crucial crossroads, as election day is only three days away.

This is high drama, with the future of the Republic and American democracy seemingly at stake.

How Can We Keep Trump from Robbing Us of Our Consciousness in These Dramatic Circumstances?

We need to pay attention and get ready to act. The first and most critical action is to vote—in a reliable manner that will ensure our vote is counted. It is already too late, in many states, to vote by mail.

Yet we also need to prepare to oppose the actions of Trump and his supporters to suppress the vote and to interfere with the counting of the votes. The latter could occur through mob action as in fact occurred in Florida in 2000 when a threatening crowd forced a halt to the counting of the ballots and the chads in one key county. (I still have vivid memories of the scenes on TV in which the mob was pounding on the windows of the office where they were counting the votes.) Or the Republicans could try to interfere with the counting of the votes by bringing endless bad-faith legal challenges against mailed-in and other ballots.

We must also be prepared to oppose any efforts by Republican-controlled state legislatures to name electors to the Electoral College who do not represent those elected by a majority of the voters. Many, if not most, states have laws which require the naming of electors representing the candidate who won a majority of the votes. But these laws can be changed, particularly in states with both Republican legislatures and Republican governors.

Finally, we must be prepared to counter any attempts by armed militias, federal "police forces," National Guard troops, or federal military units to interfere with the constitutional processes for electing and placing in office a new president.

If Trump and his collaborators should still somehow succeed in taking a case to the Supreme Court on which the outcome may depend, like *Bush v. Gore* in 2000, we must be prepared to send millions into the streets, in Washington and outside the Supreme Court. We need to make it clear to the justices that the people will not tolerate the Court's throwing the election to the Republican candidate on specious grounds, as it did in 2000.

I am a lawyer, though not a constitutional law expert. Nonetheless, I read all the Florida Supreme Court opinions in 2000, when that Court's majority decided in favor of Gore. And I read all of the U.S. Supreme Court's opinions in *Bush v. Gore*, when a majority of the Court on totally specious grounds threw the election to Bush. The majority invoked novel and unprecedented legal arguments to support their decision, while stressing that the case could not be cited as a precedent in the future. The majority decision, upon very close examination, did not pass "the smell test."

So, we need to reclaim control over our consciousness by removing Trump from office. The first step will be to vote overwhelmingly against him and for Joe Biden on November 3.

Then we will need to pay close attention to any Trump maneuvers and actions aimed at disrupting the vote count and the proper operation of the constitutional processes established to count the votes and place the winner in the White House on January 20, 2020.

Unfortunately, given this timetable, Trump is likely to command an out-sized share of our consciousness for at least the next few months, until he is removed from office and replaced. Hopefully, that will happen on January 20, 2021.

Only then will we be able to reclaim full control over our own individual consciousness.

In the meantime, we will need to remain as level-headed and analytical as possible, so that we will be able to respond in an effective manner to any efforts by Trump to successfully implement his ongoing attempted coup d'état.

To remain level-headed, we will need to be disciplined in our consumption of news, avoiding the passivity of always being glued to the TV or social media. We will need to stay informed, but with a view to taking and supporting appropriate actions to counter unconstitutional maneuvers by Trump and his Republican collaborators.

FURTHER READING

1) Farhad Manjoo, "The Fury Against Trump Has Begun a Great Democratic Awakening," *New York Times*, October 30, 2020;[177]

2) Larry Diamond, "I'm a Democracy Expert; I Never Thought We'd Be So Close to a Breakdown; Our Election Systems Were Not Built for the Modern Era; Looking Abroad Might Help," *New York Times*, November 1, 2020;[178]

3) "Will America Elect a Fascist President?" *The Trenchant Observer*, November 2, 2020.[179]

68

November 2, 2020

Trump Issues Veiled Call for the Assassination of Joe Biden

Our thanks go out to Aaron Blake, who has had the courage to report some of the truly disturbing things Trump has been saying at his rallies and in his tweets. Blake reported today,

> Speaking to supporters in Opa-locka, Fla., on Sunday night into Monday, the president, who faces potential defeat this week, began sizing up his opponent Joe Biden's physical attributes and describing how he might beat him up.
>
> "So those legs — those legs, they've gotten very thin," Trump said. "Not a lot of base."
>
> He continued, drawing his words out carefully and slowly. "You wouldn't have to close," he said, holding up a clenched fist and then releasing it, "you wouldn't have to close the fi-."
>
> ...
>
> In a similar riff the day before, Trump's sentiment was even clearer, though he again suggestively trailed off at the end: "A slight slap. You don't have to close — even close your fist."

...

Trump has also for weeks used a potentially suggestive word to describe Biden's mental state, repeatedly referring to the idea that he's "shot"— which critics suggest is a deliberate double entendre. At one point last week, he referred to the idea of Kamala D. Harris taking over, saying, "Three weeks in, Joe's shot. Let's go, Kamala, you ready?"

–*See* Aaron Blake, "On Election Eve, Trump Dances around a Powder Keg with a Lit Match," *Washington Post*, November 2, 2020 (11:13 a.m. EST).[180]

Now, Trump's dog-whistle encouragement of political violence has spilled into public view with what amounts to a dog-bullhorn call for the assassination of Joe Biden.

Blake's article should be the lead story with a large headline above the fold in today's newspapers. Instead, it is buried inside. The fact that the major newspapers will not give prominence to such an explosive story reveals that they are afraid of Donald Trump, and no longer have the courage to take him on frontally. **Nothing Could Be More Consequential Than This Story.**

Trump has developed into an art form the commission of major crimes in full sight.

Similarly, while the *New York Times* did eventually publish a comprehensive story about the Reinoehl assassination, *six weeks after it occurred*, there was no follow-up. The editors didn't task their reporters with digging into the matter further. **This was cowardice at the highest levels of journalism.**

Steve Bannon's strategy to discredit the news was always to "flood the zone with shit."

Trump's veiled suggestion that Biden should be shot goes way beyond Bannon's injunction, entering into an area which beyond any doubt constitutes another of Trump's "high crimes and misdemeanors" for which he should be impeached and removed from office. Maybe he will be.

Where are the Republicans calling Trump out for this most recent outrage? If they remain silent, they should be viewed by everyone as accomplices.

Incitement to shoot or murder a presidential candidate is a very serious felony. Once we have an independent attorney general and Justice Department, again, they should conduct a very serious investigation into this matter. If that investigation results in the indictment of Donald Trump for inciting violence against a presidential candidate, he can explain to the jury that he was "just kidding" or only meant that Biden would be "shot" in the sense of being worn out. The jury would take all of the surrounding circumstances into account in reaching its judgment.

We should remember Harvey Oswald, John Hinckley, and all of the nuts who are running around out there, excited to a fever pitch by Trump's rhetoric of violence.

Part Six

2020 – Year Four of the Trump Presidency (II):

After the Election, the Conspiracy and the Coup Unfold

69

November 11, 2020

How Trump Wins

Updated November 15, 2020

BACKGROUND

For details on how Republicans are trying to delay vote counting and certifications, *see*

1) Daniela Santamariña and Elise Viebeck, "Here's How Long It Could Take to Certify the Vote in Key States — and the GOP Efforts to Upend That Process; Legal Experts Say There Is Little That President Trump Can Do to Head Off President-elect Joe Biden's Win, But Republicans Could Seek to Delay the Process," *Washington Post*, November 12, 2020 (5:35 p.m.);[181]

2) Trip Gabriel and Stephanie Saul, "Could State Legislatures Pick Their Own Electors to Vote for Trump? Not Likely; Some Trump Allies Have Suggested That Republican Lawmakers Should Override the Will of Voters Who Elected Joe Biden the Next President," *New York Times*, November 13, 2020 (12:45 p.m. ET);[182]

3) Jamelle Bouie, "2020 Shows Why the Electoral College Is Stupid and Immoral; It Doesn't Just Distort Presidential Elections. It Infects the Entire Political Process," *New York Times*, November 13, 2020;[183]

4) Fred Hiatt, "Trump Is Putting This Country Through Something Unprecedented. Here Are Three Scenarios," *Washington Post*, November 15, 2020 (1:00 a.m. ET).[184]

What strategy are Trump and the Republicans following by trying to not recognize Biden's clear victory at the polls?

After researching the Twelfth and the Twentieth Amendments and the mechanisms of the Electoral College vote, the answer became blazingly clear.

They are trying to delay the counting of the votes at the state level by any and all means possible. This includes lawsuits, which could drag out enough to delay the final count and certification of the vote beyond the December 14 date for the meeting of the Electoral College. This meeting involves the casting of electoral votes in separate meetings in each of the states. Normally they vote for the candidate who received the highest number of votes in the respective state. Many states have laws requiring electors to vote in this manner.

However, if Biden cannot marshal a majority of 270 Electoral College votes on that date, under the terms of the Twelfth and Twentieth Amendments to the Constitution, the election of the president is thrown to the House of Representatives in what is known as a "contingent election." There, each state has one vote, which is determined by a majority of the representatives in the state.

Because there are more states with a majority of Republican representatives than there are states with a majority of Democratic representatives, the "contingent election" could result in the election of Donald J. Trump as President of the United States, provided all of the Republican states went along with the scheme.

That is the logic behind the strategy Trump and the Republicans appear to be following.

To achieve their goals, they would be using anti-democratic techniques, including bad-faith allegations of massive fraud where no fraud exists. These techniques range from the filing of spurious lawsuits in bad faith to calls by the two Republican senators of Georgia for the dismissal of the Republican secretary of state because he was doing his job in order to force him into acceding to their demands. This will probably result in further delay in the certification of vote results.

However, there is an important wrinkle. In the "contingent election" for the president in the House, "a quorum for this purpose shall consist of a member or members from two-thirds of the states, and a majority of all the states shall be necessary to a choice." The precise numbers here would have to be figured out to understand how this would work in practice with the newly constituted House.

In the "contingent election" for the vice president in the Senate, "a quorum for (this) purpose shall consist of two-thirds of the whole number of Senators, and a majority of the whole number shall be necessary to a choice."

Consequently, how Trump wins is not as clear as it might at first appear. In what looks like a legal mine field, there is probably a significant possibility that the Supreme Court could get involved.

Nonetheless, despite these quorum requirements, both House and Senate Democrats would need to be extraordinarily careful.

If a quorum of two-thirds of states with one or more representatives is present, the House could elect Trump as president.

In the Senate, a majority of the Senate could elect the vice president, provided a quorum is present. "A quorum for (this) purpose shall consist of two-thirds of the whole number of Senators, and a majority of the whole number shall be necessary to a choice."

If there is no president, the vice president could then serve as president, in the same manner as if the president had died.

For a detailed analysis, *see* Congressional Research Service, "Contingent Election of the President and Vice President by Congress: Perspectives and Contemporary Analysis, Updated October 6, 2020.[185]

The Twelfth Amendment as amended by Twentieth Amendment provides:

Election of President and Vice-President

Passed by Congress December 9, 1803. Ratified June 15, 1804.
(Note: A portion of Article II, section 1 of the Constitution was superseded by the 12th amendment.)

The Electors shall meet in their respective states and vote by ballot for President and Vice-President, one of whom, at least, shall not be an inhabitant of the same state with themselves; they shall name in their ballots the person voted for as President, and in distinct ballots the person voted for as Vice-President, and they shall make distinct lists of all persons voted for as President, and of all persons voted for as Vice-President, and of the number of votes for each, which lists they shall sign and certify, and transmit sealed to the seat of the government of the United States, directed to the President of the Senate; —the President of the Senate shall, in the presence of the Senate and House of Representatives, open all the certificates and the votes shall then be counted; —The person having the greatest number of votes for President, shall be the President, if such number be a majority of the whole number of Electors appointed; and if no person have such majority, then from the persons having the highest numbers not exceeding three on the list of those voted for as President, the House of Representatives shall choose immediately, by ballot, the President. But in choosing the President, the votes shall be taken by states, the representation from each state having one vote; a quorum for this purpose shall consist of a member or members from two-thirds of the states, and a majority of all the states shall be necessary to a choice. [And if the House of Representatives shall not choose a President whenever the right of choice shall devolve upon them, before the fourth day of March next following, then the Vice-President shall act as President, as in case of the death or other constitutional disability of the President. —]* The person having the greatest number of votes as Vice-President, shall be the Vice-President, if such number be a majority of the whole number of Electors appointed, and if no person have a majority, then from the two highest numbers on the list, the Senate shall choose the Vice-President; a quorum for the purpose shall consist of two-thirds of the whole number of Senators, and a majority of the whole number shall be necessary to a choice. But no person constitutionally ineligible to the office of President shall be eligible to that of Vice-President of the United States.

*Superseded by section 3 of the 20th amendment.

National Archives, "Founding Documents: The Constitution, Amendments 11-27," Amendment XII.[186]
See https://constitution.findlaw.com/amendment12.html.

It thus appears that in 2021, a majority of the states in the House would vote to elect Trump. There is an important wrinkle, however. Two-thirds of the members of the House must be present to constitute a quorum.

The Twentieth Amendment[187] provides:

Amendment XX
Presidential Term and Succession, Assembly of Congress

Passed by Congress March 2, 1932. Ratified January 23, 1933. The 20th Amendment changed a portion of Article I, Section 4, and a portion of the 12th Amendment.

Section 1

The terms of the President and the Vice President shall end at noon on the 20th day of January, and the terms of Senators and Representatives at noon on the 3d day of January, of the years in which such terms would have ended if this article had not been ratified; and the terms of their successors shall then begin.

Section 2

The Congress shall assemble at least once in every year, and such meeting shall begin at noon on the 3d day of January, unless they shall by law appoint a different day.

Section 3

If, at the time fixed for the beginning of the term of the President, the President elect shall have died, the Vice President elect shall become President. If a President shall not have been chosen before the time fixed for the beginning of his term, or if the President elect shall have failed to qualify, then the Vice President elect shall act as President until a President shall have qualified; and the Congress may by law provide for the case wherein neither a President elect nor a Vice President shall have qualified, declaring who shall then act as President, or the manner in which one who is to act shall be selected, and such person shall act accordingly until a President or Vice President shall have qualified.

Section 4

The Congress may by law provide for the case of the death of any of the persons from whom the House of Representatives may choose a President whenever the right of choice shall have devolved upon them, and for the case of the death of any of the persons from whom the Senate may choose a Vice President whenever the right of choice shall have devolved upon them.

70

November 18, 2020

Trump Moves to Win "Contingent Election" in House

Updated November 19, 2020

Coup d'État Underway

For the latest news reports, *see*

1) Philip Rucker, Amy Gardner, and Josh Dawsey, "Trump Uses Power of Presidency to Try to Overturn the Election and Stay in Office," *Washington Post*, November 19, 2020 (11:02 p.m. EST);[188]

2) David A. Fahrenthold, Beth Reinhard, Elise Viebeck, and Emma Brown, "Trump's Escalating Attacks Put Pressure on Vote Certification Process," *Washington Post*, November 19, 2020 (8:14 p.m. EST);[189]

3) Maggie Haberman, Jim Rutenberg, Nick Corasaniti, and Reid J. Epstein, "Trump Targets Michigan in His Ploy to Subvert the Election; In a Brazen Step, the President Invited Republican State Leaders in Michigan to the White House as He and His Allies

Try to Prevent the State from Certifying Joe Biden's Clear Victory There," *New York Times*, November 19, 2020 (8:02 p.m. ET);[190]

4) David E. Sanger, "Trump's Attempts to Overturn the Election Are Unparalleled in U.S. History; The President's Push to Prevent States from Certifying Electors and Get Legislators to Override Voters' Will Eclipses Even the Bitter 1876 Election as an Audacious Use of Brute Political Force," *New York Times*, November 19, 2020.[191]

By Thursday, November 19, 2020, news reports confirmed that the Trump strategy is to prevent state certification of Biden vote majorities, presumably with a view to denying him a majority of 270 electoral votes when the Electoral College meets on December 14. Proceeding in this manner, Trump could be "elected" president.

While there is much discussion of "faithless electors" and of Republican legislatures ignoring the popular vote and appointing Trump electors to the Electoral College, these scenarios do not appear to be even remotely plausible.

Consequently, they must be viewed as red herrings, as feints to distract attention from the only strategy that has any possibility of success. That is the strategy of denying Biden the 270 electoral votes needed on December 14 and throwing the election to the House where in a "contingent election" with each state having one vote, Trump could win the presidency.

To succeed, Republican officials would have to violate state laws requiring them to act otherwise. Should they act pursuant to the vast conspiracy of Trump and his collaborators to overturn the election results, they would be committing state and federal felonies which punish conspiracies. They might well be prosecuted, by both state and federal prosecutors, and could end up spending years in prison.

The cost for individuals who commit acts which further Trump's conspiracy to overthrow the election results, which would amount to an attempted coup d'état, could be extremely high.

Indeed, by engaging in conspiracies to violate both state and federal laws, Trump may have sealed his fate. Not even a pardon by Vice President Michael Pence of his federal crimes would protect him from state prosecutions for conspiracy to violate state laws.

Trump's collaborators, who may be expecting protection through Trump pardons, would similarly remain liable for conspiracies to violate state laws.

Any Republican official contemplating participation in Trump's conspiracy should think long and hard about his or her future.

Republican senators and other leaders must now decide: Will they join Trump's attempt at a coup d'état, or will they oppose it?

Or will they argue that they just want to see how it works out?

***

Original article, entitled "Trump and Co-conspirators Move to Sow Confusion, Delay Vote Certifications, and Win Contingent Election in the House," published in The Trenchant Observer on November 18, 2020.[192]

See,

1) Nick Corasaniti, Jim Rutenberg, and Kathleen Gray, "Threats and Tensions Rise as Trump and Allies Attack Elections Process; Confrontations Have Escalated in Swing States, with Elections Officials in Both Parties Facing Threats of Violence, as the President and Other Republicans Try to Subvert the Country's

Voting System," *New York Times*, November 18, 2020,[193] updated February 1, 2021;[194]

2) Amy Gardner, Robert Costa, Rosalind S. Helderman, and Michelle Ye Hee Lee, "As Defeats Pile Up, Trump Tries to Delay Vote Count in Last-Ditch Attempt to Cast Doubt on Biden Victory," *Washington Post*, November 18, 2020 (8:47 p.m. EST).[195]

President Trump and his co-conspirators appear to be moving forward to execute a vast conspiracy aimed at overthrowing the results of the November 3, 2020 presidential election.

Key elements include:

1) Filing numerous frivolous lawsuits with a view to delaying the certifications of the votes at the state level, which are needed in order for the state, in accordance with its laws, to appoint electors pledged to the winning candidate by December 14, the date on which the Electoral College meets (in separate meetings in each of the states) to cast their electoral votes for the president and vice president;

2) Exercising pressure on Republican state legislators to appoint the electors regardless of the popular vote, in states where Biden won but which have majority Republican legislatures;

3) Carrying out a massive campaign of lies alleging electoral fraud, when none exists in fact;

4) Ginning up an atmosphere of violence and threats against electoral officials to influence their decisions;

5) Direct intervention by Trump or his co-conspirators with state election officials in order to influence the vote (e.g., Sen. Lindsey Graham's intervention with the Georgia Secretary of State); and

6) Decapitation of the Defense Department, intelligence agencies and agencies charged with protecting the integrity of the elections, leaving the

U.S. basically defenseless against Russian and other foreign interference in the electoral process to help President Trump.

We are faced with a defeated incumbent president who is willing to use every move in the fascist authoritarian playbook to overturn the results of the 2020 presidential election, and to seize power through what amounts to a coup d'état.

The Democrats need to wake up, understand the nature of the fascist threat, and pull out all the stops in a battle to defend American democracy and the rule of law against a fascist attempt to seize power.

FURTHER READING

"When an Outgoing President Runs Amok, Is There Nothing We Can Do?" *The Trenchant Observer*, November 18, 2020.[196]

November 21, 2020

Imagine: Hitler in the White House

In our previous article imagining Adolf Hitler in the White House, published in *The Trenchant Observer* on November 9[197], we outlined the rationale for this exercise of the imagination, in the following terms:

> In order to set aside our innate American naïveté and innocent prejudices about what is and is not conceivable, it is useful to simply imagine that the fascist Leader in the American White House is Adolf Hitler.
>
> If an incumbent President Hitler had just narrowly lost an American election, in which over 70 million voters had expressed their support for him and his party of abject collaborators, what would he be capable of doing in an effort to retain his hold on power?
>
> What would he not be capable of doing, or attempting? Subject to the same moral constraints which Hitler demonstrated he was subject to in Germany, and no others.

In our chapter (written November 11) "How Trump Wins (Updated)," we included a detailed analysis of what appears to be Trump's and the Republicans' strategy to win the presidency by preventing certification of the vote tallies in time for the Electoral College meeting on December 14,

2020, thereby throwing the election to the House under the terms of the Twelfth and the Twentieth Amendments to the U.S. Constitution.

In this chapter, we combine the insights from these and other articles, and imagine how Adolf Hitler, if he were the leader in the White House today, might scheme and think about how, with over 72 million voters having backed him in the presidential election, he might use the tools of power at his disposal to secure reelection as President of the United States.

His imagined thoughts follow:

Let's see, Adolph. We won over 72 million votes in the November 3, 2020 election, and we hold all of the powers of an incumbent president. Joe Biden is reported to have won the electoral vote count and the popular vote by some six million votes.

How can I secure my hold on power?

This problem is not as difficult as it might seem. Remember how we survived the 1923 Putsch (attempted coup) in Munich. Of course I got to spend some time in jail, but jail gave me the time to express my ideas in *Mein Kampf,* which was a great propaganda success. It also pulled together, in Chapter VI, essential guidance for the use of propaganda

Remember how in Germany, with only 38 percent of the votes in the December 1932 elections, we were nonetheless the leading party and persuaded von Hindenburg to appoint me as Chancellor. Then, in March 1933, I had the brilliant idea of burning down the Reichstag and blaming it on the Communists. They never could prove I was behind it.

The Reichstag fire set the stage for our great triumph in the March 1933 elections, and the subsequent adoption of the Enabling Act, which gave me all of the dictatorial powers that I needed. Now, as president in the White House, I have extraordinary emergency powers, many of which are highly classified. Biden and his crowd will be quite surprised at their nature and extent if I have to use them.

Actually, my team is trying to achieve our goals by using my powers only as needed, in an escalating manner. If we succeed in delaying electoral votes so Biden doesn't get a majority of 270 when the Electoral College meets on December 14, I may not have to fully show my hand by using the greatest of my emergency powers, at this point in time. They can be saved for later, in my second term.

After the 1933 elections, we brought everyone into line during the period of the *Gleichshaltung*, when everyone was forced to follow the Nazi line. We executed all the generals who might have posed any opposition, and then we were firmly in control. "Ein Volk, ein Reich, ein Führer ("One People, one Empire, one Leader") became not only our slogan, but our reality.

Now, turning to America on November 21, 2020, what is the situation and what needs to be done?

First, our greatest success has been in the field of mass propaganda. Propaganda shapes the battlefield. As I pointed out in *Mein Kampf,* the key to successful propaganda is to aim it at the masses, not the intellectuals, and to limit its content to only a few issues which even the least intelligent of the masses can grasp, and to repeat these few points endlessly until even the dumbest of the masses understand the message we are imparting to them. The masses cannot remember anything for long, so the propaganda must be repeated over and over.

I have been brilliant in constantly repeating the charge that there has been massive electoral fraud, and it is only that fraud that threatens to enable the Democrats to steal the election which I won. What we are doing now is defending my victory by reversing the massive electoral fraud the Democrats have committed.

Second, our legal experts tell me that it is actually fairly simple. We need only to prevent the certification of state votes in enough states to prevent Biden from winning the majority of the electoral votes required to select a president at the meeting of the Electoral College on December 14.

The Electoral College does not meet in a single place but rather consists of separate meetings in each state. That makes things quite a bit simpler. If developments aren't going our way in the run-up to its December 14 meeting, we can resort to stronger tactics, as we did in Germany.

We can threaten and intimidate the election officials responsible for certifying the election results or those responsible for appointing the electors. We know their names, where they live, and the names and habits of their children. One kidnapped child could do a lot to persuade Republican (and even Democratic) officials to vote to not certify the election results, or to not appoint electors.

If even stronger methods are needed, we can do that.

The assassination of an election official, by individuals who could never be traced back to us, would probably persuade the other officials to vote our way. Steve Bannon, with his public call for the beheading of Nancy Pelosi and Anthony Fauci, already has our supporters riled up and ready to act. People around the country are talking about beheadings.

The risk here is not great. The main media are afraid to take me on directly. Following the Michael Reinoehl killing near Seattle on September 3, 2020, the *New York Times* didn't even write a comprehensive story for six weeks, and then didn't do any follow-up reporting. Six weeks!

The virus of hatred is out there. It is circulating. That is good for us.

The Proud Boys have already sent key individual warnings that they are being watched. "Stand down and stand by," we said when asked in the debate what we would say to these supporters. Recently, we have sent out the word to them to "Stand Up." They and other groups, including armed militias, are mobilized and ready to act when they get the signal. Bannon or someone else could just put out the word that election officials that certify the vote for Biden or appoint electors, when we oppose such action, should be beheaded.

All we have to do is to delay the vote count to ensure that it cannot be certified by December 14, in a few key states, so that Biden can't get a majority of 270 electoral votes on that day.

To slow the count, we have already launched a slew of lawsuits, and will launch more. Now that the vote is largely counted, we have turned our attention to the election officials that must certify the vote before electors can be appointed at the state level. Also, we are filing lawsuits to prevent their decisions from taking effect before December 14.

In Georgia, for example, we have gotten Senators Loeffler and Perdue to attack the Republican Secretary of State, demanding that he resign. He didn't, but their attacks should have softened him up to be more pliant in future decisions, e.g., on the recount. Earlier, Sen. Lindsey Graham, the Chair of the Senate Judiciary Committee, called election officials in Georgia to see if they could throw out some Biden votes.

It doesn't seem to have worked yet in Georgia, though we still have the recount we are requesting to play with, so that when we request a recount after the secretary of state certifies the results (a Biden win), he will accede to our demands for a very time-consuming recount, which we might be able to slow even further with additional litigation.

But we also have other ways, beyond litigation, to slow the certification of vote counts and the appointment of electors to ensure that Biden does not come up with 270 electoral votes.

We have many measures we can take, beyond those mentioned above, to prevent the appointment of 270 Biden electors by December 14. We could close down the state legislatures due to the COVID-19 threat. We could get our militias to start some arson and looting in major cities and state capitols, so that we are "forced" to invoke the Insurrection Act and send in federal troops to restore law and order.

Or there could be terrorist attacks or threats of such attacks, which might require us to send in federal troops to defend critical institutions such as state legislatures. It would then be fairly easy to deny entrance to these buildings to legislators seeking to tally the electoral votes on December 14, in their separate state meetings.

And there are many more things we could do both before and after December 14 to affect the electoral tally and the counting of electoral votes on January 6 in the joint session of congress.

But I am getting ahead of myself. We have to take this one day at a time. Still, as of today, I think that things are going pretty well and that I will win the "contingent election" in the House.

I've been underestimated before. The Democrats and others are underestimating me now. They are flush with victory and feel overconfident and complacent.

I can work with that.

FURTHER READING

"Fighting the American Fascists: Just Imagine They Are Wearing Nazi Military Uniforms," *The Trenchant Observer*, February 23, 2021.[198]

November 22, 2020

Trump's Criminal Conspiracy to Overthrow the Presidential Election

Updated December 6, 2020

See,

52 U.S.C. 10307, which provides in sections (a) and (b) the following:

52 U.S. Code § 10307 – Prohibited acts[199]

(a) Failure or refusal to permit casting or tabulation of vote
No person acting under color of law shall fail or refuse to permit any person to vote who is entitled to vote under any provision of chapters 103[200] to 107[201] of this title or is otherwise qualified to vote, or willfully fail or refuse to tabulate, count, and report such person's vote.

(b) Intimidation, threats, or coercion

No person, whether acting under color of law or otherwise, shall intimidate, threaten, or coerce, or attempt to intimidate, threaten, or coerce any person for voting or attempting to vote, or intimidate, threaten, or coerce, or attempt to intimidate, threaten, or coerce any person for urging or aiding any person to vote or attempt to vote, or intimidate, threaten, or coerce any person for exercising any powers or duties under section 10302(a),[202] 10305,[203] 10306,[204] or 10308(e)[205] of this title or section 1973d or 1973g of title 42.[1][206]

Trump's Criminal Conspiracy to Overthrow the Presidential Election Results

The statutes and the legal analysis, set forth above, directly support the headline.

President Donald Trump appears to be leading a vast criminal conspiracy to overthrow the results of the presidential election on November 3, 2020. His current strategy appears to be to influence and/or intimidate state and local Republican election officials so that they do not certify the vote totals as required by state law.

The battle of certification is part of a larger strategy to prevent Joe Biden from gaining 270 electoral votes when the Electoral College meets on December 14. If Trump succeeds in this gambit, under the Twelfth Amendment the election would be thrown to the House of Representatives and a so-called "contingent election," in which each state has one vote as determined by a majority of its representatives in the House. Because Republicans control more state delegations than Democrats, this could lead to the election of Donald Trump as the next President of the United States.

Rudy Giuliani has laid this out, as follows:

Rudy Giuliani, Trump's personal attorney, told associates that his goal is to cast enough doubt on the election that state legislatures won't certify the results for Biden. "Rudy told people he was trying to get the legislatures to flip," a source familiar with the campaign's legal strategy tells TIME. "Rudy's view of the world is if he does a good enough job inflaming the results, Pennsylvania won't certify, Wisconsin won't certify."

–Mish, "Trump's Maneuver to Intimidate Michigan Lawmakers Fails," Mish Talk, November 20, 2020.[207]

The problem with Trump's strategy is that it involves a large conspiracy*[208] to get state election officials to criminally violate state election laws.

*"conspiracy": *See* Justia, "Conspiracy to Commit a Crime & Legal Defenses," at https://www.justia.com/criminal/offenses/inchoate-crimes/conspiracy/.

A typical state law is that of Louisiana, which provides:

LA Rev Stat § 18:1461.5

§1461.5. Election offenses involving bribery, threats or intimidation of election officials or candidates; penalties

A. No person shall knowingly, willfully, or intentionally: (1) Offer money or anything of apparent present or prospective value or use, directly or indirectly, or engage in any form of intimidation to influence the action or encourage inaction of any election official with regard to the duties of his office.

...

B. Whoever violates any provision of this Section shall be fined not more than two thousand dollars or be imprisoned, with or without hard labor, for not more than two years, or both, for the first offense. On a second offense, or any subsequent offense, the penalty shall be a fine of not more than five thousand dollars or imprisonment at hard labor for not more than five years, or both.

...

Acts 2010, No. 797, §1, eff. Jan. 1, 2011; Acts 2012, No. 585, §1.

Attempting to influence a state official to violate a state law is also a federal crime for "a person employed in any administrative position by the United States or by any department or agency thereof." This would appear to apply to administrative employees at the White House and other agencies who help Trump.

See 18 U.S.C. Section 595, which provides:

18. United States Code Section 595.[209] **Interference by administrative employees of Federal, State or Territorial Governments**

Whoever, being a person employed in any administrative position by the United States, or by any department or agency thereof, or by the District of Columbia or any agency or instrumentality thereof, **or by any State, Territory, or Possession of the United States, or any political subdivision, municipality, or agency thereof,** or agency of such political subdivision or municipality (including any corporation owned or controlled by any State, Territory, or Possession of the United States or by any such political subdivision, municipality, or agency), in connection with any activity which is financed in whole or in part by loans or grants made by the United States, or any department or agency thereof, **uses his official authority for the purpose of interfering with,**

or affecting, the nomination or the election of any candidate for the office of President, Vice President, Presidential elector, Member of the Senate, Member of the House of Representatives, Delegate from the District of Columbia, or Resident Commissioner, **shall be fined under this title or imprisoned not more than one year, or both.** [emphasis added]

...

Conspiracy to intimidate or influence a state election official to violate state election law is both a state and a federal crime. There are several provisions of the U.S. Code that might apply:

The general conspiracy law, 18 U.S.C Section 371,[210] provides:

18 U.S. Code § 371 - Conspiracy to commit offense or to defraud United States

If two or more persons conspire either to commit any offense against the United States, or to defraud the United States, or any agency thereof in any manner or for any purpose, and one or more of such persons do any act to effect the object of the conspiracy, each shall be fined under this title or imprisoned not more than five years, or both.

If, however, the offense, the commission of which is the object of the conspiracy, is a misdemeanor only, the punishment for such conspiracy shall not exceed the maximum punishment provided for such misdemeanor.

(June 25, 1948, ch. 645, 62 Stat. 701; Pub. L. 103–322, title XXXIII, § 330016(1)(L), Sept. 13, 1994, 108 Stat. 2147.)

Section 371 would apply to a conspiracy to overturn the 2020 presidential election by illegally influencing the appointment of electors and their appointment by the Electoral College.

See Congressional Research Service, Federal Conspiracy Law: A Brief Overview (Updated April 3, 2020), reprinted in EveryCRSReport.com, "Federal Conspiracy Law: A Brief Overview, April 30, 2010–April 3, 2020, at https://crsreports.congress.gov/product/pdf/R/R41223/12:

Conspiracy to Defraud the United States

Section 371 has two prongs, alike but for a single exception. The first, more frequently prosecuted, requires agreement, overt act, and an underlying federal criminal offense. The elements of the second prong, sometimes styled conspiracy to defraud the United States, do not require an underlying federal criminal offense. The elements of conspiracy to defraud the United States under 18 U.S.C. § 371 are: (1) an agreement of two or more persons; (2) to defraud the United States; and (3) an overt act in furtherance of the conspiracy committed by one of the conspirators. The **"fraud covered by the statute reaches any conspiracy for the purpose of impairing, obstructing or defeating the lawful functions of any department of the Government" by "deceit, craft or trickery, or at least by means that are dishonest." The plot must be directed against the United States or some federal entity**; a scheme to defraud the recipient of federal funds is not sufficient. **The scheme may be designed to deprive the United States** of money or property, but it need not be so; **a plot calculated to frustrate the functions of an entity of the United States will suffice.** [emphasis added].

In addition, Trump's conspiracy constitutes a conspiracy to violate the civil rights of voters in general, and the rights of African American and other minority voters in Detroit in particular.

See 42 U.S. Code §1985,[211] at
https://crsreports.congress.gov/product/pdf/R/R41223/12.

Conspiracy to interfere with civil rights 42 U.S. Code § 1985 (Conspiracy to interfere with civil rights) specifically provides in Section (3) the following:

(3) Depriving persons of rights or privileges

If two or more persons in any State or Territory conspire or go in disguise on the highway or on the premises of another, for the purpose of depriving, either directly or indirectly, any person or class of persons of the equal protection of the laws, or of equal privileges and immunities under the laws; or for the purpose of preventing or hindering the constituted authorities of any State or Territory from giving or securing to all persons within such State or Territory the equal protection of the laws; or **if two or more persons conspire to prevent by force, intimidation, or threat, any citizen who is lawfully entitled to vote, from giving his support or advocacy in a legal manner, toward or in favor of the election of any lawfully qualified person as an elector for President or Vice President,** [emphasis added] or as a Member of Congress of the United States; or to injure any citizen in person or property on account of such support or advocacy; in any case of conspiracy set forth in this section, if one or more persons engaged therein do, or cause to be done, any act in furtherance of the object of such conspiracy, whereby another is injured in his person or property, or deprived of having and exercising any right or privilege of a citizen of the United States, the party so injured or deprived may have an action for the recovery of damages occasioned by such injury or deprivation, against any one or more of the conspirators.

Trump reportedly called two canvasing board officials in Michigan to influence their votes to certify the election in the Detroit area. After he spoke to them, they both sought to rescind their votes to certify the vote count, which they had cast earlier. However, the votes having been cast, they could not be rescinded.

Trump then invited seven Michigan Republican legislators to visit the White House on November 20, reportedly to urge them to ignore the vote and appoint a separate slate of electors pledged to supporting him to the Electoral College.

See, Mish, "Trump's Maneuver to Intimidate Michigan Lawmakers Fails," Mish Talk, November 20, 2020.[212] See https:// mishtalk.com/politics/trumps-maneuver-to-intimidate-michigan-lawmakers-fails/.

The author of this article quotes seven Michigan lawmakers who went to the White House at the invitation of President Trump to discuss the Michigan election results.

Even Michigan lawmakers traveled to meet with Trump for about an hour. The visit came as supporters of the president have moved in recent days to overturn the results of the state's election, which Democratic President-elect Joe Biden won by more than 154,000 votes in unofficial returns.

"We have not yet been made aware of any information that would change the outcome of the election in Michigan and, as legislative leaders, we will follow the law and follow the normal process regarding Michigan's electors, just as we have said throughout this election," House Speaker Lee Chatfield and Senate Majority Leader Mike Shirkey said in a joint statement after the meeting.

"These are simple truths that should provide confidence in our elections," they added.

Not Tiddlywinks

The White House press secretary defended the meeting: "He routinely meets with lawmakers from all across the country."

Let's get real. This was a strange meeting at the very least. *Trump did not invite Michigan legislators to the White House to play tiddlywinks or for idle chat no matter what they actually discussed.*

These are the crimes that Trump and his co-conspirators are committing as they seek to overturn the results of the 2020 presidential election.

When it becomes possible, after January 20, 2021, they should be prosecuted for these crimes, at the federal and/or the state level.

Trump's conspiracy to overturn the election results through the commission of these crimes represents perhaps the greatest assault on our democracy and Constitution since the Civil War.

It amounts to one element of what appears to be an attempted coup d'état in progress.

73

November 24, 2020

David Ignatius' Warning about the Risk of a Trump Coup d'État

Yesterday, on November 23, 2020, many of us who have been following the implementation of Donald Trump's vast criminal conspiracy[213] (see https://web.archive.org/web/20201123145801/https://trenchantobserver.com/2020/11/22/trumps-criminal-conspiracy-overthrow-presidential-election-results/) to overthrow the results of the 2020 presidential election breathed a sigh of relief, for two reasons.

First, the election officials in Michigan voted to certify the vote, by a margin of 3-0 with one abstention. Two Democrats and one Republican, who decided to follow the law and not commit a felony by joining Trump's conspiracy. The abstention was by a Republican official, who probably did commit a felony by joining the conspiracy.

Second, the General Services Administration official charged with authorizing the initiation of the transition process, who had been sitting on that decision for several weeks, issued the authorization.

Many reacted as if Trump's dramatic efforts to hang on to power through his criminal conspiracy were over. This was not exactly the case. As Trump lost support and Biden gained momentum, the risk remained of what Trump might do with his presidential powers between now and January 20, 2021.

David Ignatius, one of the very best-connected columnists with contacts in the intelligence and defense communities in Washington, published an intriguing column in the *Washington Post* today, in which he considered the possibility that Donald Trump may still be trying to carry out some kind of coup d'état to remain in power.

> *See* David Ignatius, "How Trump Could Still Disrupt the Transfer of Power," *Washington Post*, November 24, 2020 (12:24 p.m.).[214]

To be sure, after painting a harrowing picture of the possible scenarios for a coup, Ignatius reassures his readers with the following comment:

> Trump wouldn't succeed if he tried to cling to power. We know that because — well, because every responsible political leader, and, indeed, every citizen, will make sure it never happens. Still, thinking about the unthinkable can help us avoid it.

Still, thinking about the unthinkable can help us avoid it. This is more or less the rationale behind our articles asking the reader to imagine Adolf Hitler in the White House.

> *See* Chapter 71, "Imagine: Hitler in the White House," above.

74

November 25, 2020

An American Hero in Michigan, and the Inside Rot of the Republican Party

We have major challenges ahead in order to restore respect by all for our democratic processes and the rule of law. That will take time. But for now, we can simply express our gratitude for the fact that Aaron Van Langevelde and a majority of the people have successfully defended American democracy against a grave fascist threat. That should make this Thanksgiving one to remember, for the ages.

The utter corruption not only of Donald Trump but also, and perhaps more importantly, of the entire anti-democratic (Republican) party, has been in full public view for the last three weeks, since November 3, 2020.

The actions of the anti-democratic party, in supporting Donald Trump's vast criminal conspiracy to overturn the results of the presidential election on November 3, have constituted an extreme fascist threat to American democracy.

Americans have a hard time saying the word "fascist." But it is really not that hard. Just say with me, "fa shist." "Fa" with the "a" pronounced as it is in "fat." "Fa-shist." There, you've said it.

See,

Definition of "fascist":

1) Collins Concise English Dictionary © HarperCollins Publishers:

fascist /ˈfæʃɪst/ (sometimes capital)
n
1. an adherent or practitioner of fascism
2. any person regarded as having right-wing authoritarian views
adj Also: fascistic /fəˈʃɪstɪk/
characteristic of or relating to fascism

2) WordReference Random House Unabridged
Dictionary of American English © 2020

fas•cist (fash′ist),
n.
1. a person who believes in or sympathizes with fascism.
2. (often cap.) a member of a fascist movement or party.
3. a person who is dictatorial or has extreme right-wing views.
adj. Also, fa•scis•tic (fash′ist), of or like fascism or fascists. fa•s-cis′ti•cal•ly, adv.

What we have witnessed in the last three weeks demonstrates, for all who were unable to see it before, that the Republican Party has morphed into the fascist anti-democratic party of the United States. "It can't happen here," many may think, in the memorable phrase of the title of Sinclair Lewis' 1936 book.

But the transformation of the Republican Party into the fascist anti-democratic party of America *has* happened here.

Whether a democratic Republican Party can rise from the ashes of what exists now remains to be seen. At this point, prospects for that development appear to be extremely dubious.

Tim Alberta has written a brilliant article for *Politico Magazine* which lights up the dark countryside of the Republican Party, like a lightning bolt that illuminates in startling detail things that in the dark of the night could not be seen.

> *See* Tim Alberta, "The Inside Story of Michigan's Fake Voter Fraud Scandal; How a State That Was Never in Doubt Became a 'National Embarrassment' and a Symbol of the Republican Party's Fealty to Donald Trump, *Politico Magazine*, November 24, 2020 (09:00 p.m. EST).[215]

In his article, Alberta also recounts how an ordinary lawyer from Western Michigan, Aaron Van Langevelde, a 40-year-old conservative Republican, had the courage to stand up to the enormous pressures applied to him, risking his job and political career, and simply followed the law.

His vote for certification of the Michigan vote, as he was mandated to do by Michigan law, was the equivalent of that moment in the Joseph McCarthy hearings when Joseph Welch said to McCarthy, "Have you no decency, sir?"

Van Langevelde's vote represented a "profile in courage," just when the country so desperately needed to see a new "profile in courage."

Van Langevelde confirmed that the greatest weapon for the defense of American democracy lies in its people, who include many men and women who still believe in the principles our founders shared, and which they enshrined in our Constitution. For over 200 years America has been a beacon to the world, lighting the way to democracy and the rule of law.

We have just seen how countless election workers and officials, from different parties, faithfully performed their jobs in manning the election tables, and counting and tallying the votes, in accordance with the law and the Constitution. We have just seen how judges and state officials defended our democracy by doing their jobs and following the law.

We have just seen how over 150 million Americans cast their ballots and chose their president, vice president, senators and house representatives, overcoming voter suppression efforts, extremely long voting lines, and other obstacles.

We have major challenges ahead in order to restore respect by all for our democratic processes and the rule of law. That will take time.

But for now, we can simply express our gratitude for the fact that Aaron Van Langevelde and a majority of the people have successfully defended American democracy against a grave fascist threat.

That should make this Thanksgiving one to remember, for the ages.

December 11, 2020

Donald Trump and the President's Emergency Powers

Donald Trump has thrown what should be the last of his "Hail Mary" passes in the courts. On December 11, the Supreme Court summarily rejected the request for a hearing in the case brought by Texas, on the ground that Texas lacked standing to bring the suit because it had no legal interest to protect.

Even in Donald Trump's desperate mind, he must realize now that he will not succeed in his attempted coup d'état through the use of the courts.

Notwithstanding this defeat, which he may or may not have understood was extremely probable, he is not likely to give up his determination to stay in power *by any means*.

What is likely to change now are the methods and stratagems employed to continue his coup attempt.

Under the normal electoral process Joe Biden would be elected president by a majority vote of 306 electors when the Electoral College meets on Monday, December 14, 2020.

Trump appeared to be trying to delay the certifications of the votes at the state level. Were he to succeed in preventing the casting of a majority of 270 electoral votes on December 14, the election would be thrown to the House under the terms of the Twelfth Amendment, where in a "contingent election" in which each state has one vote he might be elected president.

Yet not only does Biden have 306 electoral votes, exceeding the requirement of a majority of 270, but these votes have been certified by December 8, the so-called "safe harbor" day after which they are supposed to be presumed valid and not subject to being challenged.

It therefore appears that the only way Trump could prevent the Electoral College from voting for Biden would be if he could prevent each state's electors from meeting in their respective capitals (which is what constitutes a "meeting" of the Electoral College), or at least prevent state meetings in a sufficient number of states where Biden won to bring the number of Biden electoral votes cast to less than 270.

If Biden is chosen by the Electoral College on December 14, Trump's remaining recourse under normal procedure would come on January 6, 2021 when the new Congress meets to tally the votes of the Electoral College.

There, he could try to get the Senate and the House to accept slates of his candidates named by Republican-controlled legislatures. This would involve state legislatures violating state laws which provide that the electors selected represent the winner of the popular vote in the state. While this is a long shot, Trump could hope to tie things up, and somehow get a case to the Supreme Court in an effort to prevail with his twisted interpretation of the constitutional language—arguing that the legislatures have plenary power to name electors, regardless of what laws they have passed may provide.

But we are getting ahead of ourselves.

Trump may not want to wager that any of these stratagems will succeed on their own, without a boost from his use of the president's emergency powers. On the background and extent of his emergency powers, including highly secretive powers which are classified and may include authority to declare martial law and/or seize control of communication systems (e.g., the Internet), *see,*

1) Andrew Cockburn, "The Enemies Briefcase; Secret Powers and the Presidency," *Harper's Magazine*, November 2020 issue;[216]

2) Matt Rothschild, "Trump Has Enormous 'Emergency' Powers; 1978 Law Gives President 123 Statutory Powers. He Could Round Up a Lot of People, a Lot of Groups," *Urban Milwaukee* (urban-milwaukee.com), July 27, 2020 (10:06 a.m.).[217]

Trump supporters have scheduled a mass demonstration in Washington on Saturday, December 12. Were this demonstration to evolve into violence, arson, and looting, Trump could invoke the Insurrection Act and send in federal troops to restore order.

However, the Washington police have a good record in handling demonstrations, so the predicate for any such action may not arise.

One way of looking at Trump's absolute demand for House Republicans to sign on to an amicus brief in the Texas case would be to see it as a maneuver that would compromise them, gaining their support for a counter-factual and crazy action.

Trump, who is a brilliant corrupter of politicians, could be using their fealty to soften them up so they support his next outrage.

The takeaway is that Trump is not likely to desist from his attempted coup.

We can expect that his methods will escalate, and that he will justify their use as exercises of his emergency powers, including those which are classified.

This is no time for anyone to relax.

To understand the fascist threat Trump represents, and the nature of the challenge American democracy will face in the next 39 days, just imagine Adolf Hitler in the White House, scheming and plotting to do anything that will enable him to maintain his grip on power. *Anything.*

Trump's attempted coup is continuing. We must pay close attention. This is no time to lower our guard.

FURTHER READING

Chapter 71, "Imagine: Hitler in the White House," above.

Trump Weighs Military Coup Options

Trump reportedly discussed with the duo (Michael Flynn and Sidney Powell) Flynn's idea of declaring martial law and having the military "rerun" the election — or, failing that, appointing Powell as a special counsel to probe (nonexistent) election fraud.

...Never before in U.S. history has there been a record of a president discussing a military coup to stay in office. Is there any doubt that if Trump could find any active-duty generals willing to carry out this plot against America, he would give it the go-ahead? In this instance, all that is preserving the Constitution is the military's fidelity to the rule of law.

–Max Boot, "Trump Saved the Worst for Last," *Washington Post*, December 20, 2020 (3:24 p.m. EST).[218]

President Donald Trump met with Michael Flynn on Friday, December 18, 2020 and reportedly discussed with him and Trump's own advisors Flynn's proposal that Trump use U.S. military capabilities to declare martial law and rerun the election in swing states that Biden allegedly has won. Max Boot, in the opinion piece cited above, suggests there could be little doubt that if Trump could get any generals to carry out this plot, he would give it the go-ahead.

Trump has been attempting a coup d'état for months, and in an undisguised manner since November 3 as he tries to overturn the election results.

He has led a vast conspiracy to overturn the results, pressuring state election officials, governors, and legislators to violate state law and refuse to certify elections, or even to find ways to throw out Democratic votes. He has also been pressuring U.S. senators and representatives to challenge Biden's electoral college votes (and victory)—without any factual basis— when the new Congress meets to tally and ratify the Electoral College votes on January 6, 2021.

He has, in a word, been attempting to overthrow the Constitution and the constitutional government of the United States.

That constitutes sedition, in addition to a number of state and federal felonies, including conspiracy.

He is unlikely to prevail if he invokes a self-pardon as a defense when he is indicted for these crimes by federal prosecutors. Even a straight pardon, e.g., by Mike Pence, would have no effect in any state prosecutions.

Trump would have a much better shot at escaping federal prosecution for federal crimes if he were to resign as part of a deal for a pardon with Pence.

Max Boot also notes that Trump was considering on Friday, December 18, the appointment of Michael Flynn's lawyer, Sidney Powell, as special counsel to investigate the electoral "fraud" which Trump alleges resulted in Biden's apparent election. Powell was once on Trump's legal team under Rudy Giuliani but was reportedly dropped because she was too crazy even for Giuliani and the White House.

Apparently, Powell's status with the president has improved. She may be one of the last people left telling him what he wants to hear.

As for nominating Sidney Powell to be special counsel to investigate electoral "fraud" in the election, as the French would say, *allez-y!*

Go for it!

As for the declaration of martial law and the military's rerunning the elections in swing states, if Trump tries this, we should at least learn a lot about his secret, classified emergency powers.

Trump has not had much success in carrying out his attempted coup. As the clock runs down, he is becoming increasingly desperate.

Trump does not want to spend the rest of his life in prison. But the walls are closing in.

He is apparently too crazed to act rationally, in which case he might be negotiating his pardon and resignation with Mike Pence. To avoid any surprises on the way to the airport, he would be well advised to resign from the presidency only after he has successfully relocated to a secure haven from which he is not likely to be extradited.

His situation is not unique. His co-conspirators might consider the advisability of earnestly lobbying for a pardon while Trump is still in office, and themselves traveling abroad to a secure relocation venue. If they coordinate their efforts, they could land with Trump in quite advantageous circumstances in the Bahamas, Russia, or China.

If they act quickly, they might even secure deep discounts on condos at a new Trump Tower to be built in the Bahamas, which has strong advantages being near Mar-a-Lago in Miami, or in Russia or China where the real estate and other business opportunities may be even greater.

In short, if Trump wants to appoint Sidney Powell to be a special counsel to investigate fraud in the election: *Allez-y!*

If he wants to declare martial law and have the military redo the elections in swing states, good luck with that.

Should Trump's mind turn to his likely future after noon on January 20, 2021, he might want to start studying the issues raised in our series in *The Trenchant Observer*, "Where Can Trump Go to Escape the Law?"[219]

FURTHER READING

See,

1) "Where Can Trump Go to Escape the Law? Russia?" *The Trenchant Observer*, October 17, 2020;[220]

2) "Where Can Trump Go to Escape the Law? China?" *The Trenchant Observer*, October 21, 2020;[221]

3) "Where Can Trump Go to Escape the Law? The Bahamas? *The Trenchant Observer*, Updated December 17, 2020;[222]

4) "Where Can Trump Go to Escape the Law? Will He Make It to the Airport?" *The Trenchant Observer*, December 12, 2020.[223]

The clock is ticking.

77

December 22, 2020

Should We Be Afraid of What Trump Might Do? Absolutely.

"Diplomacy is the art of saying 'nice doggie' until you can find a rock."
—Will Rogers

Should we be afraid of what Trump might do in the waning days of his presidency?

Absolutely. We should be absolutely afraid.

This is not a joke.

It is hard to imagine a more dangerous situation than the one we currently find ourselves in.

The President of the United States has gone crazy.

Loony.

Ripe for a psychiatric intervention.

Lost touch with reality.

And yet, as President of the United States, he possesses enormous powers, powers so great that it is highly questionable whether any human being should ever be entrusted with them.

The fact that some are so secret that they are classified, and even most if not all members of Congress are unaware of their existence or extent, is utterly appalling.

The existence of these powers, which nobody knows about, reveals how bad democratic governments are at controlling "secret" executive powers, secret and classified emergency powers to deal with a national emergency—as defined by the president, and not subject to any timely, serious review.

We have already seen how Donald Trump has abused emergency powers that are public, by invoking the "national security" exception to the World Trade Organization (or GATT) rules governing international trade, when he imposed tariffs on Canada and China without any valid basis in law.

These rules are contained in treaties ratified by the United States, which have the force of law.

Should we be afraid of what Trump might do in the waning days of his presidency?

ABSOLUTELY. WE SHOULD BE ABSOLUTELY AFRAID.

On Friday, December 18, the president met with Michael Flynn, convicted but pardoned criminal felon, former national security advisor and previously director of the Defense Intelligence Agency, to discuss Flynn's proposal that Trump declare martial law in the swing states that voted for Joe Biden, and that the military conduct a "rerun" of the elections in those states.

In a word, Trump met with his advisors on Friday to consider the option of carrying out a military coup in the United States.

Read those words again. Let them sink in.

Flynn's lawyer, Sidney Powell, also participated in that meeting, where she reportedly urged the President to seize voting machines in the states in question. Trump was reported to be considering her appointment as special counsel to investigate fraud in the November 3 elections.

Powell was reportedly seen at the White House on Sunday and Monday.

Should we be afraid of what Trump might do in the waning days of his presidency?

ABSOLUTELY. WE SHOULD BE ABSOLUTELY AFRAID.

This is not a joke.

In the meantime, government officials reported there had been a massive security breach of government and private computer networks, believed to have been carried out by Russian intelligence agencies. The cyber-attack amounted to the equivalent of a Pearl Harbor attack in the cyber world.

While Attorney General William Barr and Secretary of State Mike Pompeo attributed the hack to the Russians, Trump has not said a word regarding the Russians and has instead suggested that it was the Chinese who carried out the attack.

This raises a critical question:

Did Trump, whether by act or omission, give the Keys to the Kingdom to Vladimir Putin and the Russians?

What could Trump do in the next 29 days?

The military are worried.

AND YOU SHOULD BE WORRIED TOO!

What is to be done?

What can be done?

Call in the experts on dealing with a madman in a hostage situation.

Get ready for and expect *anything*.

It is time for the House of Representatives to step up to the plate and to take the steps necessary to defend the American people and our democracy from this madman.

Should we be afraid of what Trump might do in the waning days of his presidency?

ABSOLUTELY. WE SHOULD BE ABSOLUTELY AFRAID.

This is not a joke.

He is dangerous, like a wounded wild animal in a corner.

Care should be taken not to unnecessarily provoke him.

Instead, the House should quietly begin an impeachment inquiry and prepare draft articles of impeachment.

Then, if Trump commits any unconstitutional acts that seriously endanger individuals or our democracy, they should quickly pass the draft articles of impeachment and send them to the Senate. This they can do virtually, by remote vote.

Since the Senate has not yet approved remote voting, Senators would actually have to vote for Trump's removal in person. If they were adjourned, they would have to travel to Washington to cast their vote.

Should Trump order the military or other federal officials to interfere with their travel, we as a nation would have to rely on our military and other federal officials to refuse to obey any unconstitutional orders.

Should we be afraid of what Trump might do in the waning days of his presidency?

ABSOLUTELY. WE SHOULD BE ABSOLUTELY AFRAID.

This is not a joke.

78

December 26, 2020

Was the Nashville Blast Related to Trump's Attempted Coup?

An Attack on Critical Communications Infrastructure

The following article was written before we saw an article by David Ignatius on the risk of a Trump coup.

See "Until Biden's Win Is Certified, the U.S. Remains Vulnerable, *Washington Post*, December 26, 2020 (4:51 p.m. EST).[224]

Sometimes things are so blazingly obvious, right in front of you, that you can't see them.

The massive explosion in Nashville on Christmas morning has all the earmarks of an attack on critical communications infrastructure. It appears to have been part of a highly sophisticated plot aimed at taking out a major AT&T communications and re-transmission facility. The blast has disrupted communications in Tennessee and neighboring states.

See Derek Hawkins, Michael Kranish, Simone Sebastian, and Meryl Kornfeld, "63-Year-Old Anthony Q. Warner Is a Person of

Interest in Christmas Blast in Nashville, Authorities Say," *Washington Post*, December 27, 2020 at 8:10 p.m. EST.[225]

The attack could potentially be an element of President Donald Trump's apparent attempt to carry out a coup d'état in the United States which would overthrow the November 3, 2020 election results and keep him in power.

One can imagine the chaos that would be generated by 20 such explosions, on the same day, with numerous requests from Republican governors, and perhaps others, for Trump to declare a national emergency and send in federal assistance.

We should bear in mind that the United States has been under cyber-attack by Russia for months, and that Russia has probably acquired the capability to shut down key U.S. infrastructure, including telecommunications networks.

Under the president's secret, classified emergency powers, moreover, Trump may himself have "apparent" authority to seize the nation's communications networks and to shut down the Internet. The authority is "apparent" because the grant of such powers may be unconstitutional, and their use in circumstances other than the type of emergency they were created to meet (e.g., nuclear war) may itself be unconstitutional.

If indeed Trump is testing an element of a coup d'état, the action would fit into a pattern of actions that seem to have been testing one or another element of such an attempted coup.

Trump's involvement of U.S. military forces in the Lafayette Square incident, when Trump marched across the Square with the Chairman of the Joint Chiefs of Staff in military dress, while federal forces in helicopters hovered over the crowd and assisted in their unlawful dispersal, appears to have constituted one such probe.

Trump's dispatch of federal forces to Kenosha, Wisconsin may have constituted another. So it would appear did the deployment of federal "officials" under the authority of the attorney general to Portland, Oregon. And, most disturbingly, the assassination of Michael Reinoehl near Seattle, with the apparent direct involvement of both the president and Attorney General William Barr, may have been testing the ability of the White House and the Justice Department to directly take out targeted individuals.

So, one can imagine a number of Nashville-scale attacks on our communications infrastructure, and Trump trying to take over national communications networks and the Internet through invoking his secret, classified emergency powers. And one can imagine Russia assisting in this coup attempt through cyber-attacks and shutting down critical infrastructure.

One can further imagine bomb attacks in Washington, D.C., the announcement by Trump that the government is aware of imminent threats to blow up the Capitol Building, that martial law has been declared, and that, with Trump having invoked the Insurrection Act, U.S. military troops have been deployed to secure and protect the Congress and other key facilities throughout the country.

Simultaneously, Republican congressmen and senators could drag out the tallying by Congress of the Electoral College vote and the formal election of the president, on January 6, 2021, by forcing two-hours of debate in each house on whether or not to accept each challenged elector.

The above imagined scenario paints a picture of what Trump *could* try to do in the final stages of his attempted coup, and perhaps of what his brilliant and deranged advisors may be urging him to do.

He is crazy. He could do **anything**.

We should be prepared for anything and everything. After reviewing these dark scenarios, we should be prepared for, and at least not surprised by, anything Trump might try to do.

Just look at the highly improbable and unthinkable things he has already done, like pressuring state election officials not to certify vote results, pressuring governors and state legislators to ignore the popular vote in their state and to designate Trump electors, or ginning up a violent mob of his supporters who have been making death threats against officials who do not bend to his will.

Moreover, the "chaos president" may be stirring up further disorder by blocking passage of the COVID relief and federal funding bill recently approved by Congress.

If he does not sign the bill or simply allows it to expire with Congress due to a "pocket veto," civil unrest could ensue as millions of people lose their COVID unemployment benefits and massive evictions of millions of people take place.

If, added to the above, a government shutdown is underway, President Trump may well succeed in creating the kind of chaos which he may believe will aid him in his attempted coup d'état. Or at least the kind of *Götterdämmerung* he might like to see as the curtain closes on what has been a truly spectacular "reality show."

We must imagine the unimaginable in order to ensure that it never happens.

In February 1933, Germans could not imagine that someone (probably Adolf Hitler) would burn down the Reichstag building, or that the Nazis would use that event to sweep the parliamentary elections in early March, or that with their new parliamentary majority they would then pass an Enabling Act that would empower Hitler to establish a dictatorship which would only be overthrown by the victorious Allied Powers in 1945.

But in Germany, one of the most advanced countries in Europe, it happened. The unimaginable actually happened.

Each day between now and January 20, 2021 will be filled with drama.

We must be prepared to remain calm and to take forceful steps to counter each and every one of any Trump maneuvers which may be aimed at seizing and remaining in power after January 20, 2021.

This all seems far-fetched and unlikely. Let us all take precautions to ensure that it remains so.

Part Seven

2020-2021 – The End of the Trump Presidency

The Conspiracy and the Coup Accelerate

79

January 2, 2021

Trump Calls for Rally in Washington on January 6

Republicans Plot to Reject Biden Electors

Donald Trump is continuing with his attempted coup.

A number of Republican senators have now signed on to efforts to block Congress's formal recognition of the December 14, 2020 Electoral College vote, which itself only ratified the election of electors in each state that supported the victors in the state's popular vote, as required by state law.

Trump has called on his supporters to go to Washington, D.C. for a mass rally on January 6, 2021, the same day Congress is supposed to ratify the Electoral College vote.

The Republicans in Congress who support this unconstitutional rejection of Biden electors have absolutely no legal ground to stand on.

Nonetheless, we must take seriously the attempted coup which Republican President Donald Trump and Republican legislators have been attempting to carry out since November 3, 2020, if not earlier.

Trump's mass rally on January 6 seemed ominous.

See,

1) Colbert I. King, "Fourteen Days That Will Test Our Democracy," *Washington Post*, January 1, 2021 (12:39 p.m. EST).[226]

2) David Ignatius, "Until Biden's Win Is Certified, the U.S. Remains Vulnerable," *Washington Post*, December 26, 2020 (4:51 p.m. EST).[227]

3) David Ignatius, "How Trump Could Still Disrupt the Transfer of Power," *Washington Post*, November 24, 2020 (12:24 p.m. EST).[228]

It is important to track the evolution of these efforts, which strongly suggest that Trump and his co-conspirators have been following a master plan, for some time.

His attempted coup has not been working out well for Trump. As each effort has failed, he has been driven to increasingly desperate measures in seeking to remain in power while the walls are closing in. On the evolution of Trump's attempted coup d'état, *see*,

1) Chapter 75,"Donald Trump and the President's Emergency Powers," above;

2) Chapter 78, "Was the Nashville Blast, an Attack on Our Communications Infrastructure, Related to Trump's Attempted Coup?" above;

3) "This Loony President Is the Most Dangerous Man on Earth," *The Trenchant Observer*, December 22, 2020.[229]

4) Chapter 76, "Trump Weighs Military Coup Options," above.

80

January 3, 2021

Emergency Responses to a Trump Military Coup

Warning Signs Regarding a Potential Military Coup

Unfortunately, it now appears plausible that President Donald Trump is considering attempting a military coup d'état on January 6, 2021, or in the following days leading up to Joe Biden's inauguration at noon on January 20, 2021.

There is no other way to read the op-ed by ten former secretaries of defense in the *Washington Post* on January 3, 2021. Signers included Mark Esper, Trump's secretary of defense until he was fired on November 9, 2020. It must be assumed that Esper has some sense of what has been going on in the military.

In addition, the lack of cooperation between Trump defense officials and Biden transition officials is a separate but related cause of concern.

See,

1) Dan Lamothe, "The Time to Question Election Results Has Passed, All Living Former Defense Secretaries Say," *Washington Post*, January 3, 2021 (6:44 p.m. EST).[230]

"The time to question election results has passed, and there is no role for the military in changing them, all 10 of the living former defense secretaries said in an extraordinary rebuke to President Trump and other Republicans who are backing unfounded claims of widespread fraud at the ballot box."

2) Op-ed, All 10 Living Former Defense Secretaries*: "Involving the Military in Election Disputes Would Cross into Dangerous Territory," *Washington Post*, January 3, 2021 (5 p.m. EST).[231]

    *Ashton Carter
Dick Cheney
William Cohen
Mark Esper
Robert Gates
Chuck Hagel
James Mattis
Leon Panetta
William Perry
Donald Rumsfeld

3) Bryan Bender and David Cohen, "Ex-Defense Secretaries Say Military Must Stay Out of Election Battles; The 10 Who Signed on to an Opinion Column Include Two Who Served under President Donald Trump," *Politico*, January 3, 2021 (6:13 p.m. EST, updated 7:57 p.m. EST).[232]

Mark Esper served as Trump's secretary of defense from July 2019 to November 9, 2020. James Mattis served as Trump's secretary of defense from January 2017 to January 2019.

Emergency Responses

Pro-democratic forces and the incoming Biden administration need to urgently mobilize in order to meet and defeat any actions by Trump and his administration and Republican legislative leaders to carry out a military coup d'état.

Needed Steps

1. **Cancellation of demonstration permits.** Incoming officials of the Biden administration should request the immediate cancellation by D.C. and Park Service officials of all permits for demonstrations in the Washington area on January 6. These permits were secured by subterfuge (e.g., requested by women's organizations in lieu of the Proud Boys). The demonstrations represent a clear physical danger to others, as revealed by prior behavior when gangs roved through the streets looking for individuals to attack, stabbing a number. The president's tweets calling for all his supporters to come to the demonstrations, promising "It will be wild," amounts to an incitement to violence. The permits should be rescinded, and if they aren't, democratic lawyers should go to court to ensure that they are.

2. **Refusal to obey illegal orders.** Military and any public order forces should refuse to obey any commands that appear to be illegal or unconstitutional.

3. **Emergency legal advice center.** An emergency legal advice center should be set up by the incoming Biden administration, where current military officials or soldiers can call in for authoritative legal guidance on how to proceed in the event that they receive an illegal order.

4. **Spell out potential criminal charges and consequences.** Incoming officials of the Biden administration should spell out publicly, and loudly, the specific criminal charges that might be brought against individuals

who support a military coup or actions to overthrow the Constitution, and the corresponding punishments. The serious nature of such actions and their consequences should be brought home to all Trump supporters. Impunity for the commission of crimes must end on January 20, 2021.

5. **Contingency plans to impeach Trump.** The House should quietly make contingency plans to impeach Trump on or after January 6 if he attempts a coup.

6. **Contingency plans to arrest Trump.** Contingency plans should be made to arrest Donald Trump if he attempts a coup.

If Trump and his supporters are acting outside the Constitution, there is no reason raw power should not be met with raw power until the constitutional order can be re-established. The legal justification for arresting Trump could be to protect Congress' constitutional power and ability to impeach and remove a president, and to bring "high crimes and misdemeanors" to a halt pending immediate impeachment in the House and trial in the Senate.

7. **Urgent legal actions.** Democratic lawyers should be ready to bring urgent legal actions to stay any illegal or unconstitutional actions Trump or his supporters may be undertaking.

Some of the above steps should not be taken, at least publicly, until after the polls close in the Georgia run-off elections on January 5.

By early on the morning of January 6, the contingency plans to impeach Trump should be made public. That could very well get him to back off from any crazy actions he may be contemplating. It is interesting to note that when one or more legislators called for his immediate impeachment if he didn't sign the stimulus bill, he signed the bill.

Biden address to the nation. If Trump does move to carry out a military coup, Joe Biden should be prepared to address the nation immediately.

Secret and classified emergency powers. Trump, acting under color of his secret and classified emergency powers, could act to seize communications networks and even shut down the Internet. For that reason special contingency plans should be made to ensure effective communications should such a development occur.

Putin and Russia. We should bear in mind that Vladimir Putin and Russia have just carried out a devastating cyber-attack, which may have compromised thousands of networks and computer systems, and that Russia could assist Trump in any attempted military coup d'état by interfering with our communications or shutting down news sites.

Delay in congressional approval of electoral college vote. A potential military coup could be carried out in conjunction with, or at least in parallel with, attempts by Republican senators and congressmen to block approval by the Congress on January 6, 2021 of the Electoral College vote (on December 14) for Joe Biden.

Challenging Biden's electoral slates in five or six states could greatly drag out congressional approval of the Electoral College vote. Challenge by a congressman and a senator to any state's electoral slate will give rise to a two-hour debate in each House where the issue will be decided. This could easily lead to a delay of four hours per state slate challenged, or a total of 20-24 hours. Both houses must approve the challenge in order for it to succeed.

Democratic senators and congressmen should bring plenty of food and water with them on January 6 and be prepared to work through the night and the following day to bring the formal election of Joe Biden to a successful conclusion.

If the demonstrations lead to violence and Trump sends troops or other federal forces in to restore law and order, perhaps invoking the Insurrection Act, who knows what could happen amid the ensuing chaos?

If Trump reports there is a "terrorist threat" to, e.g., blow up the Capitol, or undertakes military action against Iran, a military coup could well be underway.

Trump is desperate and unhinged, surrounded by lunatic advisors who have been talking about imposing martial law for weeks.

Democrats and everyone else should take the threat of a Trump attempted military coup seriously.

Trump might not attempt a military coup. If he did, he probably would not succeed. But he is desperate enough and crazy enough to try.

The steps outlined above should be adopted, on an urgent basis.

FURTHER READING

"Contingency Planning for Military-Style Commando Action to Arrest Trump," *The Trenchant Observer*, January 12, 2021.[233]

81

January 5, 2021

Legislators Plan to Violate Electoral Count Act of 1887

BACKGROUND

1) Miles Parks, "Biden's Victory Cemented as States Reach Key Electoral College Deadline," NPR Morning Edition, December 8, 2020 (5:00 a.m. ET).[234]

Parks reports:

> Electoral College electors are scheduled to meet in states across the country on the first Monday after the second Wednesday in December (Dec. 14 this year) to cast their votes.
>
> And if a state has finalized its results six days before then, according to the ECA, then those results qualify for "safe harbor" status — meaning Congress must treat them as the "conclusive" results, even if, for example, a state's legislature sends in a competing set of results.
>
> Every state except Wisconsin appears to have met the deadline, according to The Associated Press.

Wisconsin's 10 electoral votes are still expected to be cast for Biden on Monday; he won the state by just over 20,000 votes.

"If a state can conclude its process of appointing electors by that [safe harbor deadline] then Congress is bound by federal law to accept the slate of electors that is arrived upon by that date," said Rebecca Green, the co-director of the Election Law program at William and Mary.

Both Green and Alexander, of Ohio Northern, said they expect a few "faithless electors" to vote on Dec. 14 for a different candidate than voters chose but nowhere near enough to affect the underlying result.

A majority of states have some sort of law that either removes, penalizes, or cancels the votes of such errant electors, and the Supreme Court upheld the constitutionality of such rules earlier this year.

2) Nick Corasaniti, Sydney Ember and Alan Feuer, "The Nation Reached 'Safe Harbor'; Here's What That Means; President Trump's Efforts to Overturn the Presidential Election Are Nearing the End of the Line," *New York Times*, December 8, 2020 (Updated December 13, 2020).[235]

The *New York Times* report states:

That's because election results that have been certified by the states are now considered conclusive, and by law those states' Electoral College votes must be counted by Congress. By late Monday, every state but Hawaii had certified its results, and Mr. Biden had secured more than the 270 electoral votes needed to become president.

The 1887 Electoral Vote Count Act provides, specifically, the following:

3 U.S. Code § 5 [236]

If any State shall have provided, by laws enacted prior to the day fixed for the appointment of the electors, for its final determination of any controversy or contest concerning the appointment of all or any of the electors of such State, by judicial or other methods or procedures, and such determination shall have been made at least six days before the time fixed for the meeting of the electors, such determination made pursuant to such law so existing on said day, and made at least six days prior to said time of meeting of the electors, shall be conclusive, and shall govern in the counting of the electoral votes as provided in the Constitution, and as hereinafter regulated, so far as the ascertainment of the electors appointed by such State is concerned.

(June 25, 1948, ch. 644, 62 Stat. 673.)

What this means is that the seditionist senators and congressman, on January 6, 2021, will be violating a specific law enacted by Congress which has been in effect for 133 years. They have not challenged its constitutionality in court.

They are outlaws, pure and simple, committing acts of sedition. While they are protected by congressional immunity from being prosecuted for their votes or statements they make on the floor of their respective Houses, that immunity does not protect them from criminal liability for participation in Trump's vast conspiracy to overthrow the election results and the Constitution, to the extent their actions were performed outside of Congress.

They are trying to overthrow our Constitution. They should be prosecuted, each and every one of them.

What Is Actually Going on Here

What is going on here, despite the complexities, is actually very simple. The states have informed Congress of their approved electoral slates, which, in accordance with the law and popular vote of each state, give the victory to Joe Biden. The Twelfth Amendment and the 1887 Electoral Vote Count Act determine the procedure to be followed. The Act provides a "safe harbor" deadline which, if met, protects the electoral slates from being questioned.

The seditionists plan to violate that law, without advancing any legal justification. All of the claims of fraud have been litigated and rejected by state and federal courts. The seditionists are saying these court decisions, adopted in accordance with state and federal constitutions and laws, are irrelevant, and need be given no effect.

Instead, they are saying, Congress has an overarching power to re-litigate issues of alleged fraud, unbound by any rules of procedure or evidence, without regard to the judiciary where these claims have been adjudicated, and that Congress can overturn the vote of the American people for president.

That makes Congress the super-branch of government, the branch which may declare who is king.

The argument is wholly without merit. The seditionist senators and congressmen who are participating in Trump's conspiracy to overthrow the election and the Constitution should be prosecuted for actions that constitute conspiracy and sedition, and other crimes—committed outside of Congress.

82

January 6, 2021 (12:34 p.m. PST)

Trump Military Coup in Progress

Trump's protesters in Washington have stormed the Capitol building, causing the evacuation of the building and the disruption of congressional ratification of the Electoral College vote.

This is sedition and insurrection.

It has the air of being a carefully planned plot to launch a military coup to overthrow the election and the Constitution.

Other elements that are unfolding:

There were bomb threats that briefly caused the evacuation of congressional office buildings.

Word is coming in of demonstrations planned or taking place in other cities.

Trump's next step may be to invoke the Insurrection Act and order federal troops into Washington, D.C. to regain control of the Capitol building, and into other cities where demonstrations may threaten public order.

Any federal troops ordered to intervene in this situation, which is entirely of President Trump's creation, should question whether the order is a lawful and constitutional order.

Pro-democratic forces should stay off the streets in Washington for now, to avoid feeding the disorder that Trump and his supporters are trying to create.

With his secret, classified emergency powers, Trump could declare martial law in Washington, D.C. and other cities.

The House should immediately begin an impeachment inquiry and impeach Trump within the next day or hours.

This is real. This what the ten former secretaries of defense warned against in their recent *Washington Post* op-ed piece.

Democrats should engage with amateur radio operators in order to guarantee critical communications in the event President Trump uses his secret, classified emergency powers to seize communications systems and/or shut down the Internet.

Anyone who watched Trump's speech to his followers this morning can understand that he is operating in a world of illusions that is totally divorced from reality.

This is not a joke. This is not funny.

This appears to be the real thing, following a carefully scripted plan.

FURTHER READING

1) Robert O'Harrow Jr., "Rallies Ahead of Capitol Riot Were Planned by Established Washington Insiders," Washington Post, January 17, 2021 (5:00 a.m. EST);[237]

2) Phil McCausland, Minyvonne Burke, Ezra Kaplan, and Alicia Victoria Lozano, "Protesters Gather Outside State Capitols Nationwide as Chaos Sweeps Congress," NBC News, January 6, 2021.[238]

83

*January 7, 2021
(12:17 p.m. PST)*

IMPEACH TRUMP TODAY!

After inciting insurrection and the violent mob attack on the Capitol on Wednesday, January 6, 2021, Donald Trump should be removed from office immediately.

The House of Representatives should approve one or more articles of impeachment TODAY.

If Vice President Mike Pence and a majority of the Cabinet do not act to remove Trump from the Presidency under the Twenty-fifth Amendment, the House should transmit article(s) of impeachment to the Senate for trial TOMORROW.

The House has adopted rules that permit representatives to act virtually, from remote locations. If necessary, representatives should return to Washington.

Under this scenario, the Senate should conduct an impeachment trial over the weekend and convict and remove Trump from office by Monday, January 11, 2021.

TIME IS OF THE ESSENCE.

We can no longer permit this fascist President and would-be dictator to retain the powers of the presidency, including the secret and classified emergency powers with which the president has been invested.

It looks like the attempted coup through mob action to seize the Capitol was the first step in an attempted military coup d'état.

Trump must be stopped. NOW.

Since he is acting outside the Constitution in organizing an attempted coup, limited actions outside the scope of the Constitution narrowly aimed at restoring the constitutional order, and necessary to secure that end, may be viewed as legitimate.

That means that if Vice President Mike Pence and the top legislative and military officials determine it is necessary, the authority and powers of the presidency should de facto be transferred to Pence, and even the arrest and detention of Trump would be justified.

The key point is that the constitutional order has been breached, and even extraordinary measures such as the arrest of Donald Trump would be justified if necessary to re-establish it.
Trump's late assurances that he will **now** accept the orderly transfer of power on January 20, 2021 should be given no credence. Yesterday he was acting to overthrow the Constitution of the United States.

Trump must be impeached TODAY.

If necessary to halt his ongoing attempt to carry out a coup d'état, including by military means, he should be arrested and detained.

The advice of pundits and legislators based on prior assumptions (e.g., "Impeachment would take too long," or "We tried impeachment and it doesn't work"), should be ignored.

A coup d'état is by its very nature a fast-moving event. Those who would defend democracy need to be nimble on their feet and in their thinking and be prepared to act quickly and decisively.

FURTHER READING

Updated January 7, 2021 (6:44 p.m. PST)

1) Missy Ryan and Paul Sonne, "Pentagon Put Significant Restrictions on D.C. Guard Ahead of Pro-Trump Protests," Washington Post, January 7, 2021;[239]

2) "AOC's Instagram Account of the Trauma She Experienced on January 6," The Trenchant Observer, February 2, 2021.[240]

84

January 8, 2021

Pelosi and House Democrats Should Not Falter in Impeaching Trump

When an attempted coup d'état is underway, defenders of democracy must act swiftly and decisively.

The principal instigator of the attempted coup which included the insurrectionist invasion of the Capitol, on January 6, 2021, is the President of the United States, Donald Trump.

Trump remains in office, holding all of the powers and emergency powers of the presidency, including the secret, classified emergency powers invested in his office.

So long as the instigator of the attempted coup remains in office, we should all understand that a continuing, ongoing attempted coup d'état is underway. Trump must be removed immediately in order to end this threat to American democracy.

From reports of the Democratic caucus conference call today, Friday, January 8, 2021, *House Speaker Nancy Pelosi wants to wait until there is enough support in the country to move forward on the impeachment of Donald Trump.* [Emphasis added]

To do so would be a grave mistake.

If the House does not adopt one or more articles of impeachment, if it falters, Trump will interpret that as weakness, and will be emboldened to take even more dramatic, unconstitutional actions.

It would be a huge mistake to embolden a rogue president who is orchestrating an ongoing coup d'état.

With only two days left in power, he could start a war and would still have the power to destroy the world.

He is mad and desperate to avoid prosecution and prison, the two fates that surely await him once he leaves office.

This is no time to replay the failure of Pelosi and the Democratic caucus to move on impeachment in 2019. Had they begun a broad impeachment inquiry in April or the summer of 2019, and used that inquiry to educate the American people about the nature and extent of Trump's crimes and abuses of power, it is possible that we would have never come to **the EMERGENCY SITUATION in which we find ourselves today.**

Instead, Pelosi led the Democratic caucus to a narrow impeachment inquiry focused solely on Ukraine, leading to the wholly foreseeable acquittal of Trump in the Senate.

Predictably, Trump was emboldened by his acquittal and proceeded to commit increasingly flagrant abuses of power and "high crimes and misdemeanors," culminating in his attempted coup d'état since November 3, 2021, and his incitement of a mob on January 6, 2021 to march on the Capitol. The invasion of the Capitol was carried out in conjunction with efforts by Republicans in the Senate and the House to derail the ratification of the Electoral College vote.

Trump orchestrated the gathering of the mob ("Be there. It is going to be wild."). Then, in a fiery speech, he incited the mob to march on the

Capitol in order to thwart congressional ratification of the December 14 Electoral College vote.

A policeman and a demonstrator were killed in the riot, and three other people died of natural causes.

Trump must be viewed as a criminal who is armed and dangerous.

He is armed with all of the powers of the presidency, including his secret, classified emergency powers and his powers as commander-in-chief of the armed forces, and commander of federal authorities under the Department of Justice and the Department of Homeland Security.

He has the authority to deliver critical classified information to Russia and Vladimir Putin, such as the identities of CIA personnel and other clandestine operatives, including Russian agents in Russia working for the United States. Such information could also include details for access to defense, intelligence, and communications systems.

Ralph Waldo Emerson is frequently quoted as saying, "When you strike at the king, you must kill him."

This is ancient wisdom. The quote itself comes from an exchange with Oliver Wendell Holmes, Jr. who was publishing an article critical of Plato. Nonetheless, the idea behind the quote has stood as ancient wisdom for thousands of years.

> *See* Martin Pengelly, "Trump Quotes Emerson: 'When You Strike at the King, You Must Kill Him'; President Retweets Quote from Pre-Impeachment *Times* Article," *The Guardian*, February 15, 2020 (20:51 GMT).[241]

Pengelly writes,

Quoting Times White House correspondent Peter Baker, Trump wrote: "Ralph Waldo Emerson seemed to foresee the lesson of the Senate Impeachment Trial of President Trump. 'When you strike at the King,' Emerson famously said, 'you must kill him.'"

The king in this case is mad, unconstrained by any moral or legal considerations, and fully aware of the Emerson quote, which he took to heart after his acquittal in the Senate in 2020.

To end the ongoing coup, the king must be removed from office.

This is no time for Nancy Pelosi and the House Democratic caucus to falter.

FURTHER READING

"Pelosi and House Democratics Should Not Falter in Impeaching Trump," The *Trenchant Observer*, January 8, 2021.[242]

85

January 9, 2021

Remove and Arrest Trump

Donald Trump has incited a mob to invade the Capitol, resulting in the deaths of one Capitol police officer, one demonstrator, and three other people who appear to have died from "natural causes" such as a heart attack. All five would still be alive if it were not for Donald Trump and the mob riot he incited.

If any person other than the President of the United States had incited such a riot, with such consequences, he or she would by now have been arrested and put in jail.

Yet Donald Trump is no ordinary criminal. As long as he occupies the office of President of the United States, he poses a uniquely dangerous threat to the country and to American democracy.

Notwithstanding the statement he read recently referring to an orderly transfer of power on January 20, 2021 (which also contained a repetition of the Big Lie that he won the November election, and which appeared to praise the rioters), he continues to instigate his followers to further violence, and has not renounced by actions his ongoing efforts to overthrow the election results and the Constitution of the United States.

He is engaged in an "auto-coup" or "self-coup" or "auto-golpe," or in plain language, a "coup d'état" or "Staatsstreich."

Intellectual pundits may debate whether he is engaged in a true "coup d'état," as if their intellectual distinctions were relevant here. They and their distinctions are irrelevant, when what counts is who has the guns and the power, and what they are doing with them.

Those who have observed other coups in other times and places understand precisely what is relevant to the defense of our democracy.

There are also those who argue that the niceties of constitutional government must be observed in seeking to counter forces that are operating outside of the Constitution and seeking to overthrow it. In a raw struggle for power in which the future of the Constitution and democratic government is itself at issue, they are both correct in their instincts and mistaken in the extreme case. We are living through the extreme case at this minute and will be until Trump is removed from or otherwise leaves power.

In the extreme case, it does not make sense to try to ensure that every "t" is crossed and every "i" is dotted. While every effort should be made to act within the Constitution, it would be a grave error to insist on formalities that would delay decisive action that might save it, while delay might lead to its overthrow and to disaster.

Again, this is not an intellectual argument we should engage in while, at least figuratively, tanks are on the move.

Trump is a criminal who is armed and dangerous, and on the loose.

He should be removed from office immediately.

House Democrats should not get cute with their impeachment plans and falter in the effort to actually remove him from power. There is talk that they may impeach him by the middle of next week, but delay sending the articles of impeachment to the Senate.

Their goal should be to impeach him at the earliest possible moment, in order to secure his immediate removal from office.

That means they should immediately transmit the approved articles of impeachment to the Senate and should even this weekend constitute the team that will prosecute the case in the Senate. That is their constitutional duty, "to uphold and defend the Constitution of the United States."

At this moment, all representatives and senators need to put aside any and all political considerations and act swiftly, without hesitation, and decisively to remove Trump from office.

The question remains of when Trump should be arrested.

If his actions reveal a clear and irrevocable intent to desist from his ongoing attempted coup d'état, if he desists from repeating the Big Lie that he won the election—itself, in these circumstances, an incitement to further violence—the question of his arrest may be left until after January 20, 2021.

If he engages in any actions to further his ongoing attempted coup, he should be immediately arrested and brought before a judge.

In any event, an order for his arrest should be issued, to prevent him from fleeing the country.

How and when he should be arrested, if before noon on January 20, 2021, is a delicate issue which all potential actors should now consider on an emergency basis.

86

January 27, 2021

Democrats Should Use the Impeachment Trial to Educate the Public

See,

1) Mike DeBonis and Paul Kane, "Democrats Consider One-Week Impeachment Trial, Censure Resolution after GOP Signals Likely Acquittal of Trump," *Washington Post*, January 27, 2021 (8:00 p.m. EST);[243]

2) Timothy Snyder, *On Tyranny: Twenty Lessons from the Twentieth Century*, New York: Crown Publishing Group, 2017, Chapter 1;

3) "Unity with Fascists? NEVER!" *The Trenchant Observer*, January 26, 2021.[244]

Timothy Snyder describes how democrats in any country can make concessions to tyrants that even the latter could not imagine possible. This is a phenomenon he calls "anticipatory obedience." In Chapter 1 of *On Tyranny*, Snyder writes:

Chapter 1 Do not obey in advance

Most of the power of authoritarianism is freely given. In times like these, individuals think ahead about what a more repressive government will want, and then offer themselves without being asked. A citizen who adapts in this way is teaching power what it can do.

...

Anticipatory obedience is a political tragedy. Perhaps rulers did not initially know that citizens were willing to compromise this value or that principle. Perhaps a new regime did not at first have the direct means of influencing citizens one way or another....

The Democrats in Congress now propose to hold a quick trial in the Senate which will neither convict ex-President Trump nor educate the American people as to the nature of his crimes and his attempted coup d'état.

What will future authoritarian leaders learn from the Senate trial, and the zeal with which the Democrats prosecute the case against Trump?

The Republicans' greatest weapon over the years has been the stupidity and cowardice of their Democratic opponents, who never seem to lose an opportunity to snatch defeat from the jaws of victory.

Real Democrats need to stand up and call out the stupidity and cowardice of Democratic colleagues who support a censure resolution or a quickie trial that fails to present the evidence, educate the American people, and burst Trump's propaganda bubble.

They need to band together and pledge to never vote for, support, or endorse any Democratic senator who votes for censure or who fails to use the trial of Donald Trump to educate the electorate and to hold Trump's Republican co-conspirators and apologists in his attempted coup to account.

Like the signers of the Declaration of Independence in 1776, they should solemnly swear, *"We Mutually Pledge To Each Other Our Lives, Our*

Fortunes, And Our Sacred Honor" to uphold the Constitution and defend American democracy from the Republican fascist threat.

They must take on Trump and his fascist supporters, frontally, in what may be a life-or-death struggle to defend a world built on facts and truth, the Constitution, and the rule of law.

Democrats need to understand that what is at stake is not whether or not Trump is convicted in the Senate impeachment trial, but rather whether that trial can be used to lay out all the facts of his treasonous attempt to overthrow the Constitution and the government, and of all of his major crimes. They must fight tooth and nail for his conviction for the "high crimes and misdemeanors" he has committed, in the Senate itself if possible.

But if conviction with the help of decent, principled Republican senators is not possible in the Senate, they must nonetheless strive to achieve conviction at least in the court of public opinion and in the longer time frame of history.

My greatest fear has always been that, in his Quixotic quest for bipartisanship in a world that has radically changed, Biden would be too soft, too forgiving, and in effect pursue an illusory "Munich Pact" with American fascists, which places our democracy in great peril.

In the spring and summer of 2019, the House Democrats were too afraid of Trump and his supporters to conduct a broad impeachment inquiry into his many crimes. These included the obstruction of justice cases laid out in exquisite detail in the Mueller Report, which many appeared never to have read in close detail.

They knowingly sent narrow articles of impeachment relating to Ukraine to the Senate and to certain acquittal in the impeachment trial. This narrow and doomed effort enabled them to avoid taking on Trump, frontally, for the broad range of crimes he had committed and was committing.

Predictably, Trump was only emboldened by his acquittal.

We all saw how that worked out.

If we are to defeat not only Trump but the fascist appeal of Trumpism, the Democrats in both the Senate and the House must resolve to use every ounce of their energy and power to convict Trump, in the Senate if possible, and in any event in the court of public opinion and in future elections if not.

Biden and the Democrats are suffering from a fatal illusion if they think for a moment that they will more quickly advance their programs by going into the impeachment trial in the Senate with the expectation of defeat.

FURTHER READING

"Weak-kneed Democrats on Verge of Blowing It Again," *The Trenchant Observer*, January 23, 2021.[245]

87

February 1, 2021

Senate Oaths of Office and as Juror in Impeachment Trial

"So Help Me God"

Perhaps the most important issue in the Senate impeachment trial of Donald J. Trump is whether senators will honor their oath of office and their oath to serve as impartial jurors in the trial, to "do impartial justice according to the Constitution and laws."

Do these oaths mean anything? If they don't, the trial is a sham, just like the trial of Alexei Navalny in Moscow this week.

If their oaths are meaningless and the trial is a sham, then the Constitution has lost its force and in important respects has also become a sham.

The procedural vote on whether or not to proceed to a trial, in view of the objections of most Republicans that the Constitution does not permit the trial of a president who has left office, failed by a vote of 45-55. Those opposed were all Republicans.

The decision on this procedural vote, like all procedural votes in the Senate, is binding on all senators.

All senators are bound to uphold their oath of office to "support and defend the Constitution of the United States against all enemies, foreign and domestic... (and to) well and faithfully discharge the duties of the office on which I am about to enter."

Among those duties is the duty to "do impartial justice according to the Constitution and laws," in the words of their impartial juror oath.

Consequently, senators by their oaths are bound to consider impartially the charges and facts argued before them in the trial.

They cannot, while still honoring their oaths, refuse to convict Donald Trump on the ground that the trial is not constitutional. They lost that procedural vote, which did not go to the merits of the trial.

All senators are bound by the Senate's decision, by a vote of 55-45, that the trial is constitutional.

Therefore, there are two critical questions being addressed in the Senate trial of ex-President Donald J. Trump.

First, will all senators honor their oaths of office and their oaths to serve as impartial jurors?

Second, is Donald Trump guilty of the "high crimes and misdemeanors" charged in the article of impeachment approved by the House of Representatives?

The first of the two questions may well be the more important of the two. All federal officers take an oath to uphold the Constitution. If senators are not bound by that oath, then logically neither are they.

The oath of office of senators is essential to their constitutional role and function. It is not a separable clause of the Constitution.

Yet a curious and alarming thing has happened in recent years. Some senators no longer take their solemn oaths of office or their oaths to serve as an impartial juror in an impeachment trial seriously.

They act as if their oaths are meaningless.

Are they? Are they subordinate to the cult of opportunism in Washington?

Are they meaningless in a Godless America, in which there is nothing that is sacred anymore?

Can the Constitution serve to guarantee our democracy when no one really pledges their allegiance and their sacred honor to uphold and defend it, "against all enemies foreign and domestic"?

The Declaration of Independence of 1776[246] concludes with the following words: "And for the support of this Declaration, with a firm reliance on the protection of divine Providence, **we mutually pledge to each other our Lives, our Fortunes and our sacred Honor**" [emphasis added]

The solemn oaths sworn by members of the United States Senate are the following:

1. The Oath of Office

I do solemnly swear (or affirm) that I will support and defend the Constitution of the United States against all enemies, foreign and domestic; that I will bear true faith and allegiance to the same; that I take this obligation freely, without any mental reservation or purpose of evasion; and that I will well and faithfully discharge the duties of the office on which I am about to enter: So help me God.

2. The Oath to be an impartial juror in an impeachment trial

I solemnly swear (or affirm, as the case may be) that in all things appertaining to the trial of the impeachment of Donald J. Trump, now pending, I will do impartial justice according to the Constitution and laws, so help me God.

FURTHER READING

1) "Will 'Godless' Senate Republicans Break Their Oaths to God, and Acquit Trump?" *The Trenchant Observer*, February 4, 2021;[247]

2) Michael Zeldin, "How Senators and the Chief Justice Can Ensure a Full and Fair Trial (Opinion by CNN Legal Analyst), CNN, January 21, 2020 (Updated 10:24 p.m. ET).[248]

88

February 12, 2021

The Cancer on the American Body Politic

Let there be no doubt about it. The American body politic is infected by a cancer. That cancer threatens the existence and survival of American democracy. Currently all of the antibodies and forces defending the body politic are fully engaged in fighting the cancer.

The cancer on the American body politic must be killed, with the political equivalents of chemotherapy, radiation, and even surgery where necessary.

Unlike a human body, the American body politic does not have the expected lifespan of a single human being. In the case of an individual fighting cancer, remission for five or ten years might, in some cases, be regarded as a "success." This is not the case with the American body politic, however. A five-or-ten-year remission of the cancer would not be sufficient to save the life of a democracy that is already 244 years old.

The cancer on the American body politic is represented by the current Republican Party, and most but not all of its senators and representatives in Congress.

The cancer is represented by the overwhelming majority of Republican voters, throughout the country, who have been seduced by a false god who demands idolatrous obeisance to his absolute will.

It is represented by the universe of lies and delusions to which Republican voters have subscribed, and by the determination of these same cult followers to impose their will, the leader's will, on their elected senators and congressmen.

The Trial of 50 Republican Senators

The guilt of ex-president Donald J. Trump for the high crimes and misdemeanors for which he is being tried in the Senate, following his impeachment by the House of Representatives, has been clearly established by the House impeachment managers. His defense team has not resorted to serious legal argument. We know that there can be no defense for the actions he has taken, in full sight, and which have been shown to us in video and slides and other evidence in the last three days.

We know that the Republican Party is already guilty of having supported Trump's attempted coup and remained silent or endorsed his Big Lie that he won the November 3 election.

Two of these 50 Republican senators reportedly helped lead the insurrection on January 6, which included not only the mob action in invading the Capitol but also the legislative rebellion of Republican congressmen and senators who, without the slightest legal justification, tried to block the certification of the Electoral College vote which named Joe Biden President.

Josh Hawley will forever be remembered for his raised fist in the air as the insurrectionist mob headed toward the Capitol. Sitting in the gallery of the Senate during the trial of Donald Trump, ostentatiously ignoring the proceedings, a man of high intelligence and low moral character, he must know that his political career is over. Ted Cruz, another of the ringleaders, has already begun to take on the appearance of a grizzled old man who, at the moment of truth, chose to step on the wrong side of history and to betray his country.

Moments of Truth

There have been some incredible moments of truth during and since the Capitol Insurrection. U.S. Capitol Police Officer Eugene Goodman, confronting a mob of insurrectionists in the Senate corridors, chose to act with courage in the face of great potential harm and single-handedly led the mob away from the Senate Chamber. He also ran to head off Senator Mitt Romney from walking into the mob and into great danger as he was moving forward.

Goodman had but a split second to make his choice. Almost instinctively, he chose to act with courage and honor, with heroism really. Hawley and Cruz had more time to make their choice, between honor and country, on the one hand, and cowardice, treason and betrayal of country, on the other. They made the wrong choice.

Now, 50 Republican senators face a similar moment of truth. Will they honor their oaths of office to uphold the Constitution and to defend their country against all enemies foreign and domestic "so help me God"? Will they honor their solemn oaths to do impartial justice in accordance with the Constitution and laws in the impeachment trial of Donald J. Trump, "so help me God"?

Or will they betray their oaths, the American people, and their country, kowtowing and genuflecting instead before the false god who threatened our democracy, who attempted to stay in power through a coup d'état, the last act of which was the Capitol Insurrection?

As a columnist, you wish you had the power to craft words that would sway Republican senators to honor their oaths of office and their oaths to serve as impartial jurors in the impeachment trial. But you know that they have sold their souls to the Devil, that they have entered into Mephistophelean bargains they hope will give them continued political life, just as Goethe's Faust sought to prolong his earthly life.

You know they have sold their souls to the false god Trump and his "base" of idolaters. You know also that they live in fear, fear of the Trump mob, fear of the fascist leader and his fascist followers. You know also that this is no excuse.

Once honorable men and women perhaps, most of them have now followed Trump's path as co-conspirators, as men and women who, observing monstrous lies and great evil, looked away and said nothing.

Their place in the history books is almost secure. Their individual names will long be forgotten, like the names of the corrupt Tammany Hall gang that once ruled New York. But their actions will live forever in infamy.

One Last Shot at Redemption

These 50 Republican senators have one last shot at redemption: they can honestly evaluate the charges in the article of impeachment and weigh the evidence, which will lead them ineluctably to a decision to convict Donald Trump for his attempted coup and the Capitol Insurrection on January 6, 2021.

With a vote for conviction, they will also be voting to excise the source of the cancer from the American body politic.

Will they do it? The odds are long against such an epiphany at this late hour. But who knows?

The final decision is one which each person can make only in the innermost recesses of their own heart and soul. As did Officer Eugene Goodman, they face a moment of truth, a fateful decision involving political danger if not the danger of life or death. They can choose between courage and their country, honoring their oaths, on the one hand, and cowardice and treason, on the other.

Their decisions will mark their lives and careers for all time. It is as if their children and grandchildren, and further descendants could read on their tombstones, "He (or she) voted to honor his (or her) oaths and to save the Republic," or "He (or she) voted to betray the Constitution and his (or her) country, and for the false god Donald Trump." Which will be their epitaph?

Throughout their lives, they will have to face their children and grandchildren, and everyone they know or may come to know, and answer that question.

If they make the wrong choice, the shame of that choice will mark them for the rest of their days.

FURTHER READING

1) "In Memoriam: The Republican Party (March 20, 1854-February 13, 2021)," *The Trenchant Observer*, February 16, 2021;[249]

2) "Fascism in America Is Here NOW, in the Republican Party," *The Trenchant Observer*, May 20, 2021;[250]

3) Michael Gerson, "The Threat of Violence Now Infuses GOP Politics. We Should All Be Afraid," *Washington Post*, May 20, 2021 (2:48 p.m. EDT).[251]

89

February 13, 2021

Democrats Blow Huge Educational Opportunity at Impeachment Trial

BACKGROUND

See Mike DeBonis and Tom Hamburger, "Late-Night Talks and a Moment of Chaos: Inside the Democrats' Eleventh-Hour Decision to Forgo Impeachment Witnesses," *Washington Post*, February 13, 2021 (4:07 p.m. EST).[252]

After brilliantly prosecuting the case against Donald Trump in his Senate impeachment trial and winning a vote to allow the calling of witnesses, the Democrats snatched defeat from the jaws of possibility Saturday afternoon, falling for a defense ploy that destroyed their chances of putting on witnesses, winning the trial by a larger margin in the court of public opinion, and potentially even putting the vote to convict into play.

They became very confused just after winning their vote to call witnesses. The defense offered to enter a stipulation to enter into evidence an affidavit by the witness the Democrats wanted to call, in exchange for giving up the victory they had just won in the vote to call witnesses. Forgetting that the most important court was the court of public opinion, they fell for the ploy.

What was certain when they made this decision was that they would fail to gain the two-thirds vote needed to convict Trump.

What was uncertain was how the twists and turns of a trial with witnesses might open up new opportunities to win the public over.

They were obviously divided over whether or not to call witnesses. They were reportedly unprepared to call further witnesses and were following a game plan before Friday night that did not involve witnesses.

A number of senators were ready to go home for a week in their home districts. And there was no nimble, clear-eyed strategist among them who could take firm control of their boat in stormy, uncharted waters, and steer them safely to their destination.

So, they followed their original plan. They gave away a major chance to shake up the whole trial in a way that might have enabled them to achieve their larger goals, in exchange for the opportunity to go home for Valentine's Day and a week of working from their districts, which would lead to certain defeat.

Above all, they fell into a pattern of hurried and scatter-shot decision-making which prevented them from carefully considering their new options.

The result was a disaster, a fact which will be increasingly appreciated in the coming months and years.

The main mistake they made was that they lost sight of who their main audience should have been.

Since the spring of 2019, they have failed to understand that the greatest threat facing the country has been the phantasmagorical world Donald Trump and many others have created, a world of big lies, massive propaganda, and enormous delusions. It is a world in which perhaps 35 percent of the population live, an alternative universe where truth is not recognized or valued, and whose fascist inhabitants are increasingly willing to use violence, and even kill people, to impose their and their leader's will.

The great political challenge we all now face is to find a way to dismantle Trump's propaganda bubble and alternative universe, so that rational people, no longer fearful of fascist mobs and voters, can participate in a politics of reason.

The advantage of a broad impeachment inquiry in 2019 would have been that it might have served as a huge educational project in which daily hammers of truth might have chipped away at Trump's propaganda wall of lies and distortions. Such an inquiry might have helped to break Trump's hold on the minds of his cult-like followers, and also on the minds of Republican politicians ruled by fear.

The Democrats didn't get it.

Instead, they went for Nancy Pelosi's ploy of impeaching Trump on two narrow grounds related to the Ukraine affair, sending articles of impeachment to the Senate for a removal trial they knew beforehand they could not win. This maneuver helped Pelosi resist demands to conduct a broad impeachment inquiry into Trump's crimes and abuses of power.

On February 13, 2021, the Democrats made a similar mistake. Viewing their goal solely in terms of convicting Trump, they lost sight of the broader challenge America faces and the opportunity they had just created to call witnesses and to demolish, in front of a national television audience, the last remnants of Trump's wall of lies and delusions, puncturing the propaganda bubble that feeds and sustains him.

The arguments that were heard yesterday, such as senators were ready to vote and wanted to get home for Valentine's Day, or Republican senators were ready to vote and if the proceedings were delayed for witness testimony, the Democrats might lose a couple of Republican votes for conviction, sound ludicrous today, and will be ridiculed by future historians.

"You threw away your chance to transform the trial through witness testimony when the future of the Republic was at stake, so senators could get home for Valentine's Day?" "You blew this opportunity because you were afraid you'd lose a couple of Republican votes for conviction as senators were restless and wanted to go home?"

History will be a merciless judge.

Yet let us not lose sight of the great success of the House impeachment managers in presenting a compelling case. Let us also not lose sight of the fascist challenge that America faces, and the hard work that remains to be done to overcome it.

Building on the brilliant presentation of the evidence by the House impeachment managers, Democrats and all American (small "d") democrats must now turn their attention to the project of civic education and de-programing of Trump's cult followers.

Important components of this project will be establishing a 9/11 style commission tasked with investigating Trump's crimes and abuses of power, including his attempted coup d'état which culminated in the Capitol Insurrection on January 6, 2021.

It is important, however, that the inquiry is not limited to the January 6 Capitol Insurrection, or even the attempted coup d'état whose origins probably go back to at least June 2020. It is also important to show Trump's four-year pattern of obstruction of justice, including the very actionable cases set forth in great detail in the Mueller Report.

Intimidation of witnesses and subornation of perjury were part and parcel of Trump's *modus operandi* throughout his four years in office. It is important that the commission investigate these facts and leave no doubt as to their occurrence.

A second key component will be the prosecution of Trump and his co-conspirators for the many crimes he and they committed during what was, in effect, a four-year crime spree.

Because Trump's fascist supporters continue to threaten and use violence against legislators and officials who oppose the leader's will, so that they not only fear political consequences but also physical harm to themselves and their families, it is critically important that all those who make such threats or commit such actions be prosecuted, convicted, and sent to prison. Such prosecutions will have an important deterrent effect.

In pursuit of the broader educational project, Democrats and all democratic Americans will need to wield their hammers and jackhammers of truth in tearing down Trump's wall of lies and deceptions, just like the East Germans tore down the Berlin Wall in November 1989. Those Republicans of principle who remain must join with Democrats in demanding, like Ronald Reagan did to Mikhail Gorbachev,

"TEAR DOWN THAT WALL!"

Part Eight

2021 – Year One of the Biden Presidency

The Threat of Fascism and the Battle to Defend Democracy Continue

90

February 16, 2021

Forget Bipartisanship: Extirpate the Fascist Threat and Defeat All Fascists

Sometimes it is too hard to look an existential threat directly in the eye. Sometimes it is too hard to call out by its rightful name a phenomenon which we see clearly before our very eyes.

Today that existential threat in America is the threat of fascism, represented by the Republican Party and the 35 million or more Americans who still support their fascist Leader, even after he has led an attempted coup d'état which culminated in the Capitol Insurrection on January 6, 2021.

Seventy-four million people voted for the Leader, some seven million fewer than those who voted for Joe Biden. So the estimate of 35 million fascist supporters could be low.

Human beings have a natural desire to avoid looking at hard realities because a clear-eyed understanding of hard truths could place extraordinarily hard demands on these human beings—to do something, to deal with those hard realities, and to act to avert disaster or at least to make things better. Republican responses to climate change illustrate this point.

That is the situation we find ourselves in now. We live in a country filled with fascists, who still exhibit cult-like adulation of and obeisance to their fascist Leader.

In Europe, in the 1920s and 1930s, political leaders looked away for too long from what was immediately before their eyes, making the mistake of believing that they could work with Mussolini and Hitler, and their minions. The Munich Pact in October 1938 was the result of one such effort. Some Jewish leaders in 1933 believed they could work with Adolf Hitler and the Nazis.

In their brief efforts at bipartisanship, it quickly became apparent which partisan party would gain the upper hand. Too late, they came to understand that they had lost their freedom, having fallen into the hands of violent and ruthless partisans, who were fascists.

In the United States, in 2021, is it possible to work in a "bipartisan" manner with the fascist Republican Party of the fascist Leader Donald Trump?

Mistakes could be made by democrats if they fail to recognize the nature of the threat they face. For example, they could make great mistakes if they were to think that they are dealing with the party of Everett Dirksen or Bob Dole, when in fact they are dealing with the American equivalent of a European fascist party in Italy or Germany in the 1920s and 1930s.

Democrats and supporters of democracy should never **choose** to work in a "bipartisan" manner with the fascists.

Rather, they should work with them only when 1) they are forced to in order to achieve some important strategic goal; and 2) in order to wean individual fascists away from their allegiance to their fascist party, leader, or goals.

Both sides will pursue strategic goals:

The fascists will pursue the goal of obtaining and keeping power, tolerating violence if necessary, and with no regard for law or facts if they block their quest for power.

The strategic goal of the Democrats and "little d" democrats will be to defend the Constitution and the rule of law, and to do so above all by defeating the fascists and the fascist threat that would do away with both altogether.

Is "bipartisanship" between democrats and fascists possible?

Only occasionally, without losing sight of the strategic goal, which for democrats is to destroy the fascists and the fascist threat.

See Chapter 74, "An American Hero in Michigan, and the Inside Rot of the Anti-Democratic Republican Party," above, for the definitions of fascism.

FURTHER READING

"Unity with Fascists? NEVER!" *The Trenchant Observer*, January 26, 2021.[253]

91

February 21, 2021

Penalize Advertisers Who Support Programs That Invite Liars Back

"A Boycott for Truth"

BACKGROUND

See Brian Stelter, *Network of Lies: The Epic Saga of Fox News, Donald Trump, and the Battle for American Democracy*, Simon and Schuster, 2023.

Brian Stelter published today an account of what we all know to be true: the media, even the so-called liberal media, are continuing to fuel the Big Lie that Trump won the November 3, 2020 election and many other lies that the fascist Republican Party and its leaders continue to spread, by giving air time to those same lying Trump apologists. (The article appeared on the CNN Business website as "The Big Lie Lives," Reliable Sources," February 21, 2021, but was taken down after Stelter was fired in August 2022.)

The media fuel this lie by inviting lying guests to appear on their programs. They justify doing so by arguing that they cross-examine their guests and don't let them tell their lies unchallenged. This is self-serving b.s. They are giving the liars a platform from which to spread their lies. What the cable channels and TV networks are pursuing is not truth but rather viewers and ratings, i.e., money from advertisers.

Let us never forget that the primary goal of these cable channels and TV networks is to sell soap and to make money.

Given these realities, how can we break the media's connivance in spreading the monstrous lies of Donald Trump and his co-conspirators and apologists, who supported an attempted coup d'état and the Capitol Insurrection, in addition to Trump's routine intimidation of witnesses and obstruction of justice throughout his four-year term of office?

These Trump co-conspirators and apologists no longer support democracy and the rule of law, if they ever did. How can we slow their spread of lies and disinformation?

There is actually a simple idea that could produce that result if enough people would join in.

That is **A Boycott for Truth**.

We should simply boycott all the advertisers who sponsor programs that invite known liars to appear for interviews, to make statements, or for any other purpose. For example, the sponsors of any program that invites a guest to appear who denies that Biden won the election should be boycotted. The same rule should be applied to any program that shows news video in which such statements are made.

In other words, if a program invites a guest to appear who is known for telling monstrous lies or invites a guest back who has lied on the program, the public should boycott all of the advertisers who support that program.

In a word, we propose a program of **Truth or Consequences**.

If the idea catches on, it could have a huge impact.

92

March 21, 2021

Biden's Looming Foreign Policy Catastrophe in Afghanistan

Revised March 23, 2021

On February 29, 2020, the United States under Donald Trump and the special ambassador he appointed to lead the "peace" negotiations with the Taliban, Zalmay Khalilzad, signed a "peace agreement" calling for the withdrawal of all American and allied forces from Afghanistan by May 1, 2021.

The commitments were one-sided: the U.S. agreed that it and its allies would withdraw all of their forces from Afghanistan in exchange for a "commitment" by the Taliban to enter into "intra-Afghan" negotiations with the democratically elected government of Ashraf Ghani, and to not let the territory of Afghanistan be used to attack the security of the United States and its allies. One of the items on the agenda of the "Intra-Afghan" negotiations was to be the establishment of a ceasefire.

The Agreement essentially amounted to a surrender agreement, by which the Americans would "cut and run" from Afghanistan, turning their backs on all the promises of supporting democratic government and human rights in Afghanistan made since it overthrew the Taliban government in 2001, following the September 11, 2001 attacks orchestrated from Afghan territory.

See "Agreement for Bringing Peace to Afghanistan between the Islamic Emirate of Afghanistan Which Is Not Recognized by the United States as a State and Is Known as the Taliban and the United States of America," February 29, 2020.[254] Signed in Doha, Qatar, "in Pashto, Dari, and English languages, each text being equally authentic."

The agreement is an abomination. It reflects a policy of Donald Trump which was aimed primarily at giving him an advantage in the 2020 presidential election.

The agreement pursues the wrong goal and was negotiated by the wrong people. It is strongly opposed by the Afghan Government of Ashraf Ghani, leading experts, and many allies whose forces (primarily from the NATO countries, in addition to the U.K and Canada) have fought and died alongside American and Afghan soldiers. Their assistance, both military and civilian, was given in pursuit of what the U.S. held out to be the goal of establishing a democratic state governed by law in Afghanistan.

Now, the United States has joined with Russia in convening a conference in Moscow to be attended by Russia, China, Iran (invited), Pakistan, and Turkey. Notoriously *uninvited and absent* were the Europeans and the NATO members who helped make up the International Security Assistance Force (ISAF) in Afghanistan from 2001-2014, and since 2014 its follow-on successor, "Operation Resolute Support." The latter, in principle, has been focused on training.

The reason the Europeans were not invited is blazingly clear: They would never go along with a settlement which sells out the democratic government of Afghanistan, established pursuant to elections in 2018 (legislative) and 2019 (presidential), and made up of a coalition of the two leading presidential candidates in 2019 and their supporters. *Nor would the Europeans be likely to go along with a settlement that surrenders the future of Afghan women to the Taliban.*

The stated U.S. objective in the "peace" agreement is the promise by the Taliban not to let the territory of Afghanistan be used by any group to conduct attacks against the security of the U.S. or its allies.

The Wrong Goal

A fatal flaw in U.S. policy in Afghanistan in recent years, and perhaps as far back as 2001, has been the stated goal of getting out of Afghanistan. This makes no sense since to withdraw U.S. and Allied forces will, in all likelihood, lead to the fall of the democratically elected government of Ashraf Ghani and a takeover by the Taliban. The U.S. and its allies have worked hard, with considerable success, to build up the Afghan military. But without U.S. air and logistical support, the ability of the Afghan military to hold the cities and other territory the government controls is dubious at best.

The goal of getting out of Afghanistan makes about as much sense as saying that the goal of the United States in the Korean Peninsula should be to get all of its forces out of Korea, or to say that its goal in NATO should be to get all of its forces out of Germany. The United States has forces stationed and deployed in many countries around the world, to secure important foreign policy objectives. Should our goal in Africa be to get all American and French troops out of Africa, and simply leave the nascent democracies there to deal with Islamic terrorists on their own? What foreign policy objectives would this achieve?

The problem is that Joe Biden, like Donald Trump, is letting his foreign policy objectives be determined by domestic politics.

The Wrong Negotiators

Why in the world did Secretary of State Antony Blinken and Joe Biden leave Zalmay Khalilzad in place as Trump's point man to negotiate an

American withdrawal. This was a huge mistake, and one which needs to be corrected immediately.

Biden must replace Khalilzad forthwith. If he needs his advice, Blinken can sign him on as a consultant. Zalmay Khalilzad is an Afghan and now also an American whose interests and objectives are not always clear. He has reportedly considered running for the presidency of Afghanistan in the past.

See, Pamela Constable and Sayed Salahuddin, "Afghans Are Rooting for Zalmay Khalilzad to End Up in Trump Administration," *Washington Post*, November 19, 2016.[255]

The authors, after discussing Khalilzad's background, including the positions of ambassador to Afghanistan and ambassador to Iraq under George W. Bush, observe the following: "(H)e also has been criticized as a lone operator who 'freelanced' or skirted official limits as a diplomat. He also reportedly considered running for president of Afghanistan in 2009 and 2014."

The Wrong "Peace" Agreement

The U.S. must make it clear that they are not leaving Afghanistan until a ceasefire is established—and observed—and a reconciliation process is put into motion that allows for some real possibility of Afghans working together in governing the country.

Many possibilities exist, e.g., allowing the Taliban to govern territory they presently control, and allowing the Ghani government to govern the cities and other areas under its control, with negotiated compromises in contested areas.

But let the Taliban know that the United States is prepared to stay for 50 years, if that is what it takes, to reach an equitable peace agreement that protects the human rights achievements, particularly those relating to women, and other achievements they have secured over the last 20 years.

Stop Implementing a Trump Policy

After saying that its goal in Afghanistan was to strengthen and defend the democratic government of the country, almost since the beginning, the United States is now following Donald Trump's plan to "cut and run" from Afghanistan, and to leave the Afghan democratic forces we have supported for almost 20 years to fend for themselves, without the air and other logistical support that—up until now—has prevented the government from falling to the Taliban.

This is a Trump policy, which was designed to help him win the election in 2020. Why Joe Biden and Secretary of State Antony Blinken are following the craven policy of Donald Trump, negotiated by Zalmay Khalilzad, George Bush's ambassador to Afghanistan (2002-2005) and Iraq (2005-2007), and Donald Trump's ambassador charged with getting him out of Afghanistan (2018-2021, continuing since January 2021 under President Joe Biden), is anyone's guess.

My guess is that Biden and Blinken have been preoccupied with other priorities and haven't taken the time to think through Trump's "cut and run" policy and its likely consequences. Biden is familiar with the challenges and complexities of Afghanistan, having participated in Barack Obama's excruciatingly slow and analytical review of Afghan policy in 2009.

What positions Biden and Blinken took then are extremely revealing and raise the question of whether there has been any fresh thinking, or if they are simply regurgitating their positions from 2009. In the 2009 policy review, Biden reportedly favored a minimal presence in the country. They may not have updated his views with information about the current situation. The latter possibility is suggested by their decision to keep Khalilzad on as the point man on the withdrawal negotiations with the Taliban.

See, Peter Baker, "Biden No Longer a Lone Voice on Afghanistan," *New York Times*, October 13, 2009.[256]

Baker quotes Thomas Ricks, a leading military authority on Afghanistan, and others, as follows:

> (O)thers, more harshly, argue that Mr. Biden's judgment on foreign policy has often been off base. They point out that he voted against the successful Persian Gulf war of 1991, voted for the Iraq invasion of 2003, proposed dividing Iraq into three sections in 2006 and opposed the additional troops credited by many with turning Iraq around in 2007.
>
> "When was the last time Biden was right about anything?" Thomas E. Ricks, a military writer, wrote in a blog on September 24.

For an incisive account of Biden's views on Afghanistan and other countries over the years, *see*

Greg Jaffe, "The War in Afghanistan Shattered Joe Biden's Faith in American Military Power; 'I Am Not Sending My Boy Back There to Risk His Life on Behalf of Women's Rights!' the Vice President Shouted," *Washington Post*, February 18, 2020.[257]

Another reason to replace Khalilzad is that he is an Afghan, with multiple interests and objectives all of which are not entirely clear.

The fact that Biden and Blinken are planning to sell out the democratic forces in Afghanistan could not be made clearer than by their failure to invite NATO and the Europeans to participate in the international peace process which the conference in Moscow on March 18 has been intended to kick off.

The Iranians and Pakistanis were invited to participate, but not NATO and the Europeans? What greater tip-off to Biden's and Blinken's dishonorable intentions could there be?

See Jacques Follorou and Jean-Pierre Stroobants, "Joe Biden inflige un camouflet aux Européens sur le dossier afghan; Première donatrice civile, l'Union européenne est mise à l'écart par Washington du règlement diplomatique final de la crise en Afghanistan," *Le Monde*, March 17, 2021 (11:18; Updated March 18, 2021 at 10:03).[258]

The United States is pressuring the government of Ashraf Ghani to give up power to a new coalition government with the Taliban before his term of office ends and without prior elections. They have pressured the Afghan government to participate in the intra-Afghan negotiations on a coalition government, without insisting on a halt to Taliban attacks on Afghan forces and civilians.

The Trump policy behind the U.S. withdrawal agreement, and the May 1 deadline, never made any sense. It was always a surrender agreement designed to give Trump an election argument that he had ended foreign wars, as he had promised in 2016.

Nonetheless, we are where we are.

Now, how can the U.S. get out of the May 1, 2021 deadline for withdrawal of all of its troops?

The Taliban have undercut the logic of a peace agreement by continuing to attack Afghan forces and civilians, in the most brutal way, during the period in which they were supposed to be negotiating the terms of a power-sharing coalition government. They have not negotiated in good faith. That is reason enough to delay any withdrawal, and to insist on a ceasefire and balanced commitment from the Taliban before any further withdrawal of U.S. forces.

Good faith is a fundamental principle underlying all international agreements. By continuing their war against the Afghan government, its military forces, and Afghan civilians, the Taliban have undercut the essential preconditions for negotiation of an equitable peace agreement which might actually advance the cause of peace in Afghanistan. By doing so, they have transformed the February 29, 2020 "peace" agreement into a roadmap leading to the early rapid collapse of the Ghani government and the return to power of a movement driven by an extremist religious ideology.

President Biden and Secretary Blinken and Secretary of Defense Lloyd Austin, who is in Afghanistan today (March 21), need to act energetically to prevent this looming catastrophe from happening.

If they don't, the catastrophe could help sink Biden's presidency.

See Julian E. Barnes, Thomas Gibbons-Neff and Eric Schmitt, "Officials Try to Sway Biden Using Intelligence on Potential for Taliban Takeover of Afghanistan; If U.S. Troops Leave before any Deal between the Taliban and the Afghan Government, the Militant Group Will Take over Much of the Country, an Intelligence Assessment Predicted, *New York Times*, March 26, 2021.[259]

On the rapidly deteriorating situation in Afghanistan by early July 2021, *see*

"The Afghan Government Could Fall Quickly," *The Trenchant Observer*, July 5, 2021.[260]

93

May 2, 2021

When Will Trump Be Indicted?

When will Trump be indicted?

We have an apparent serial felon on the loose, hanging out at or near Mar-a-Lago in Palm Beach, Florida.

He is the unnamed "Individual One" in the indictment of Michael Cohen, who is currently serving out a sentence after pleading guilty, on August 21, 2018, to campaign finance violations, tax fraud, and bank fraud. Numerous reports from reliable sources point to Trump as "Individual One," who the Cohen indictment said had ordered Cohen to commit the crimes. It should have been a simple matter to unseal the identity of "Individual One" in the Cohen indictment, and to simply fill in Donald Trump's name and indict him. Why hasn't that happened?

Robert Mueller in his report lists at least ten cases where Trump appears to have committed obstruction of justice. The evidence Mueller cites sounds convincing. Why have indictments not been issued in these ten cases?

Donald Trump was impeached in 2019 for obstruction of justice, which included a number of crimes. During and after the House impeachment investigation, Trump appears to have committed further crimes involving obstruction of justice, including witness tampering and retaliation against witnesses for truthfully testifying in the House investigation. Why has Trump not been indicted for these crimes?

In December 2020, Trump was impeached a second time for his actions related to inciting an insurrection that included, but was not limited to, the invasion of the Capitol by a mob, which resulted in the deaths of at least five people. Why has Trump not been indicted for the crimes that lay at the heart of his impeachment for the Capitol Insurrection?

The political decision by Republican senators not to remove him from office constituted a violation by them of their oaths of office and their oaths to render "impartial justice" as jurors in the impeachment trial. But their decisions, which were politically motivated, in no way absolved Trump of criminal responsibility for the crimes he apparently had committed.

From the summer of 2020 until November 3, 2020, Trump engaged in a number of actions that would appear to have been serious crimes

After the election, on November 3, 2020, Donald Trump appears to have engaged in multiple crimes, ranging from attempts to corrupt election officials responsible for counting and tallying the votes, and attempts to persuade legislators and governors to violate election laws and constitutional provisions for the election of the president. These actions culminated in the Capitol Insurrection on January 6, 2021, and the president's own apparent incitement to insurrection on that day. His failure to send National Guard troops to protect the lives of Vice President Mike Pence, House Leader Nancy Pelosi, and other legislators and their staffs—withholding such assistance for some three hours—evidenced not only his callous indifference but probably also his intent to promote the insurrection.

Putting all of these actions together, it appears that Donald Trump led a vast conspiracy in which he enlisted the support and cooperation of Republican federal, state, and local legislators and officials, to overthrow the results of the November 3 presidential election and, consequently, the Constitution of the United States.

Why have we heard virtually nothing about federal or state grand juries investigating these alleged crimes?

There have been only a few exceptions, such as the grand jury in Atlanta where a courageous prosecutor is investigating a blatant case of apparent election interference for which there is recorded and public evidence.

Why indeed has former President Donald Trump not yet been indicted for the many crimes he has apparently committed? When will he be indicted?

Moreover, when will his many Republican co-conspirators and accomplices in these apparent crimes be investigated and themselves indicted?

What is going on?

We are all tired of thinking about Trump and his crimes. However, democracy is a very fragile flower, and we have just seen how close we can come to losing it, to seeing it crushed. If America's first fascist president, and the many members of the Republican Party who engaged in a vast conspiracy to overthrow the Constitution, are not held accountable before the courts for the very numerous crimes which they appear to have committed, the lesson of political impunity will not be lost on others, while these unpunished actors, apparent criminal co-conspirators, will remain in power to commit further crimes in the future, whether in 2022 or 2024.

Americans who are too cowardly to defend American democracy by prosecuting, and insisting on the prosecution of, those who have committed criminal acts in furtherance of the Republican conspiracy to overthrow the Constitution, will have only themselves and their own passivity to blame if that democracy is lost.

FURTHER READING

1) "The U.S. Doesn't Need Investigations or Commissions. It Needs Prosecutions, *The Trenchant Observer*, May 28, 2021;[261]

2) Laurence H. Tribe, "Trump's Crime Spree Must Not Escape Investigation; The Presidency Must Never Become a Get-Out-of-Jail Free

Card for All Crimes Committed in One's Lifetime," *Boston Globe*, Updated January 4, 2021 (4:30 p.m.);[262] See also Laurence H. Tribe, Barbara McQuade, and Joyce White Vance, "Here's a roadmap for the Justice Department to follow in investigating Trump," Washington Post, August 5, 2021 (9:10 a.m. EDT);[263]

3) Ankush Khardori, "What the DOJ Isn't Telling Us about Jan. 6; Merrick Garland Can and Should Be More Forthcoming about Investigating the Insurrection," *Politico*, July 6, 2021 (12:00 p.m. EDT).[264]

4) "Trump's Future," *The Trenchant Observer*, January 18, 2021.[265] This article cites Anne Applebaum's interview in *Die Welt* on January 18, 2021, in which she declares, "Trump's adventure is over. He will spend the rest of his life in court."

5) Laurence H. Tribe, Barbara McQuade, and Joyce White Vance, "Here's a roadmap for the Justice Department to follow in investigating Trump," Washington Post, August 5, 2021 (9:10 a.m. EDT);[266]

6) Laurence H. Tribe, "Merrick Garland must investigate Donald Trump's attempted coup — not for retribution but for deterrence; For nearly all of us, a solid factual basis that one has committed a federal crime — much less inciting an insurrection against the government itself — would trigger a criminal investigation. So why the hesitation by the US attorney general?" Boston Globe, Updated August 20, 2021 (2:49 p.m.);[267]

94

May 6, 2021

Liz Cheney and the Republican "Gleichschaltung"

BACKGROUND

Update

See,

1) Peggy Noonan, "Liz Cheney Confronts a House of Cowards; House Republicans Are about to Demonstrate They Can't Handle the Truth about 2020 and Jan. 6," *Wall Street Journal*, May 6, 2021 (7:11 p.m. ET).[268]

2) "Trump and the Republican 'Gleichschaltung'," *The Trenchant Observer*, May 13, 2020.[269]

There is a movement afoot in the House of Representatives to strip Liz Cheney (R-Wyoming) of her post in the House Republican leadership. Her opponents are furiously trying to remove her because she has refused to endorse the Big Lie that Donald Trump won the November election, and that it was stolen from him by massive fraud.

Cheney survived a similar challenge a few weeks ago, but she has apparently lost the support of House Republican Minority Leader Kevin McCarthy (R-California) and is being challenged by a proponent of the Big Lie and everything Trump. Cheney says she will not tell lies to keep her position. The whole development reminds one of what took place in Germany in the 1930s.

See, Adam Serwer, "Liz Cheney Has Only Herself to Blame: The Representative from Wyoming Is Taking a Stand Against an Authoritarian Streak in the Republican Party That She Helped Cultivate," *The Atlantic*, May 6, 2021 (1:25 p.m. ET).[270]

The *Gleichschaltung* in Nazi Germany

After Adolf Hitler became Chancellor of Germany on January 30, 1933, he immediately began actions aimed at seizing absolute power. In February he launched a terror campaign against Communists and other opponents. The Reichstag Fire on February 27, which Hitler claimed was the work of the Communists, led the following day to the Reichstag Fire Decree, which allowed Hitler to arbitrarily arrest his opponents. Elections were held on March 5, in which despite the terror the Nazis obtained less than a majority of the vote (43.9 percent). In the last free elections, in November 1932, the Nazis won 33 percent of the vote, the Social Democrats 20 percent, the Communist Party 17 percent, and the Center Party just short of twelve percent of the vote.

–Wikipedia, "July 1932 German Federal Election"[271] and "November 1932 German Federal Election."

Nonetheless, with the support of other parties, the Reichstag or parliament adopted the Enabling Act on March 23, 1933, which gave Hitler full dictatorial powers.

He soon began implementing a policy of "compelled political conformity," which was known as the *Gleichschaltung*. During this process, university rectors, professors, political opponents, and others who did not march in lockstep with Nazi views, were removed from positions of influence or suffered worse fates.

There are many translations of the term *Gleichschaltung*. The German word is often used in English to refer to its specifically Nazi connotations. Among the translations are synchronization. like getting on the same frequency. In the specific historical context of Germany in the 1930s, *Gleichschaltung* meant the synchronization of all views with those of the Nazi Party. The literal meaning in German is a switch to the same or identical gear or value.

How Are We to Understand the Republican Fury Directed against Liz Cheney?

She voted to impeach President Trump after the Capitol Insurrection on January 6, 2021.

She has steadfastly refused to accept the Big Lie that the Democrats stole the November election through fraud.

In general, she has refused to repeat the lies that have now become Republican orthodoxy. Indeed, willingness to repeat the Big Lie and other Republican lies about the November election and the January 6 insurrection appears to have become a virtual litmus test of good standing in the Republican Party. People like Marjorie Taylor Greene (R-GA), Matt Gaetz (R-FL), and Lauren Boebert (R-CO) now command attention in the party, while Senate Leader Mitch McConnell (R-KY) and House Leader Kevin McCarthy (R-CA) stand aside and are silent.

Washington Has Moved into The Twilight Zone

Washington and the media seem to have moved into The Twilight Zone. President Joe Biden and the Democrats are like a homeowner who can only talk about the new kitchen he is installing, seemingly oblivious to the fact that the roof, in another section of the house, is on fire.

The Democrats haven't even indicted Trump for any of his many apparent crimes.

They are operating on "Prosecutor Time," like Robert Mueller did, unmindful of the fact that the nation is moving on "Political Time," and that that time is running out for those who hope to influence the 2022 elections.

Republican Elise Stefanik (R-NY), who is actively campaigning to replace Cheney in the Republican leadership in the House, has been an ardent defender of the Big Lie and other Republican lies championed by Donald Trump and his supporters.

See,

1) Colby Itkowitz, "Stefanik Emphasizes Support for False Election Claims, Trump Movement Ahead of Leadership Vote," *Washington Post*, May 6, 2021 (7:37 p.m. ET);[272]

2) Catie Edmondson and Luke Broadwater, "Stefanik Resurfaces False Election Claims as She Moves to Oust Cheney; Republicans Say Liz Cheney, Their No. 3, Is Being Targeted Because She Won't Stay Quiet about Donald J. Trump's Election Lies. Her Would-be Replacement Is Campaigning on Them," *New York Times*, May 6, 2021 (7:06 p.m. ET).[273]

Why is there such Republican fury against Cheney and other Republican legislators who insist on telling the truth, or at least not telling lies?

The answers to this question are not logical, but rather psychological and political in nature.

To maintain the strength of a cult and of the belief system of cult members, deviation from the official beliefs of the cult cannot be permitted.

When the beliefs of the cult are manifestly divorced from reality, to allow deviant views would be to allow a mortal threat to the cult's belief system. If the belief or propaganda bubble of the cult is pierced, the beliefs in the leaders of the cult could come crashing down to the ground, and with them the entire power structure and power of the cult's leaders.

This accounts for the phenomenon whereby dissident members of a political cult or movement are often dealt with more harshly than opponents from outside the group or party.

A second psychological factor that plays a major role in maintaining unity or identity of thought within a cult or a cult-like political movement is that members who have accepted, incorporated, and repeated the big lies of the cult that are at variance with observed reality, or accepted moral values they used to believe were wrong, are themselves in a state of acute cognitive dissonance. In this state, they are torn between the irrational beliefs which they now hold, and the facts and values rational people can observe or affirm. One way to reduce the stress of this cognitive dissonance is to vilify those who reject the beliefs or values of the cult's followers.

Trumpism has become a political cult which is in many respects similar to the cult of Adolf Hitler and the Nazi Party in Germany in the 1930s. Trump supporters will reject this view, which is precisely what you might suspect from members of a political cult such as that referred to. Readers should examine the facts and catalogue for themselves the similarities and the differences.

A third component of the cult-like behavior we are observing among the Republicans in Congress is that current Republicans unwilling to speak the truth have surrendered to their worst fears, that they will lose their seats and also their membership in Republican political society—future jobs, invitations to banquets and parties, personal political friends—if they oppose the cult, its most extreme spokesmen, or the cult's leader, Donald Trump.

They have made their deals with Mephistopheles (the Devil), as it were, and they are now all locked together, synchronized, and will share their fates with their fellow opportunists, cult followers, and the cult leader himself.

95

June 2, 2021

Sleepwalking in the Garden of Fascism: "Merrily We Roll Along!"

Merrily We Roll Along
by Eddie Cantor

Merrily we dance along while facing the sun
Merrily our slogan is: 'say, don't we have fun?'
We live in style, with a smile and a song
As we merrily roll along!

Reading the newspapers and watching cable news, one would think that life is moving along, merrily moving along, and that all is well in the United States.

President Joe Biden is pushing his initiatives, while he appears to have that old-fashioned belief that good deeds and policies will be rewarded by voters at the polls.

The House Democrats are continuing merrily along their path, now planning some kind of further investigation into the Capitol Insurrection on January 6.

At the Justice Department, prosecutors are moving merrily along with their endless investigations into what are essentially peripheral matters.

Attorney General Merrick Garland, who at his confirmation hearings swore that he would not allow political considerations to influence the work of the Justice Department, and in particular decisions whether or not to prosecute individuals, seems to be moving merrily along.

Newspapers have relegated threats to American democracy to the periphery of their attention, while op-eds seem to focus on secondary subjects, the kind of subjects that would merit attention if everything in America were moving merrily along.

This is the way the guardians of democracy, in the press, in the Congress, and in the White House, appear to be moving merrily along.

What could possibly go wrong?

Republicans are working hard, in seeming unison, to pass voter suppression laws and electoral laws that would give state officials and legislators the power to overthrow the results of popular elections, as some Republican officials tried to do in 2020.

Democratic and non-Trump-compliant Republican officials appear to be influenced by threats of physical harm to themselves and their families. The threat of political violence in the country seems to lie just below the surface, while mass shootings appear to have become almost a daily occurrence.

What could be wrong?

What could possibly go wrong?

Former President Donald Trump and numerous co-conspirators and presumptive felons run around freely, with no fear of arrest or prosecution.

Everyone seems quite undisturbed by the non-prosecution of politicians in high places who have committed serious and blatant crimes, in broad daylight.

Trump introduced the normalization of the unthinkable, and the normalization of the unforgivable.

The Biden administration and Attorney General Garland are now introducing the normalization of impunity for politically motivated crimes at the highest levels.

House Democrats should forget the immense distraction of conducting yet another investigation of the insurrection on January 6.

Instead, they should be holding hearings into why the Biden administration and the Justice Department are not prosecuting serious felonies committed by the former president and his Republican co-conspirators, who sought to overthrow the election and the Constitution of the United States.

The country faces a stark choice between prosecuting the presumptive criminals, who committed their crimes in broad daylight, or accepting the normalization of impunity for political crimes at high levels, as the country rolls merrily along.

If America chooses the second path, what could possibly go wrong?

96

June 21, 2021

The Normalization of Impunity: The Most Important Story No One Will Cover

When will Trump be indicted?

Why are we asking this question five months after Democratic President Joe Biden has been in office?

A Pulitzer Prize is waiting for the newspaper or magazine that will field a news team to take this story on.

The Biden administration and Merrick Garland's Justice Department have not convened grand juries and indicted Donald Trump and his Republican co-conspirators for the many electoral crimes and other crimes they committed in what amounted to a vast Republican conspiracy to overthrow the election and the Constitution.

All the attention has been diverted to the insurrection on January 6 and the violent demonstrators who seized the Capitol. Attention of the media has focused on the foot soldiers and not the generals who sent them into battle. Trump and his Republican co-conspirators committed many acts of intimidation of election officials and other acts of obstruction of justice. Why have Biden and Garland not prosecuted these crimes?

Many of these questions can be summarized in a single question:

Why has Trump not been indicted?

Yet there is perhaps an even more important question in a fading democracy with a weakened press whose priorities are set, at least on cable TV stations, by how much soap the TV programs can sell.

Why isn't the press reporting on the failure of Biden and Garland to investigate and prosecute Donald Trump and his co-conspirators?

See, "America Has Become a Country of the Absurd," *The Trenchant Observer*," June 6, 2021.[274]

There, we observed,

"It is as if some foreign country that is an enemy of democracy had launched a massive missile attack on the United States that unleashed a tasteless, odorless gas on the entire population, causing total amnesia regarding certain tenets of democracy and the rule of law.

"One such bedrock principle of the rule of law is that crimes must be punished, suspected criminals must be indicted and tried, and, when found guilty, sent to prison.

"In the absurd country which America has become, however, the feckless Democrats have become complicit in *the NORMAL-IZATION OF IMPUNITY* for high public officials who commit political crimes while in office.

"If Trump gave us *the Normalization of the Unthinkable* and *the Normalization of the Unforgivable*, President Joe Biden and Attorney General Merrick Garland have given us *the Normalization of Impunity.*"

Which newspaper or magazine or news team will go after the Pulitzer that is just sitting there, like on a table, waiting for someone to pick it up?

97

July 6, 2021

Denazification and Detrumpification

Updated November 2, 2021

The United States faces a problem similar in many ways and different in many ways to the problem faced by Great Britain, France, and the United States after the defeat of Adolf Hitler and the Nazis in May 1945.

Denazification

In their respective occupation zones—which included parts of Berlin—England, France, and America faced the daunting task of governing a population whose thinking and world view had been altered by 12 years of Nazi lies and propaganda and the terror with which the Nazi regime had ruled as it seized all positions of power and influence in the country.

The cult of Adolf Hitler was very strong. The Western Allies needed to de-program the German population in their respective occupation zones as a first step toward laying the groundwork for a future democratic state and society.

The Western Allies held certain advantages, including military occupation and control over all governmental decisions in the British, French, and American zones of occupation and their respective sectors in Berlin.

Importantly, they also held control over all means of mass communication, including newspapers and radio.

With these advantages, they launched a program of what was known as denazification, portrayed brilliantly in the movie "Judgment at Nuremberg." In addition to the trials of the major war criminals in Nuremberg, they held denazification trials of Nazi leaders and other officials in 12 different sectors of government. Leon Jaworski, the prominent Houston lawyer who later became the famous Watergate Prosecutor, was an American prosecutor in one or more of the lower-level trials of Nazi war criminals.

The Saturday Night Massacre

On Saturday, October 20, 1973, President Richard Nixon ordered Attorney General Elliot Richardson to fire Special Prosecutor Archibald Cox. Richardson refused and resigned effective immediately, as did Deputy Attorney General William Ruckelshaus when he was ordered to fire Cox. These events produced a firestorm of reaction. The impeachment proceedings against Nixon began ten days later, on October 30, 1972, and Leon Jaworski was sworn in as the new Watergate Special Prosecutor on November 1, 1973.

Detrumpification

The situation in the United States in July 2021 is vastly different from the situation the Western Allies faced in Germany in 1945.

Nonetheless, there is a strong need to carry out a program of detrumpification.

While Donald Trump and the Republicans were defeated at the polls on November 3, 2020, Trump refused to admit his defeat, launching the

Big Lie that he won by a landslide and that the election was "stolen" by Biden and the Democrats through massive fraud.

The official results showed that Trump was defeated in the Electoral College by a vote of 306-232 electors. The popular vote results were 81,283,098 votes for Joe Biden, or 51.3 percent of the votes cast. Trump won 74,222,958 votes, or 46.8 percent of the votes cast.

See James M. Lindsay (The Water's Edge blog), "The 2020 Election by the Numbers," *Council on Foreign Relations*, December 15, 2020 (5:00 p.m. EST).[275]

Every electoral process aimed at verifying the results of the elections, including decisions by some 60 courts, have completely rejected all arguments of fraud on any scale that might have remotely affected the outcome of the elections. Interestingly, the Republicans do not challenge the elections that gave them 50 Senate seats and a pickup of a number of seats in the House of Representatives.

On January 6, 2021, even after the Capitol Insurrection, eight Republican senators voted against certification of the electoral votes of Arizona and/or Pennsylvania, while 128 Republicans in the House of Representatives opposed certification of the electoral votes of one or more states, notwithstanding the certification by the Electoral College vote on December 14, 2020. Before the Capitol Insurrection, some 14 senators and 140 Republican members of the House were reportedly planning to vote against certification.

See,

1) Jenny Gross and Luke Broadwater, "Here Are the Republicans Who Objected to Certifying the Election Results," *New York Times*, January 7, 2021 (Updated January 8, 2021);[276]

2) Li Zhou, "147 Republican Lawmakers Still Objected to the Election Results after the Capitol Attack; Congress Has Certified President-Elect Joe Biden as the Winner of the Election — but Some Republicans Still Objected," *Vox* (vox.com), Updated January 7, 2021 (3:28 p.m. EST).[277]

Li Zhou reports, "In a vote Wednesday evening, six Republicans in the Senate and 121 in the House backed objections to certifying Arizona's electoral outcome, while seven Senate Republicans and 138 House Republicans supported an objection to certifying Pennsylvania's electoral outcome."

Gradually, all but a very small minority of Republican senators and congressmen came to endorse the Big Lie and to adopt it as a litmus test for good standing in the Republican party. The Republican caucus expelled Wyoming Representative Liz Cheney from her position as the third-ranking member of the House Republican leadership because she refused to endorse the Big Lie. She was replaced by Elise Stefanik (R-New York), a shameless Trump sycophant who did.

Republicans at the state level have also endorsed the Big Lie and plan to "primary" those who haven't done so in the upcoming 2022 elections.

The corruption of the Republican party has been almost complete, including at the state level and among Republican candidates for election to state-wide political office.

Far from controlling the news media as the Western Allies did in Germany after World War II, the victorious Democrats face a mass media machine headed by Fox News, which propagates the Big Lie and spreads many other lies to tens of millions of Trump and Republican supporters every day. Since the deregulation of television and radio in 1996, under a plan put through by Democratic President Bill Clinton, and the auction of TV and radio frequencies to broadcasters, the Federal Communications

Commission (FCC) no longer enforces fairness rules or any semblance of what used to be known as "the fairness doctrine."

Indeed, the FCC and the Federal Government seem powerless to regulate the lies and disinformation which, in the case of the pro-Trump media machine, feeds Trump supporters and Republicans a steady diet of anti-Democratic propaganda and lies, upholding and propagating further the Big Lie that Trump won the election and that Biden stole it.

The Big Lie myth is vaguely analogous to the "Stab-in-the-back" (*"Dolchstoss"*) myth Hitler and the Nazis spread in the 1920s and early 1930s in their drive to take power, which was ultimately successful in 1933. The "Dolchstoss" or "stab-in-the-back" myth spread the totally false belief that Germany had lost World War I only as the result of betrayal by civilians on the home front, especially Jews, revolutionary socialists, and other republican politicians.

After losing the election on November 3, 2020, President Trump and his co-conspirators appeared to commit many election-related crimes aimed at overturning the results of the presidential election, whether by tampering with vote counts or pressuring election officials to find fraud where none existed; or by refusing to recognize or certify voting results, which they were obligated to do under statutory procedures designed to guarantee the accuracy of vote counts and the fairness of elections.

These apparent crimes culminated in the Capitol Insurrection on January 6, 2021, and Republican votes against certification, described above, in what was a conspiracy to deny Joe Biden the presidency. They planned to do this by refusing to vote for the congressional certification of the Electoral College vote count, as provided for in the Twelfth Amendment to the Constitution.

This is the situation Democrats and other constitutionalists face in the United States today.

Detrumpification: What Can Be Done?

What can be done? What can we learn from Germany's experience?

A complete answer to these questions cannot be provided here.

However, any effective plan of detrumpification might include the following key elements:

First, public trials will be necessary to unmask the crimes of the criminals. These trials should benefit from great media attention and be televised in whole or in part, to the full extent permitted by court regulations. The effect of the Nuremberg trials on the German population in 1945-1946 was great.

Second, the detrumpification plan should proceed from the understanding that members of the cult of Trump, like members of the cult of Adolf Hitler, will not be easy to de-program. Drastic measures are likely to be required, such as the adoption of laws and regulations to take down, or at least de-fang, the pro-Trump media machine, including, in particular, Fox News.

Legislation should be adopted to this end. One measure would be to introduce tax benefits (reductions) for real news organizations who put on objective, fact-based news programs. These benefits would not be available to propaganda operations like Fox News. Objective reporting and fairness standards could be introduced under the regulations governing administration of the tax breaks.

Third, civil penalties should be adopted to sanction the deliberate or reckless dissemination of lies and disinformation. The legal norms set forth in the Supreme Court case of *New York Times v. Sullivan (1964)* and its progeny would provide the governing legal standards, to ensure that speech protected by the First Amendment is not sanctioned.

Detrumpification will not be easy.

But it is as essential for the maintenance and growth of a vibrant democracy in the United States today as denazification was for the growth of democracy in Germany after 1945.

98

August 25, 2021

Joe Biden, Captain of the Titanic, Which Just Hit the Iceberg of Afghanistan

Sometimes a metaphor can help us understand a complicated reality, highlighting the most important features so that we can keep them clearly in mind.

With respect to Afghanistan, the metaphor that comes to mind is that of President Joe Biden as Captain of the Titanic.

Biden Steered the Ship Directly toward the Iceberg

A big difference from the historical example is that unlike the captain of the real Titanic, this time Captain Joe steered the ship directly toward the iceberg, despite all the warnings of his top officers and their urgings to change course.

To be sure, President Trump set the ship on a course headed toward the iceberg. But it was Captain Joe who, after being provided all of his bearings and with ample time to change course, decided to steer the Titanic directly toward the iceberg.

The Titanic Hit the Iceberg, and Is Going Down

The Titanic hit the iceberg. As the ship is sinking, Captain Joe has dug in and is insisting he made the right decision to steer toward the iceberg.

He and his officers go on television frequently to defend his decision to hit the iceberg.

Now, Captain Joe is working hard to ensure that all of the first-class passengers get into lifeboats and safely away from the sinking ship.

Captain Joe and his officers are on television touting the fact that the crew is doing an outstanding job in getting the first-class passengers into the lifeboats and safely away from the ship.

He has promised that he will get all of the passengers in steerage who have worked for his company into lifeboats, which will be supplied by other ships coming to the area to help in rescue efforts. The only problem is that those ships are days away, and the Titanic is sinking fast. It looks like they will not arrive before the Titanic goes down.

The world, glued to their television sets, is focused on how many of the first-class passengers are finding places in the lifeboats, and the race between the ships bringing additional lifeboats and the inexorable progress of the ship going down.

Accountability for the Disaster

Captain Joe and his officers point to the great job they have done in getting first-class passengers into lifeboats and safely away from the ship.

Relatives and friends of those in steerage are not satisfied with this explanation and demand accountability.

Other captains and some leaders of the industry are demanding that Captain Joe and his officers be held accountable for the decision to steer directly into the iceberg.

This is the debate.

Future reports on television are likely to show the ship going down with those who are in steerage still aboard.

Scenes such as those in the movie *Dunkirk*, which graphically showed sailors drowning, are expected.

Updated August 28, 2021

Further Reports and Commentary on Biden's Catastrophic Withdrawal from Afghanistan

See,

1) Ayaan Hirsi Ali, "Joe Biden Is Deaf, Dumb and Blind to the Chaos the US Has Unleashed; The Administration Is Ignoring History by Putting Blind Faith in the Goodwill of the Murderous Taliban," *The Telegraph*, August 28, 2021 (9:30 p.m.).[278]

2) Jacques Follorou, "Vingt ans après leur intervention en Afghanistan, les Américains s'en vont sur un sentiment d'échec," *Le Monde*, May 28, 2021 (Updated May 30, 2021 at 16:07).[279] *Detailed historical overview.*

The catastrophic nature of the decisions the Biden administration has made and is making relating to the U.S. withdrawal from Afghanistan is jaw-dropping, or as Ayaan Hirsi Ali puts it, "blind, deaf and dumb." We are witnessing the enormous damage an incompetent foreign policy team, under a stubborn president guided not by reason but by emotion, can do to the strategic position and foreign policy interests of a nation. Democrats must either require a reconstitution of Biden's foreign policy team or start packing their bags as they look to the 2022 and 2024 elections.

FURTHER READING

1) "Joe Biden's Foreign Policy Judgment: You Can't Fill a Bucket with a Hole in It," *The Trenchant Observer*, August 31, 2021;[280]

2) Peggy Noonan, "The Afghan Fiasco Will Stick to Biden; It Hit at His Reputational Core. He No longer Comes Across as Empathetic, Much Less Serious," *Wall Street Journal*, September 2, 2021 (6:23 p.m. ET);[281]

3) "Afghanistan Faces Famine, Economic Collapse as International Community Poses Conditions for Aid," *The Trenchant Observer*, September 15, 2021.[282]

99

September 10, 2021

Trump's Coup Continues, While Democrats Are Afraid to Act

BACKGROUND

See Kevin D. Williamson, "The Trump Coup Is Still Raging," *New York Times*, September 10, 2021.[283]

The headline screams out, "The Trump Coup Is Still Raging."

Yes. And Republicans are plotting to successfully carry it out.

What are the Democrats doing to stop it? Virtually nothing. They haven't even passed one of the Voting Rights bills.

The Democrats have decided not to prosecute Trump for any of the electoral crimes or other felonies he appears to have committed.

Their approach to countering the American fascist threat by Trump and his acolytes, far from weakening them, has only served to make them stronger.

The Democrats need to rethink their strategy.

Impunity for Trump and his co-conspirators in his attempt to overthrow the 2020 election and the Constitution has only emboldened Republicans, who are contemplating the commission of similar crimes in the future.

If the Democrats continue to grant Trump and his co-conspirators impunity, as they have to date, surely Republicans setting the stage for new electoral crimes will have nothing to fear in the future.

Democrats: Your strategy for saving our democracy, if you have one, is not working.

Look at the facts. Stare at the facts and their implications.

Then act!

FURTHER READING

"On the Ballot in Virginia on Tuesday: Fascism v. Democracy," *The Trenchant Observer*, October 31, 2021.[284]

100

September 23, 2021

A Parable of Our Time: "Our Democratic House Is on Fire!"

BACKGROUND

See Robert Kagan, "Our Constitutional Crisis Is Already Here," *Washington Post*, September 23, 2021 (3:32 p.m. EDT).[285]

Parable

There is a man running up and down the street, with his hair all frazzled and his eyes filled with terror, shouting, "The house is on fire! Our house is on fire! Our whole democratic city is on fire!"

Outside a cafe, on a bright sunny morning, a number of people sit calmly drinking their coffee. A few, but not as many as in the past, are reading their newspapers.

"Help! Help!" the screaming man implores. "Don't you know, the whole city is on fire!"

The seated individuals proceed calmly to drink their coffee and chat among themselves.

"Don't you know?" the wild man implores again. "The whole city is on fire!" Different individuals respond variously.

"You exaggerate," one says. "We don't see any flames."

"The houses in the next street are on fire," the wild man rejoins.

"Don't worry," another replies. "Someone will take care of it."

"Fake news!" another shouts out, aggressively.

"What about you newspaper readers?" the wild man screams, in exasperation.

"We know," one of them replies. "But what do you expect us to do about it? Someone will take care of it."

Another newspaper reader says, "I haven't read anything about it in my newspaper or heard anything about it on television."

"Of course not, John," another cajoles. "Look at the newspapers you read and the television stations you watch."

Another man, a thoughtful-looking gentleman, declaims, "You're right. Something is going on. We ought to launch an investigation to see who started the fire."

A teenager, sitting with her parents at the cafe, leaps to her feet and shouts out, "We know who started the fire, and who the arsonists are who have been pouring gasoline on it!"

"In this town," the wild man screams, "we have a volunteer fire department. You are all members of our volunteer fire department."

"Don't get so excited," a senior member of the group rejoins. "Someone will take care of it."

"The alarm bell at the fire department hasn't even rung," says another.

"Who disarmed the bell?" the teenager shouts out and is ignored.

"The wild man, with growing terror in his eyes, screams, "Our democratic town will be destroyed if we don't act to save it!"

"Go on, get out of here. You are disturbing our morning coffee," one man yells back as other coffee drinkers join in. "Yes, go on, get out of here. You're disturbing our morning coffee."

The screaming man yells, "The whole town is on fire and half of its citizens are pouring gasoline on the fire!

One might ask, "Does this parable have anything to do with current politics or democracy in America?"

One thinks of Katherine Anne Porter's brilliant novel, *Ship of Fools (1962)*—made into a movie[286] of the same name in 1965. In the final scene of the movie, the protagonist, a dwarf, is watching the other passengers get off the ship, including those who had argued vociferously in the movie in defense of Adolf Hitler and the Nazis.

Looking directly into the camera, he says. "You are thinking, what does all this have to do with us?' He then says, "Nothing." He chuckles, then laughs. Puffing on his cigar, he turns and walks out of the station. The movie ends.

101

November 10, 2021

J'accuse

On January 13, 1898, French novelist Émile Zola published his famous letter entitled, "J'accuse" (I accuse), addressed to the President of the Republic, in which he denounced the government and its military command and their antisemitic leaders for prosecuting Alfred Dreyfus, a Captain of Jewish descent, on trumped up charges of treason. Dreyfus had been convicted in 1894. Zola's letter had a decisive impact on democracy and the rule of law in France.

See Douglas O. Linder, "J'accuse" by Emile Zola (Texts in English, UMKC School of Law, Famous Trials).[287]

In the United States, we now face a similar moment in which the rule of law is at stake. It is a moment in which anti-Semitic and racist militants are actively participating in a fascist conspiracy to overthrow the Constitution and the rule of law. In these circumstances, the following letter is addressed to "Democrats" and political leaders in the United States, calling on them to act, vigorously and effectively, to defend American democracy.

J'accuse

J'accuse. I accuse Joe Biden, Merrick Garland, and the House Democrats of putting our democracy at risk by not prosecuting, or demanding prosecution of, Donald Trump and his co-conspirators for their plot and attempt to overthrow the Constitution of the United States.

J'accuse. I accuse Attorney General Merrick Garland of putting our democracy at risk by not acting expeditiously on the House criminal referral of prosecution of Steve Bannon for defying a House subpoena to appear before the Special Committee investigating the Capitol Insurrection on January 6, 2021.

J'accuse. I accuse Attorney General Merrick Garland of putting our democracy at risk by not prosecuting individuals making threats of violence against federal and state legislators and public officials who do not bow down before the will of Donald Trump and his Republican supporters.

J'accuse. I accuse President Joe Biden of putting our democracy at risk by ignoring the de facto impunity granted to Trump and his allies for the crimes they have committed, often in full public view, both before and since the November 3, 2020 elections.

J'accuse. I accuse Nancy Pelosi and the House Democrats of putting our democracy at risk by not pursuing a broad impeachment inquiry into the full range of Donald Trump's "high crimes and misdemeanors" committed while in office.

J'accuse. I accuse the Democrats in Congress of putting our democracy at risk by not acting effectively to safeguard voting rights and democratic procedures for counting and certifying votes in accordance with the Constitution and the rule of law.

J'accuse. In sum, I accuse the Democrats, Joe Biden, and the Biden administration of putting our democracy at risk by failing to act vigorously and effectively to defend it.

Part Nine: Conclusion

The Republican Conspiracy to Overthrow the Constitution

102

August 2, 2021

Should Trump Be Indicted?

Updated August 23, 2021

We have set forth the considerations which we believe argue strongly for the indictment and prosecution of Donald Trump for his election-related crimes and others, and for the prosecution of his Republican co-conspirators who joined him in what constitutes a vast conspiracy to overthrow the election and the Constitution of the United States.

See,

1) Chapter 96, "The Normalization of Impunity: the Most Important Story No One Will Cover," above;

2) "IMPUNITY: The triggest and most important story no one will cover," *The Trenchant Observer*, June 21, 2021;[288]

3) "America Has Become a Country of the Absurd," *The Trenchant Observer*, June 6, 2021;[289]

4) Chapter 95, "Sleepwalking in the Garden of Fascism: 'Merrily We Roll Along,'" above.

The basic argument is quite simple: Trump and others appear to have committed serious crimes, often in full public view, and he and they should be indicted and prosecuted for committing them.

A fundamental norm of a democratic state governed by law is that the authors of serious crimes must be prosecuted and sent to prison if found guilty. This rule should apply no matter who they are.

President Joe Biden and Attorney General Merrick Garland have solemnly stated (Garland under oath) that they would not let political considerations influence Department of Justice decisions on whether or not to prosecute individuals.

Both Biden and Garland have violated these promises, in a most egregious and blatant manner, by refusing to prosecute Donald Trump and his co-conspirators.

There appears to be an iron-clad agreement between President Biden, Attorney General Garland, and Democrats in Congress, not to raise this issue, that is, not to even talk about it.

Republicans, for their part, have bowed to Trump in supporting the Big Lie that he won the 2020 election and can hardly be expected to push for his prosecution.

A Democratic Conspiracy of Silence

We are faced with a Democratic conspiracy of silence regarding whether Trump should be indicted. It is not a criminal conspiracy, like Trump's conspiracy to overthrow the election and the Constitution, but it is a conspiracy in the broader sense of the term.

The news media, perhaps out of deference to Democratic desires, or perhaps due to their inability to think independently and outside the box of daily "breaking news" stories, have failed to raise this question in any systematic way. Why they haven't is a great mystery, one of the great mysteries of mass psychology and mass political propaganda, which future historians of the press and mass media will be challenged to figure out.

Why Do Biden, Garland, and the Democrats Refuse to Indict Trump and His Co-conspirators?

Let us now consider the arguments for not prosecuting Trump and his co-conspirators. We have focused on the rule of law and the mandatory requirements of a rule-of-law state to prosecute the authors of serious crimes, even when they are present or former high government officials. But what are the arguments against prosecuting Trump and his Republican co-conspirators?

All but one of these arguments are not legal arguments, and the one legal argument—related to the requirement of proving intent—is a spurious legal argument made by politicians playing lawyer, not by serious lawyers. However inadvertently, these politicians and pundits have assumed the role of defense attorneys, making arguments for the defense, however weak. If any Justice Department lawyers are making these arguments, or even raising them in background conversations with journalists, they are doing so in bad faith.

Nonetheless, aside from the "intent" argument, the other non-legal arguments against indicting Trump must be seriously considered because they have apparently persuaded Biden, Garland, and the Democratic leaders to forego prosecuting Trump and his allies for the serious electoral and other crimes they have apparently committed.

What, indeed, might be the arguments against prosecuting Trump and his Republican co-conspirators?

First, Democrats may be making the political calculation that they can retain control of the Senate and the House if they just focus on their economic and other programs, which are aimed at improving the lives of voters.

The assumption seems to be that potential Trump voters will be rationally persuaded to vote for Democrats in 2022 and 2024 when they see how their lives have improved under Biden (e.g., child credits, management of the coronavirus pandemic, unemployment assistance, and jobs).

This assumption is of dubious validity, as indicated by the polls in August 2021 that show over 60 percent of the voters give Biden credit for managing the COVID-19 pandemic well, but only 49-50 percent believe that he is doing a good job as president. The job approval numbers are taken from the Rasmussen polls, which have been quite accurate on this issue.

The assumption fails to take into consideration how political propaganda, the existence of a Trump cult, and the creation of an alternate universe enveloping Trump's followers affects the likelihood of rational calculations in deciding for whom to vote.

Second, Biden and the Democrats seem to be afraid of taking on Trump and his supporters directly, particularly by indicting him. They seem to believe that indicting Trump and his cronies for the crimes they appear to have committed would inflame public opinion and strengthen support for Trump and the Republican Party, contributing to Republican victories in the congressional elections in 2022 and 2024, and the presidential election in 2024.

Republican legislators, almost to a man or a woman, have hitched their stars to Donald Trump, and appear to believe that allegiance to Trump and his alternate universe of propaganda and lies is their best bet for getting reelected in 2022 and beyond.

Third, the Democrats may be afraid of the violence indicting Trump could unleash against them personally, and against their families. Threats against Republican officials and Democratic legislators and officials who opposed Trump were widespread after the November 3, 2020 election, when Trump and his supporters were trying to overthrow the presidential election. There have been reports that legislators' votes are being influenced by fears of violence against them and their families.

See,

1) Michael Gerson, "The Threat of Violence Now Infuses GOP Politics. We Should All Be Afraid," *Washington Post*, May 20, 2021 (2:58 p.m. EDT);[290]

2) "Three Immediate Steps to Stop Threats of Assassination and Other Acts of Political Terror," *The Trenchant Observer*, January 14, 2021;[291]

3) Chapter 54, "Rehearsal for a Coup d'État? Violence in American Cities and 'the Chaos President'," above.

Fourth, the Democrats may fear that prosecuting Trump and other Republicans would lead to widespread civil unrest which would ultimately help Trump and the Republicans win the elections in 2022 and 2024.

Fifth, Biden, Garland, and Democratic leaders may be afraid of what is known as "jury nullification." Jury nullification occurs when one member of the jury, despite overwhelming evidence of guilt, simply refuses to vote to convict, resulting in a hung jury.

Jury nullification was once a problem in trying to get convictions of white defendants accused of committing terrorist crimes against black victims, e.g., in the Jim Crow South. Even today it can be a problem in seeking convictions of white police officers for committing crimes against black victims, and even affect prosecutorial decisions on whether or not to bring charges, or what charges to bring. It has been a problem in trying mob leaders, where jurors may either be under the influence of the mob or directly intimidated by mob threats of violence.

Nonetheless, in all of these kinds of cases, the demand for justice has led to prosecution of the defendants, often resulting in convictions. Prosecutors have sophisticated ways of challenging jurors who might vote to acquit despite the evidence. Lying during questioning in the jury selection process, however difficult to prove, is itself a crime for which a prospective juror may be prosecuted.

Still, prospective jurors who are ardent Trump supporters may lie during jury selection and then vote to acquit Trump or one of his co-conspirators. That is also true in trying a case against a white police officer for a crime against a black victim.

Finally, the Democrats may be calculating that the House Special Committee investigation into the January 6 insurrection will bring out evidence that will weaken Trump.

However, there is a timing problem. The impact of the investigation and its findings on Trump's propaganda bubble and alternate universe may come too late to significantly impact voters' attitudes in the 2022 primaries and elections.

Fortunately, there is no reason to have to choose between a course of active prosecutions, on the one hand, and supporting the House Special Committee inquiry, on the other. The Democrats and supporters of our democracy are in an all-out struggle with the Republicans for power. They must deploy all available non-violent and constitutional weapons if they hope to prevail in that struggle.

The Disadvantages of Not Prosecuting Trump and His Co-conspirators

As there has been virtually no public discussion of the reasons that have led the Democrats to refrain from indicting Trump and his co-conspirators for their apparent crimes, the disadvantages of this course of action have not been articulated or discussed seriously in the media.

One disadvantage may be that by failing to prosecute Trump, the Democrats are foregoing the most promising course of action that could burst Trump's propaganda bubble and bring down his illusory alternate universe, anchored by the Big Lie. Potentially, prosecution of Trump could free some Republican legislators from Trump's hold over them and the Republican Party. So long as Trump retains his iron grip on the allegiances of his cult followers and the Republican Party, the chances of a return to a more normal functioning of Congress will remain negligible.

A second disadvantage of the Democrats' current timid approach to prosecuting Trump may be that the army of insurrectionists who sought to overthrow the 2020 presidential election will remain in place, following a playbook informed by an understanding of all the critical decision points where they were thwarted in 2020. Now, through state legislation and other actions, they are earnestly trying to fix these critical decision points so that the next attempt to overthrow the election and the Constitution will succeed.

A third disadvantage may be that by revealing their weakness and lack of resolve to punish electoral and other crimes, Democrats may be giving a green light to Republicans and Trump cult-followers to attempt a coup d'état again in 2024, and even to manipulate the results of legislative elections in 2022. With strength on the Republican side and weakness on the Democratic side, such efforts could be successful.

Republicans have abandoned the democratic creed and any belief they may have had in the past in democracy and the rule of law. Those who are leading the ongoing insurrection, with the acquiescence of virtually all other Republican officials, are engaged in a raw struggle for power at any cost.

The Democrats would do well to reflect on whether their current strategy of not prosecuting Trump and his co-conspirators, for the many serious crimes they appear to have committed, will ultimately benefit the Republicans or the Democrats and other defenders of democracy in that power struggle.

Reader's Comment on Biden's and Garland's Dilemma

In a comment on the original publication of this article on *The Trenchant Observer*, one reader forcefully stated the dilemma which Biden and Garland seem to face:

SHOULD TRUMP BE INDICTED? . . . A likely scenario: — Indict Trump; go to trial; pick a jury (on which it is inevitable at least one Trumpist will sit); get a hung jury; 2nd trial; 2nd hung jury . . . ad infinitum. Political fallout: Trump crows, "See, I won!" Biden's and country's attention is diverted. New deal #II crashes. USA eats crow. Growing worldwide authoritarianism blossoms further. Russia, China, Taliban cheer. Earth continues to warm. Science and scientists disappear. Quantum theory becomes meaningless. Klingons attack.

In response to this reader, several points may be stressed.

First, if we allow prospects of jury nullification to determine whether to prosecute present or former high officials for serious crimes, we have essentially abandoned the rule of law for the rule of the mob. In doing so, we may have given political movements led by criminals strong incentives for stirring up their supporters in order to ensure the impunity of their leaders. This will inevitably foster civil unrest.

Second, even if we defer the prosecution of Trump—but not beyond the statute of limitations—jury nullification would be less of a risk in indicting some of Trump's co-conspirators.

Third, beginning prosecution of some of the older apparent crimes by Trump, such as the ten obstruction of justice cases outlined in the Mueller Report, would make good sense, because the older cases don't involve the passions of the January 6 Capitol Insurrection, wouldn't interfere—even theoretically—with the House Select Committee's investigation, and would in fact prevent the statutes of limitation from running out.

Ultimately, while the reader highlights the nature of our dilemma, even if he exaggerates the threat of a Klingon attack, rising to the challenge to defend the rule of law and our democracy is something our predecessors have found the courage to do on many occasions, from the Revolutionary War to the Civil War, World War II, and the Civil Rights Movement.

What Can We, as Citizens, Do to Change This Situation?

In the face of this broad conspiracy of silence among Democratic officials and leaders, and mass hypnosis among the press and the media, what can we, as citizens, do to affect the situation?

When there is a conspiracy of silence, or mass forgetfulness, the most important actions will be aimed at breaking that silence. Suggestions for immediate action:

1) Citizens should contact their congressmen and senators to push for open discussion of these issues;

2) Citizens should urge their House representatives to push for hearings on these issues in order to hold Biden and Garland to account for their promises not to allow political considerations to influence prosecution decisions;

3) Citizens should contact journalists at their local and at national newspapers, and cable news hosts (like Rachel Maddow), and urge them to cover these issues intensively;

4) Citizens should write letters to the editor demanding news coverage of these issues;

5) Finally, citizens can hold demonstrations to demand that Trump and his co-conspirators be prosecuted.

Others may have additional ideas. However, these actions would represent a good start.

Whatever one may think should be done, there is virtually no case for not talking about the issues raised above.

FURTHER READING

1) Donald Ayer and Norman Eisen, "Trump's Conduct Needs a Federal Investigation, CNN, August 20, 2021, (Updated 3:08 p.m. ET.)[292]

2) "The Indictment of Trump: The Democratic Wall of Silence Begins to Break," *The Trenchant Observer*, August 3, 2021.[293]

103

December 29, 2021

Three Urgent Actions Needed to Save American Democracy

Sometimes political situations and their implications are very clear to the objective observer, someone like the author who is far removed from the buzz of Washington, Twitter, and the latest "breaking news" on the cable news networks. The author is a keen and unbiased commentator who reads many newspapers, both American and foreign, and who has been paying attention to political developments in the United States for a long time.

Drawing on this experience and his own original analysis, the author believes that there are three major problems that pose a challenge to American democracy, and that there are three active measures that the Democrats and "little d" democrats should take, now, in order to save the Republic.

The Three Problems

1. The propagation of lies and misinformation

The first and greatest problem is that perhaps up to 40 percent or more of the population no longer access reliable newspapers, television channels, and websites to inform themselves of the facts of what is going on in the country and the world. As a result, they live in an alternate universe in which the truth is often ignored and lies and disinformation are transmitted to them instead. Fox News, One America News and a number of right-wing media operations and social media accounts propagate this false information and maintain what is in effect a propaganda bubble which serves to prevent people from understanding the facts and events that define the universe in which they live.

Donald Trump and legions of his Republican supporters have either willingly contributed to the creation and maintenance of this false universe of lies and disinformation, or have simply acquiesced in limiting themselves to the media and narratives of the tribe they are comfortable in.

The core of the problem is that media companies are allowed to, and are complicit in, the transmission of the disinformation and lies, and deliberate omissions, that create and maintain the alternate universe of propaganda which enshrouds an alarming percentage of the population. The fact that individuals and politicians, including elected officials, contribute to and magnify this propaganda bubble, is a related but separate problem.

2. The failure to indict Donald Trump and his Republican enablers

The second problem is that, despite all the hard work done for and hopes placed in Democratic candidates in the November 2020 elections, Attorney General Merrick Garland has not indicted Donald Trump and his co-conspirators in what was in fact a conspiracy to overthrow the November 3 presidential election and the Constitution.

Trump and his supporters clearly appear to have committed numerous electoral crimes, while Trump himself clearly appears to have committed numerous felonies involving obstruction of justice, including the intimidation and retaliation against witnesses in the Ukraine impeachment proceedings in 2019 and 2020, and in his impeachment and trial in

2021 for abuse of power including his support of the January 6, 2021 Capitol Insurrection.

3. The failure to enact Voting Rights legislation

In an emergency situation in which all but a few Republican congressmen and senators either support or acquiesce in the Big Lie espoused by Donald Trump that Joe Biden did not win the November 3, 2021 presidential election, but instead secured the presidency through massive fraud, the Democrats and "little d" democrats have failed to enact legislation to protect voters' rights and ensure fair elections in 2022, 2024, and beyond.

Republicans in many and indeed most states have been busy enacting laws that suppress voting and that place key positions in the electoral machinery in the hands of politicians, including state legislators who are being given control over the selection of electors for the Electoral College in the 2024 presidential elections. It is evident to even the most casual observer that the Republicans are hell-bent on setting up the electoral machinery that will enable them to refuse to certify or to overturn the popular vote in upcoming elections.

The Three Urgent Actions

1. Congress should pass legislation prohibiting the knowing propagation of lies and disinformation

The Democrats and other little "d" democrats in Congress have a powerful weapon they can use to fix our current broken communications system. They can and must pass legislation prohibiting, and establishing liability for, the knowing transmission of lies and other misinformation on television and radio and cable news channels. This is an important first step, which can be taken now, whereas federal regulation of the transmission of such content on social media platforms raises more complicated issues and may be considered at a later stage.

This is analytically simple. The Democrats may have to amend the Senate filibuster rule to be able to pass the legislation, 51-50 with Vice President Kamala Harris' tie-breaking vote. This can be done. This must be done. Now.

2. Indict Donald Trump now

Why Attorney General Merrick Garland has not indicted Donald Trump for his many apparent felonies is a mystery which future historians may be left to ponder.

By this inaction, Garland and the Democrats have granted Donald Trump and his Republican co-conspirators effective impunity from the rule of law.

This impunity has enabled Trump and the Republicans to perpetuate the Big Lie, and to run around the country organizing the anti-democratic forces of the Republican Party to run on a platform of lies and disinformation in congressional races in 2022, and in the presidential race in 2024.

Democrats appear to be afraid to take Trump and his supporters on directly by indicting him and seeking to enforce the law. This appears to be a fatal error on their part, however.

3. Enact Voting Rights legislation

The third action, which must be taken on an urgent basis, is the enactment of legislation to protect voting rights, both to prohibit the blatant forms of voter suppression Republican state legislatures have been enacting, and to safeguard the fair and impartial operation of our electoral machinery, which Republican-controlled legislatures have also been trying to weaken in order to ensure that they can successfully overturn the election results as they tried but failed to do in 2020.

This is not the time for "perfect" electoral reforms or remaking the entire federal electoral system. Democrats should be willing to peel back their ambitions to the extent necessary to secure the votes of Joe Manchin and Kyrsten Sinema, and to reform the filibuster if that is what is needed to pass the essential voting rights legislation.

Taking down Trump is the single most important action the Democrats can undertake to safeguard American democracy in 2022 and 2024. Together with passing legislation prohibiting the knowing transmission of lies and disinformation on television and radio, and enacting Voting Rights legislation, indicting Trump is a critical action in any program to protect American democracy from the anti-democratic and authoritarian threat Trump and his supporters represent.

These three problems represent the greatest challenges to American democracy today. These three urgent actions represent our best hopes for beating back the anti-democratic challenge before it is too late.

Afterword

Dispatch from an Imagined Future: The Fascist Victory in America, 2021-2025[294]

Costa Rica, From an Imagined Future. Writing today, on June 4, 2025, it is hard to believe what has happened in the United States in the last few years. It wasn't easy to uproot my life and move abroad, as a refugee from the fascism which has taken over in the United States.

With my mastery of foreign languages and cultures and history of working in many foreign countries, I have had, and have, many options in terms of countries to which I might move. At the moment, I am in Costa Rica, where I lived for three years half a century ago.

I am in Costa Rica for a number of reasons, including financial reasons, though the country meets my main criterion of being a functioning democracy governed by the rule of law, and indeed I love the country and could well end up living here permanently.

As Medicare does not cover treatment outside the U.S. and its territories, beyond a short period of 60 days or so, I'm still considering moving to Vancouver, British Columbia, which would be near U.S. medical services covered by Medicare. Ideally. I'd like to live in France, Portugal, or Germany, countries where I speak the language.

It was foreseeable that politics in the United States would be headed in a direction leading to fascism. The Capitol Insurrection on January 6, 2021 represented an obvious attempted coup d'état by the cult followers of Donald Trump and his Republican co-conspirators. This failed coup was Trump's last desperate attempt to hold on to power after losing the November 2020 election.

By the summer of 2021, it had become clear that, with 60-70 percent of Republicans believing the Big Lie that Trump had won the 2020 presidential election, America had a problem.

President Joe Biden and the Democrats placed their bets on the proposition that enacting programs that enhanced the lives of voters, even Republican voters, would lead to Democratic victories at the polls in 2022 and 2024.

In retrospect, it is now clear that they made two huge mistakes.

First, they assumed that the political playing field would remain pretty much as it had been in the past, with opposing candidates making rational arguments and voters acting more or less rationally, in the aggregate, to choose their leaders and representatives at the polls.

These assumptions were not borne out in fact. The Republicans, acting in virtual unison, changed the laws in states where they controlled the legislatures and governorships or could override the veto of a Democratic governor. They made little effort to conceal the fact that they were acting in bad faith and had abandoned belief in democracy in favor of a "no holds barred" grab for power at any cost.

The Republicans adopted two kinds of laws. The first kind was aimed at suppressing the Democratic vote, particularly among African American and other minority voters in critical states, such as Georgia, where the Republicans had lost close Senate elections to Jon Ossoff and Rev. Raphael Warnock on January 5, 2021, and with those seats, the Senate.

The Democrats had passed bills in the House of Representatives which imposed federal standards and Justice Department pre-clearance requirements for legislative changes in Southern states, as had existed before the Supreme Court overthrew this part of the Civil Rights Law of 1965, in its decision in the *Shelby County Alabama* case in 2013.[295]

These bills, however, did not gain Senate approval, primarily because Senator Joe Manchin (D-West Virginia) and Senator Kyrsten Sinema (D-Arizona) refused to vote to reform or abolish the Senate filibuster rule, which in practice requires 60 votes to advance draft legislation for discussion and approval or rejection by a majority of the senators.

In effect, the filibuster rule, originally a rarely used procedure that served as a kind of safety valve and a time-out device, had by the 2020s become a supermajority voting requirement. This meant that no legislation could pass without 60 votes except for some legislation on economic issues that could be adopted using a special budget reconciliation procedure.

The second huge mistake the Democrats made was that they failed to prosecute Donald Trump and his co-conspirators in a timely manner for the many electoral crimes and other felonies they apparently had committed. Attorney General Merrick Garland failed to proceed against Trump for almost two years. Finally, in November 2022, he appointed Jack Smith as a special prosecutor to investigate and prosecute Trump. Smith succeeded in securing indictments against Trump and others for his involvement in the attempted coup on January 6, 2021, and for his illegal retention of classified documents, some involving highly sensitive nuclear secrets.

The U.S. Supreme Court issued decisions to hear Trump's immunity claim and then to uphold presidential immunity for the president's "official acts,"[296] and Aileen Cannon, a federal judge in the Southern District of Florida, dismissed Jack Smith's case against Trump regarding classified documents, on the ground that he was not properly appointed and confirmed by the Senate.[297] These decisions helped ensure that Trump would not be tried on the federal charges before the election.

The biggest challenge the Democrats faced was Trump's propaganda bubble and alternate universe, fueled and encouraged by a right-wing media universe made up of Fox News and other radio, television and news outlets, and buttressed by a rabid social media machine that helped spread the propaganda churned out by Trump and his supporters.

How the Democrats arrived at the thought that they might pierce Trump's propaganda bubble without taking him on and prosecuting him and his co-conspirators was never clear and in retrospect defies understanding.

House Leader Nancy Pelosi and the Democrats in Congress, Joe Biden, and Attorney General Merrick Garland seemed to have entered into some kind of conspiracy of silence.

Not only did the Justice Department not proceed to prosecute Trump and his co-conspirators for almost two years, but there seemed to be a taboo among Democrats against even discussing the issue. When Laurence Tribe, Harvard Law School's emeritus professor and perhaps the leading constitutional law scholar of his generation, published a carefully-worded op-ed in the *Washington Post* urging Garland and the Justice Department to begin an investigation of these crimes on August 5, 2021,[298] Garland distracted attention from Tribe's article by himself publishing an op-ed in the *Washington Post* later that same day, at 6:09 p.m. EDT, entitled, "It is Time for Congress to Act Again to Protect the Right to Vote."[299] The *Post's* editors can only be viewed as complicit in this blatant ploy. They could easily have published Garland's op-ed the following day.

Closing ranks, the Democratic response to Tribe's op-ed was a deafening silence.

Since the Democrats would not even allow discussion of the issues related to the non-prosecution of Trump and his co-conspirators, there was virtually no public discussion of their strategy for nearly two years.

Proceeding with this strategy of not challenging Trump directly by indicting him and his co-conspirators, the Democrats lost the House in 2022. Joe Biden's domestic initiatives then hit a brick wall.

During 2023 and 2024, Trump's propaganda bubble and alternate universe continued to grow in size and power.

Two events shook up the presidential race in the summer of 2024.

In the first, on July 13, 2024, an attempt was made to assassinate former President Trump. Fortunately, the would-be assassin missed by a couple of inches, merely grazing Trump's ear.

In the second, President Joe Biden, yielding to enormous pressure from Democratic Congressional leaders and donors, announced on July 21 that he was withdrawing from the presidential campaign. Within days, Democrats had rallied around the candidacy of Vice President Kamala Harris.

Her campaign unleashed an initial burst of enthusiasm and campaign contributions which led many to hope that she might lead the Democrats to victories not only in the presidential race but also in the House and the Senate in November.

In the ensuing three months, however, vicious attacks on Harris based on her race (African American and Indian), her gender, and her background as a liberal from San Francisco ate into her support, particularly in the battleground states which were critical to secure an Electoral College victory.

Moreover, there was an "October surprise" in the form of some huge, unexpected event which was so traumatic that my memory of it is completely blurred. Was it that the Internet was shut down for five days just before the election? Or was it that an all-out regional war broke out in the Middle East? Or was it that Vladimir Putin, feeling that Russia was on the verge of defeat, used a tactical nuclear weapon in Eastern Ukraine? The event was so traumatic that I can't remember exactly what it was. It undoubtedly had an impact on the election, swinging many voters to cast their ballots for Trump and the Republicans.

In the 2024 presidential election, amid widespread cries of "fraud" by Republicans and the refusal by Republican electoral officials and legislatures to certify voting results in favor of the winning Democratic candidate, an Electoral College majority in favor of the Democratic ticket was not achieved.

Following the procedures set forth in the Twelfth Amendment, the House and the Senate voted to elect the Republican candidate to the presidency. Democrats challenged the elections in several states whose Republican representatives and senators cast votes for the Republican-backed slates of electors when voting to recognize the Electoral College results or not. This threw the election into the House where in a so-called "contingent election" under the terms of the Twelfth Amendment, a majority of Republican-controlled state delegations voted to elect Donald Trump as president. While these Republican maneuvers and votes were challenged in the courts, they were ultimately upheld by the U.S. Supreme Court.

On January 20, 2025, Donald Trump took office. With the election of a Republican Senate and a Republican House, the Trumpists had returned to power. They promptly set about passing laws which curtailed freedom of the press and other civil liberties.

Within days of the inauguration, I boarded my flight to Costa Rica.

I must say that the country agrees with me. I speak fluent Spanish, so I am quite at home here. With the Internet, I am still able to publish my weekly Substack column on political, cultural and international affairs.[300] My readership has expanded, and my column is now read by government officials, university professors, researchers, and informed citizens throughout the world.

Since publication of *The Rape of American Democracy* in 2024, I have been working on other projects, including a sequel to this book (*The Rape of American Democracy: The Fascist Triumph, 2022-2025*), a children's book, and a book on Ukraine ("Russian Aggression in Ukraine and the Battle to Save Civilization").

As I sit watching a stunning Pacific sunset in the late afternoon on a Costa Rican beach, I am happy to be living in a democracy with no fascist threat which is a proud member of a growing community of democratic states.

Who said the United States is the best country in the world? It ranked high once and may one day do so again. In the meantime, there are other countries.

[A friendly voice] *"Honey, wake up. You seemed like you were having a nightmare. Remember, we have to leave for the fundraiser in an hour."*

Endnotes

1 James P. Rowles, *Law and Agrarian Reform in Costa Rica* (Boulder, Colorado: Westview Press, 1985).

2 James Rowles, *El conflicto Honduras–El Salvador de 1969 y el orden jurídico internacional* (*The Honduras-El Salvador Conflict of 1969 and the International Legal Order*) *(San Jose: Editorial Universitaria Centroamericana* [EDUCA], 1980).

3 Karl Jaspers, *The Question of German Guilt*, New York: Fordham University Press, 2000 (E.B. Ashton transl.), 1947), 93.

4 https://www.govinfo.gov/content/pkg/GPO-J6-REPORT/pdf/GPO-J6-REPORT.pdf

5 https://www.justice.gov/archives/sco/file/1373816/dl

6 https://web.archive.org/web/20220121164431/https:/trenchantobserver.com/2021/12/24/democrats-should-impeach-attorney-general-merrick-garland-updated-december-24-2021/

7 The *Internet Archive*, also known as the *Way Back Machine* (https://archive.org//) makes regular back-ups of Internet pages. Since The Trenchant Observer was hacked, we have found it to be enormously useful in providing URL's where *Trenchant Observer* articles cited in the text can be found. These include a number of articles which complement analyses in chapters in the book The Internet Archive is an extraordinarily valuable resource for authors and readers in general and for journalists, academics, and researchers in particular.

8 José Otega Y Gasset, The Revolt of the Masses, paperback ed. (New York, W.W. Norton, 1964). Original Spanish ed. published in 1930. original W.W. Norton English ed. 1932

9 Robert D. Putnam, *Bowling Alone: The Collapse and Revival of American Community*. (New York: Simon and Schuster Paperbacks, rev. ed., 2000).

10 Tom Nichols, The Death of Expertise: *The Campaign Against Established Knowledge and Why It Matters*, 2nd ed. (New York: Oxford University Press, 2024).

11 Richard Hofstadter, *Anti-Intellectualism in American Life* (New York: 1966). *See also* Susan Jacoby, *The Age of American Unreason in a Culture of Lies*, 2nd ed. (New York: Vintage Books, 2018); and Matthew Motta, *Anti-Scientific Americans: The Prevalence, Origins, and Political Consequences of Anti-Intellectualism in the US* (New York: Oxford University Press, 2024).

12 Richard Haass, *The World: A Brief Introduction* (New York: Penguin Books, 2020), xv-xxii.

13   Franklin Foer, *World Without Mind: The Existential Threat of Big Tech* (New York: Penguin Press, 2017).

14   Timothy Snyder, *On Tyranny: Twenty Lessons from the Twentieth Century* (New York: Tim Duggan Books, an imprint of Crown Publishing, a subsidiary of Penguin Random House 2017), 65-71.

15   Snyder, On Tyranny, 65.

16   Snyder, 66-69.

17   See Victor Klemperer, *The Language of the Third Reich: LTI—Lingua Tertii Imperii— A Philologist's Notebook*, Martin Brody transl., Bloomsbury Revelations ed. (London: Bloomsbury, 2013).

18   Neil Postman, *Amusing Ourselves to Death: Public Discourse in the Age of Show Business*, 20th ed., New York: Penguin Books, 2006. This edition with a Foreword by Andrew Postman. [Originally published by Viking in 1985, and by Penguin Books in 1986.]

19   Postman, *Amusing Ourselves to Death*, 155-156.

20   *See* Melissa Murray and Andrew Weissmann, *The Trump Indictments: The Historic Charging Documents with Commentary* (New York: W.W. Norton & Company, 2024).

21   Sam Levine, "'A Different Level Than 2020': Trump's Plan to Steal Election Is Taking Shape" *The Guardian*, August 12, 2024.qq (06.00 EDT). https://www.theguardian.com/us-news/article/2024/aug/12/trump-overturn-result-presidential-election-vote

22   https://trenchantobserver.com/2020/04/28/h-l-mencken-s-memorable-quote-prophecy/

23   http://www.moroccoworldnews.com/2015/12/175861/donald-trump-the-ugly-face-of-america/

24   https://www.washingtonpost.com/opinions/trumps-flirtation-with-fascism/2016/03/07/340cc798-e4ac-11e5-b0fd-073d5930a7b7_story.html?hpid=hp_no-name_opinion-card-e%3Ahomepage%2Fstory

25   https://www.bbc.com/news/election-us-2016-36232271?zephr-modal-register

26   http://www.faz.net/aktuell/politik/ausland/wahlkampf-in-amerika-die-medien-haben-ihren-auftrag-vergessen-14470037.html

27   https://www.washingtonpost.com/lifestyle/style/its-time-for-tv-news-to-stop-playing-the-stooge-for-donald-trump/2016/09/16/bc66812e-7c28-11e6-ac8e-cf8e0dd91dc7_story.html

28   https://trenchantobserver.com/2016/10/07/vice-presidential-debate-pence-pushes-kaine-and-clinton-on-military-action-in-syria/

29   https://web.archive.org/web/20161105211553/http:/trenchantobserver.com/2016/09/26/syria-russias-military-assault-on-western-civilization/

30   https://www.wsj.com/articles/
      only-hillary-clinton-is-prepared-for-the-nuclear-threat-1477261646

31   http://www.nytimes.com/2016/10/27/opinion/playing-with-fear-russias-war-card.html?_r=0

32   https://www.washingtonpost.com/opinions/global-opinions/why-is-trump-suddenly-talking-
      about-world-war-iii/2016/10/28/be44cc0e-9d24-11e6-a0ed-ab0774c1eaa5_story.html?utm_
      term=.a17bfff41972

33   https://web.archive.org/web/20201021141200/https:/trenchantobserver.com/
      putin-playing-chicken-in-syria-and-the-risk-of-escalation-to-nuclear-war/]

34   http://www.zeit.de/politik/ausland/2016-11/us-wahl-donald-trump-praesident-wahlergebnis

35   http://www.zeit.de/politik/ausland/2016-11/us-election-donald-trump-president-result

36   http://www.nytimes.com/2016/11/06/opinion/sunday/the-end-is-nigh.html

37   https://www.washingtonpost.com/news/worldviews/wp/2016/11/09/
      angela-merkel-congratulates-donald-trump-kind-of/

38   http://mobile.nytimes.com/2016/12/03/world/americas/alt-right-
      vladimir-putin.html?rref=collection%2Fbyline%2Fandrew-higgins&actio
      n=click&contentCollection=undefined®ion=stream&module=stream_
      unit&version=latest&contentPlacement=4&pgtype=collection&_r=0&referer=http://www.
      nytimes.com/by/andrew-higgins

39   https://www.washingtonpost.com/politics/inside-trumps-financial-ties-to-russia-and-his-
      unusual-flattery-of-vladimir-putin/2016/06/17/dbdcaac8-31a6-11e6-8ff7-7b6c1998b7a0_
      story.html

40   https://www.washingtonpost.com/opinions/2017/01/25/e59a8ab6-e34a-11e6-ba11-
      63c4b4fb5a63_story.html?tid=a_inl&utm_term=.cdb315510bd9

41   http://www.huffingtonpost.com/entry/
      ex-kgb-spy-cited-in-the-trump-blackmail-dossier-just_us_588e3f0de4b0cd25e4904a24

42   https://www.nytimes.com/2017/01/27/world/europe/russia-hacking-us-election.html?_r=0

43   https://www.nytimes.com/2017/01/25/world/europe/sergei-mikhailov-russian-
      cybercrimes-agent-arrested.html?rref=collection%2Fbyline%2Fandrew-e.-krame
      r&action=click&contentCollection=undefined®ion=stream&module=s
      tream_unit&version=latest&contentPlacement=4&pgtype=collection

44   http://www.mcclatchydc.com/news/nation-world/national/national-security/
      article129262849.html

45   http://www.telegraph.co.uk/news/2017/01/27/
      mystery-death-ex-kgb-chief-linked-mi6-spys-dossier-donald-trump/

46   https://sethjhettena.wordpress.com/2017/01/31/a-mole-in-the-white-house/

47   https://web.archive.org/web/20210615194705/https:/trenchantobserver.com/2017/03/01/
president-trumps-speech-to-congress-and-his-proposed-37-cut-in-the-state-departments-
budget/

48   https://www.washingtonpost.com/opinions/global-opinions/why-is-trump-suddenly-talking-
about-world-war-iii/2016/10/28/be44cc0e-9d24-11e6-a0ed-ab0774c1eaa5_story.html?utm_
term=.a17bfff41972

49   https://www.theguardian.com/commentisfree/2017/jan/14/
donald-trump-not-normal-president-congress-theresa-may

50   https://www.theguardian.com/commentisfree/2017/feb/07/
trump-disempower-institutions-protect-truth

51   https://www.washingtonpost.com/blogs/post-partisan/wp/2017/02/07/
joe-scarborough-trumps-dangerous-lie-about-russia/?utm_term=.8680898a213d

52   https://www.washingtonpost.com/news/true-crime/wp/2017/02/07/trump-makes-false-
statement-about-u-s-murder-rate-to-sheriffs-group/?hpid=hp_hp-more-top-stories_trump-
murderrate-0408pm%3Ahomepage%2Fstory&utm_term=.58d2905ed153

53   https://web.archive.org/web/20210615194422/https:/trenchantobserver.com/2017/03/11/
the-level-of-analysis-problem-in-assessing-and-reacting-to-trumps-assault-on-american-
democracy/

54   https://web.archive.org/web/20210416024754/https:/trenchantobserver.com/2019/11/22/
democrats-need-sue-trump-republican-apologists-defamation/

55   https://web.archive.org/web/20210518055147/https:/trenchantobserver.com/2017/02/02/
technical-adjustment-on-russian-sanctions-may-involve-more-than-meets-the-eye/

56   http://www.towleroad.com/2017/03/trump-russia-collusion/

57   https://www.thenation.com/article/archive/
rex-tillersons-jaw-dropping-testimony-just-completely-disqualified-him/

58   https://www.nytimes.com/2017/02/20/world/europe/churkin-russia-ambassador-un-death.
html?_r=0

59   http://www.cbsnews.com/news/
nyc-medical-examiner-says-more-study-needed-in-death-of-russian-diplomat/

60   https://www.nytimes.com/2017/03/10/world/americas/vitaly-churkin-united-nations.html

61   https://www.passblue.com/2017/03/12/
us-mission-to-the-un-do-not-release-vitaly-churkins-autopsy-report/

62   http://www.passblue.com/2017/02/20/
vitaly-churkin-64-russias-longtime-ambassador-to-the-un-dies-suddenly/

63   https://www.buzzfeed.com/kenbensinger/these-reports-allege-trump-has-deep-ties-to-russia?utm_term=.qvPOQe12k

64   https://web.archive.org/web/20140703004942/http:/trenchantobserver.com/

65   https://www.wsj.com/articles/exxon-seeks-u-s-waiver-to-work-in-russia-despite-sanctions-1492620677

66   https://www.nytimes.com/2017/04/19/business/energy-environment/exxon-mobil-russia-sanctions-waiver-oil.html

67   https://www.theguardian.com/us-news/2017/apr/21/donald-trump-marine-le-pen-french-presidential-election

68   https://www.france24.com/en/20180220-frances-jean-marie-le-pen-defends-vichy-leader-memoirs

69   https://www.brookings.edu/topic/human-rights/

70   http://www.politico.com/story/2017/05/10/trump-tillerson-russia-238191

71   https://web.archive.org/web/20210515164538/https:/trenchantobserver.com/2017/06/28/trumps-attitude-of-appeasement-toward-russia-makes-big-inroads-among-republican-voters/

72   https://www.washingtonpost.com/opinions/get-ready-for-the-impeachment-election/2017/05/23/9e93c4fe-3ff5-11e7-9869-bac8b446820a_story.html?utm_term=.9992d1476328

73   https://www.reuters.com/article/us-ukraine-crisis-rebels-declaration-idUSKBN1A31AX

74   http://theduran.com/donetsk-alexander-zakharchenko-declares-new-state-malorossiya/

75   https://en.wikipedia.org/wiki/Magnitsky_Act

76   https://www.nytimes.com/2017/08/18/opinion/the-test-of-nazism-that-trump-failed.html?rref=collection%2Ftimestopic%2FHolocaust%20and%20the%20Nazi%20Era&action=click&contentCollection=timestopics®ion=stream&module=stream_unit&version=latest&contentPlacement=7&pgtype=collection&_r=0&GLS=1503775278%7COmefl%2B5I7SE42%2Fc4Qn1%2BDUVv8iJLbLhOASR4cmk7fEU%3D

77   https://www.buzzfeed.com/kenbensinger/these-reports-allege-trump-has-deep-ties-to-russia?utm_term=.qvPOQe12k

78   https://web.archive.org/web/20210515071510/https:/trenchantobserver.com/2017/03/07/more-on-the-golden-showers-dossier-prepared-by-former-mi6-agent-christopher-steele/

79   https://www.justsecurity.org/44697/steele-dossier-knowing/

80   https://en.wikipedia.org/wiki/Steele_dossier

81   https://web.archive.org/web/20210514094644/https:/trenchantobserver.com/2017/05/19/human-rights-in-saudi-arabia-will-trump-look-the-other-way/

82 https://www.newyorker.com/news/news-desk/the-saudi-royal-purge-with-trumps-consent

83 https://www.thedailybeast.com/trump-after-saudi-palace-coup-weve-put-our-man-on-top

84 https://web.archive.org/web/20210514103030/https:/trenchantobserver.com/2019/04/11/
america-lose-soul/

85 https://www.lawfareblog.com/irony-nunes-memo

86 https://www.nytimes.com/2018/04/13/opinion/trump-hitler-europe.html

87 http://uscode.house.gov/view.xhtml?path=/prelim@title18/part1/chapter73&edition=prelim

88 https://www.washingtonpost.com/lifestyle/media/restoring-voice-of-america-post-
trump/2020/12/11/d1088ba6-3bb7-11eb-bc68-96af0daae728_story.html

89 https://web.archive.org/web/20210415232211/https:/trenchantobserver.com/2018/10/24/
khashoggi-affair-murder-foul/

90 https://web.archive.org/web/20210415232211/https:/trenchantobserver.com/2018/10/24/
khashoggi-affair-murder-foul/

91 https://web.archive.org/web/20210416015756/https:/trenchantobserver.com/2018/11/18/
news-reports-cia-concludes-saudi-crown-prince-ordered-kashoggi-assassination/

92 https://web.archive.org/web/20200811092223/https:/trenchantobserver.com/2018/11/19/
american-policy-khashoggs-assassination-human-rights-international-law/

93 https://web.archive.org/web/20200815142823/https:/trenchantobserver.com/2018/11/21/
khashoggi-value-cost-one-human-life/

94 https://web.archive.org/web/20210302072241/https:/trenchantobserver.com/2021/03/01/
khashoggi-assassination-really-sanction-mbs-minimize-u-s-allied-dealing/

95 http://www.rasmussenreports.com/public_content/politics/trump_administration/
trump_approval_index_history

96 https://www.washingtonpost.com/graphics/2019/politics/read-the-mueller-report/

97 https://web.archive.org/web/20210518044012/https:/trenchantobserver.com/2019/07/17/
democrats-already-lost-2020-elections-part-ii/

98 http://www.rasmussenreports.com/public_content/politics/trump_administration/
trump_approval_index_history

99 https://theintercept.com/2019/09/26/impeachment-trump-ukraine-democrats/

100 https://web.archive.org/web/20210515072919/https:/trenchantobserver.com/2019/09/24/
impeachment-inquiry-tool-educating-american-people-electorate/

101 https://web.archive.org/web/20210615194345/https:/trenchantobserver.com/2019/11/16/
scope-impeachment-elizabeth-drew-supports-broad-inquiry/

102 http://www.rasmussenreports.com/public_content/politics/trump_administration/
trump_approval_index_history

103 https://web.archive.org/web/20210615195338/https:/trenchantobserver.com/2019/11/15/
house-democrats-stampeding-like-buffaloes-heading-toward-cliff/

104 https://web.archive.org/web/20200812113902/https:/trenchantobserver.com/2018/12/05/
republicans-white-knuckle-tactics-limiting-governors-seal-image-anti-democratic-party/

105 https://www.amazon.com/Fear-Trump-White-Bob-Woodward/dp/1501175513/
ref=sr_1_4?keywords=fear&qid=1579998055&sr=8-4

106 https://www.amazon.com/Profiles-Courage-John-F-Kennedy/dp/0060530626/
ref=sr_1_1?crid=1JM2IP8B1LEN3&keywords=profiles+in+courage+by+
john+f.+kennedy&qid=1579991232&sprefix=profiles+in+courage%2Caps%
2C222&sr=8-1

107 https://www.amazon.com/Question-German-
Perspectives-Continental-Philosophy/dp/0823220699/
ref=sr_1_1?keywords=the+question+of+german+guilt&qid=1580447200&s=books&sr=1-1

108 https://www.amazon.com/Tyranny-Twenty-Lessons-Twentieth-Century/dp/0804190119/
ref=sxin_0_sxwds-bia-wc1_0?cv_ct_cx=on+tyranny&keywords=on+tyranny&pd_
rd_i=0804190119&pd_rd_r=eee76e4f-5c82-4a8e-9bf4-bc3e7adb576b&pd_
rd_w=6RLPS&pd_rd_wg=4iiNm&pf_rd_p=e308a38c-3620-4845-b486-
18a551828bb6&pf_rd_r=JB75PABRY31T31408CTM&psc=1&qid=15804467
94&sr=1-1-e1d37225-97ae-4506-b802-4ca5ff43ebe6

109 https://www.nytimes.com/2020/04/03/technology/coronavirus-masks-shortage.
html?action=click&module=Top%20Stories&pgtype=Homepage

110 https://web.archive.org/web/20200815134823/https:/trenchantobserver.com/2020/07/15/
trump-impeached-removed-office-now-save-100000-lives-200000/

111 https://web.archive.org/web/20200925203415/https:/trenchantobserver.com/2020/09/12/
covid-19-u-s-can-grasp-significance-200000-deaths/

112 https://web.archive.org/web/20201029011930/https:/trenchantobserver.com/2020/10/12/
trumps-failure-protect-american-people-coronavirus/

113 https://www.salon.com/2020/06/12/come-november-a-us-coup-detat_partner/

114 https://www.washingtonpost.com/nation/2020/07/17/portland-protests-federal-
arrests/?hpid=hp_hp-top-table-high_mm-portland-810am%3Ahomepage%2Fstory-ans

115 https://www.washingtonpost.com/national-security/white-house-intensifies-effort-to-
install-pentagon-personnel-seen-as-loyal-to-trump/2020/06/25/1bfeee3a-9f86-11ea-9d96-
c3f7c755fd6e_story.html

116 https://www.nytimes.com/2020/06/25/us/politics/esper-trump-defense-military.
html?action=click&module=News&pgtype=Homepage

117 https://www.politico.com/news/magazine/2020/06/06/
the-guardrails-are-off-the-us-military-303959

118 https://www.thenation.com/authors/elie-mystal/

119 https://www.thenation.com/article/politics/
the-question-isnt-whether-trump-will-go-full-authoritarian-its-how-well-respond/

120 https://www.nytimes.com/2020/06/06/opinion/coronavirus-covid-19-lockdown.
html?action=click&module=Opinion&pgtype=Homepage

121 https://web.archive.org/web/20201027085016/https:/trenchantobserver.com/2020/06/02/
demonstrators-made-point-now-play-trumps-campaign-narrative/

122 https://web.archive.org/web/20201025045927/https:/trenchantobserver.com/2020/06/10/
elephant-room-russias-role-demonstrations/

123 https://web.archive.org/web/20201025045927/https:/trenchantobserver.com/2020/06/10/
elephant-room-russias-role-demonstrations/

124 https://www.cnn.com/2020/06/07/opinions/trumps-unidentified-security-forces-putins-
little-green-men-vinograd/index.html

125 https://www.theguardian.com/commentisfree/2020/jul/23/
trump-authoritarianism-portland-cbp-election

126 https://www.salon.com/2020/06/12/come-november-a-us-coup-detat_partner/

127 https://www.washingtonpost.com/nation/2020/07/17/portland-protests-federal-
arrests/?hpid=hp_hp-top-table-high_mm-portland-810am%3Ahomepage%2Fstory-ans

128 https://www.washingtonpost.com/opinions/2020/07/17/whats-happening-portland-shows-
trump-is-ignoring-constitution-attacking-america/?hpid=hp_save-opinions-float-right-4-0_
opinion-card-b-right%3Ahomepage%2Fstory-ans

129 https://www.latimes.com/opinion/story/2020-07-17/
federal-agents-trump-portland-protesters

130 https://www.lawfareblog.com/what-heck-are-federal-law-enforcement-officers-doing-portland

131 https://www.nytimes.com/2020/07/24/opinion/trump-germany.html

132 https://thehill.com/homenews/
administration/516020-trump-says-he-would-put-down-riots-on-election-night-very-quickly

133 https://web.archive.org/web/20201127034047/https:/trenchantobserver.com/2020/08/10/
arent-house-democrats-preparing-articles-impeachment-trump/

134 https://thehill.com/homenews/
administration/516020-trump-says-he-would-put-down-riots-on-election-night-very-quickly

135 https://www.mediamatters.org/roger-stone/
     roger-stone-calls-trump-seize-total-power-if-he-loses-election

136 https://www.washingtonpost.com/health/2020/09/14/michael-caputo-coronavirus-cdc/

137 https://www.washingtonpost.com/health/joe-biden-coronavirus-plan/2020/09/11/002b972c-
     eecc-11ea-99a1-71343d03bc29_story.html?itid=lk_inline_manual_20

138 https://www.theguardian.com/commentisfree/2020/sep/04/
     trump-democracy-voting-process-elected

139 https://elpais.com/opinion/2020-09-02/un-bolchevique-en-la-casa-blanca.html

140 https://web.archive.org/web/20201202060822/https:/trenchantobserver.com/2019/01/10/
     international-law-trump/

141 https://web.archive.org/web/20210126031044/https:/trenchantobserver.com/2019/01/25/
     trump-steers-dangerous-course-venezuela/

142 https://web.archive.org/web/20210518035926/https:/trenchantobserver.com/2019/01/26/
     stupid-incompetent-foreign-policy-towards-venezuela-intervention-protect-nationals/

143 https://www.cbsnews.com/news/
     michael-reinoehl-suspect-portland-shooting-killed-federal-task-force/

144 https://www.theguardian.com/us-news/2020/sep/04/
     man-linked-to-death-of-far-right-protester-in-portland-shot-deadby-us-marshals-reports

145 https://www.nytimes.com/2020/09/03/us/michael-reinoehl-arrest-portland-shooting.
     html?action=click&module=RelatedLinks&pgtype=Article

146 https://www.nytimes.com/2020/09/04/us/portland-shooting-michael-reinoehl.html

147 https://www.justice.gov/opa/pr/
     statement-attorney-general-william-p-barr-tracking-down-fugitive-michael-forest-reinoehl

148 https://www.wsj.com/articles/attorney-general-praises-law-enforcement-after-pursuit-killing-
     of-michael-reinoehl-11599245921

149 https://www.cnn.com/2020/09/04/us/portland-protest-suspected-killer/index.html

150 https://www.nytimes.com/2020/09/04/us/michael-forest-reinoehl-portland.html

151 https://www.oregonlive.com/crime/2020/09/witness-says-officers-never-gave-commands-
     before-firing-at-michael-reinoehl-outside-wa-apartment.html

152 https://www.washingtonpost.com/nation/2020/09/10/
     reinoehl-portland-antifa-killing-police/

153 https://www.leftvoice.org/michael-reinoehl-was-executed-by-the-police

154 https://www.rollingstone.com/politics/politics-news/
     eyewitness-disputes-federal-killing-accused-portland-shooter-barr-reinoehl-1058049/

155   https://www.vox.com/2020/9/14/21436216/
      trump-michael-reinoehl-protests-portland-shooting

156   https://www.nytimes.com/2020/09/14/opinion/trump-antifa-civil-liberties.html

157   https://www.theolympian.com/news/local/article245823195.html

158   https://www.wweek.com/news/2020/09/17/sheriff-says-michael-reinoehl-suspected-in-
      portland-protest-killing-was-armed-when-officers-shot-him/

159   https://nypost.com/2020/09/18/
      michael-reinoehl-pointed-handgun-at-officers-during-arrest-cops/

160   https://www.nytimes.com/2020/10/13/us/michael-reinoehl-antifa-portland-shooting.html

161   https://web.archive.org/web/20201129112902/https:/trenchantobserver.
      com/2020/10/28/27423/

162   https://en.wikipedia.org/wiki/Killings_of_Aaron_Danielson_and_Michael_Reinoehl

163   https://www.washingtonpost.com/elections/2020/10/17/trump-biden-live-updates/

164   https://web.archive.org/web/20201129112839/https:/trenchantobserver.com/2020/10/20/
      can-trump-go-escape-law-bahamas/

165   https://web.archive.org/web/20201129111948/https:/trenchantobserver.com/2020/10/21/
      can-trump-go-escape-law-china/

166   https://web.archive.org/web/20210118233132/https:/trenchantobserver.com/2020/12/12/
      can-trump-go-escape-law-will-make-airport/

167   https://web.archive.org/web/20210118235658/https:/trenchantobserver.com/2020/12/17/
      can-trump-go-escape-law-bahamas-2/

168   https://web.archive.org/web/20210118232821/https:/trenchantobserver.com/2020/12/24/
      can-trump-go-escape-law-israeli-settlements-west-bank/

169   https://www.vox.com/2020/9/14/21436216/
      trump-michael-reinoehl-protests-portland-shooting

170   https://www.nytimes.com/2020/10/13/us/michael-reinoehl-antifa-portland-shooting.html

171   https://www.washingtonpost.com/opinions/2020/10/30/
      its-up-people-foil-trumps-plot-against-democracy/

172   https://mailchi.mp/worldjusticeproject/egi-launch-437266?e=312811fc67

173   https://www.washingtonpost.com/technology/2020/10/30/
      trump-twitter-domestic-disinformation/

174   https://www.nytimes.com/2020/09/15/opinion/caputo-trump-2020.
      html?action=click&module=Opinion&pgtype=Homepage

175   https://trenchantobserver.com/2020/09/17/27000/

176 https://www.nytimes.com/2020/10/29/opinion/trump-arts-culture.
html?action=click&module=Opinion&pgtype=Homepage

177 https://www.nytimes.com/2020/10/30/opinion/trump-democracy-apathy.
html?action=click&module=Opinion&pgtype=Homepage

178 https://www.nytimes.com/2020/11/01/opinion/election-vote-2020.
html?action=click&module=Opinion&pgtype=Homepage

179 https://web.archive.org/web/20201129094437/https:/trenchantobserver.
com/2020/11/02/27495/

180 https://www.washingtonpost.com/politics/2020/11/02/
election-eve-trump-dances-around-powder-keg-with-lit-match/

181 https://www.washingtonpost.com/elections/2020/11/12/
vote-certification-deadlines-ga-mi-wi-nv-az-pa/?arc404=true

182 https://www.nytimes.com/article/electors-vote.html?action=click&module=Top%20
Stories&pgtype=Homepage

183 https://www.nytimes.com/2020/11/13/opinion/biden-trump-electoral-college.
html?action=click&module=Opinion&pgtype=Homepage

184 https://www.washingtonpost.com/opinions/trump-wants-to-overturn-the-results-of-a-
free-and-fair-election-theres-a-word-for-that/2020/11/13/cb94b77e-25b6-11eb-952e-
0c475972cfc0_story.html

185 https://fas.org/sgp/crs/misc/R40504.pdf

186 https://www.archives.gov/founding-docs/amendments-11-27

187 https://constitutioncenter.org/interactive-constitution/amendment/amendment-xx

188 https://www.washingtonpost.com/politics/trump-uses-power-of-presidency-to-try-
to-overturn-the-election-and-stay-in-office/2020/11/19/bc89caa6-2a9f-11eb-8fa2-
06e7cbb145c0_story.html

189 https://www.washingtonpost.com/politics/trumps-escalating-attacks-put-pressure-on-vote-
certification-process/2020/11/19/42f5fd76-2aa5-11eb-8fa2-06e7cbb145c0_story.html

190 https://www.nytimes.com/2020/11/19/us/politics/trump-michigan-election.
html?action=click&module=Spotlight&pgtype=Homepage

191 https://www.nytimes.com/2020/11/19/us/politics/trump-election.html

192 https://web.archive.org/web/20201129094203/https:/trenchantobserver.com/2020/11/18/
trump-co-conspirators-move-sow-confusion-delay-vote-certifications-win-contingent-
election-house/

193 https://www.washingtonpost.com/politics/trump-election-strategy/2020/11/18/94fbe50e-
29c9-11eb-92b7-6ef17b3fe3b4_story.html

194 https://www.nytimes.com/2020/11/18/us/politics/trump-election.
html?searchResultPosition=1

195 https://www.washingtonpost.com/politics/trump-election-strategy/2020/11/18/94fbe50e-
29c9-11eb-92b7-6ef17b3fe3b4_story.html

196 https://web.archive.org/web/20201129101705/https:/trenchantobserver.com/2020/11/18/
outgoing-president-runs-amok-nothing-can/

197 https://web.archive.org/web/20201129100803/https:/trenchantobserver.com/2020/11/09/
imagine-adolf-hitler-white-house/

198 https://web.archive.org/web/20210303223606/https:/trenchantobserver.com/2021/02/23/
fighting-american-fascists-just-imagine-wearing-nazi-military-uniforms/

199 https://www.law.cornell.edu/definitions/uscode.
php?width=840&height=800&iframe=true&def_id=52-USC-3625706-244965480&term_
occur=999&term_src=title:52:subtitle:I:chapter:103:section:10307

200 https://www.law.cornell.edu/uscode/text/52/subtitle-I/chapter-103

201 https://www.law.cornell.edu/uscode/text/52/subtitle-I/chapter-107

202 https://www.law.cornell.edu/uscode/text/52/10302

203 https://www.law.cornell.edu/uscode/text/52/10305

204 https://www.law.cornell.edu/uscode/text/52/10306

205 https://www.law.cornell.edu/uscode/text/52/10308

206 https://www.law.cornell.edu/uscode/text/52/10307

207 https://www.thestreet.com/mishtalk/politics/
trumps-maneuver-to-intimidate-michigan-lawmakers-fails

208 https://www.justia.com/criminal/offenses/inchoate-crimes/conspiracy/

209 https://codes.findlaw.com/us/title-18-crimes-and-criminal-procedure/18-usc-sect-595.html

210 https://www.law.cornell.edu/uscode/text/18/371

211 https://www.law.cornell.edu/uscode/text/42/1985

212 https://www.thestreet.com/mishtalk/politics/
trumps-maneuver-to-intimidate-michigan-lawmakers-fails

213 https://web.archive.org/web/20201123145801/https://trenchantobserver.com/2020/11/22/
trumps-criminal-conspiracy-overthrow-presidential-election-results/

214 https://www.washingtonpost.com/opinions/how-trump-could-still-disrupt-the-transfer-of-
power/2020/11/24/42e4e3ee-2e68-11eb-96c2-aac3f162215d_story.html

215 https://www.politico.com/news/magazine/2020/11/24/
michigan-election-trump-voter-fraud-democracy-440475

216 https://harpers.org/archive/2020/11/the-enemies-briefcase-secret-powers-of-the-presidency/

217 https://urbanmilwaukee.com/2020/07/27/op-ed-trump-has-enormous-emergency-powers/

218 https://www.washingtonpost.com/opinions/2020/12/20/trump-saved-worst-last/

219 https://web.archive.org/web/20201028173629/https:/trenchantobserver.com/2020/10/17/27316/

220 https://web.archive.org/web/20201129105441/https:/trenchantobserver.com/2020/10/17/can-trump-go-escape-law-russia/

221 https://web.archive.org/web/20201129111948/https:/trenchantobserver.com/2020/10/21/can-trump-go-escape-law-china/

222 https://web.archive.org/web/20201129112839/https:/trenchantobserver.com/2020/10/20/can-trump-go-escape-law-bahamas/

223 https://web.archive.org/web/20210118233132/https:/trenchantobserver.com/2020/12/12/can-trump-go-escape-law-will-make-airport/

224 https://www.washingtonpost.com/opinions/2020/12/26/until-bidens-win-is-certified-us-remains-vulnerable/

225 https://www.washingtonpost.com/national-security/2020/12/26/after-nashville-blast-tennessee-governor-asks-trump-emergency-disaster-declaration/

226 https://www.washingtonpost.com/opinions/fourteen-days-that-will-test-our-democracy/2020/12/31/7a59d6d6-4b96-11eb-a9f4-0e668b9772ba_story.html

227 https://www.washingtonpost.com/opinions/2020/12/26/until-bidens-win-is-certified-us-remains-vulnerable/

228 https://www.washingtonpost.com/opinions/how-trump-could-still-disrupt-the-transfer-of-power/2020/11/24/42e4e3ee-2e68-11eb-96c2-aac3f162215d_story.html

229 https://web.archive.org/web/20210118232421/https:/trenchantobserver.com/2020/12/22/loony-president-dangerous-man-earth/

230 https://www.washingtonpost.com/national-security/former-defense-secretaries-rebuke-trump-election/2021/01/03/1c708f64-4de5-11eb-b2e8-3339e73d9da2_story.html

231 https://www.washingtonpost.com/opinions/10-former-defense-secretaries-military-peaceful-transfer-of-power/2021/01/03/2a23d52e-4c4d-11eb-a9f4-0e668b9772ba_story.html

232 https://www.politico.com/news/2021/01/03/defense-secretaries-military-trump-election-454334

233 https://web.archive.org/web/20210226181052/https:/trenchantobserver.com/2021/01/12/contingency-planning-military-style-commando-action-arrest-trump-part-one/

234 https://www.npr.org/2020/12/08/942288226/bidens-victory-cemented-as-states-reach-deadline-for-certifying-vote-tallies

235 https://www.nytimes.com/2020/12/08/us/politics/election-safe-harbor-deadline.html

236 https://www.law.cornell.edu/uscode/text/3/5

237 https://www.washingtonpost.com/investigations/capitol-rally-organizers-before-riots/2021/01/16/c5b40250-552d-11eb-a931-5b162d0d033d_story.html

238 https://www.nbcnews.com/news/us-news/protesters-gather-outside-state-capitols-nationwide-chaos-sweeps-congress-n1253125

239 https://www.theday.com/article/20210107/NWS21/210109574

240 https://web.archive.org/web/20211206154822/https:/trenchantobserver.com/2021/02/02/aocs-instagram-account-trauma-experienced-january-6/

241 https://www.theguardian.com/us-news/2020/feb/15/donald-trump-new-york-times-grievance-persecution-resentment-daytona-500

242 https://web.archive.org/web/20211025230840/https:/trenchantobserver.com/2021/01/08/pelosi-house-democrats-not-falter-impeaching-trump/

243 https://www.washingtonpost.com/politics/democrats-consider-impeachment-alternatives-censure/2021/01/27/fdfd9b6c-60bd-11eb-afbe-9a11a127d146_story.html

244 https://trenchantobserver.com/2021/01/26/unity-fascists-never/

245 https://web.archive.org/web/20211203093959/https:/trenchantobserver.com/2021/01/23/weak-kneed-democrats-verge-blowing/

246 https://www.archives.gov/founding-docs/declaration-transcript

247 https://web.archive.org/web/20211206144655/https:/trenchantobserver.com/2021/02/04/will-godless-senate-republicans-break-oaths-god-acquit-trump/

248 https://edition.cnn.com/2020/01/16/opinions/senators-abide-by-your-impeachment-oath-zeldin/index.html

249 https://web.archive.org/web/20211016175441/https:/trenchantobserver.com/2021/02/16/memoriam-republican-party-march-20-1854-februart-13-2021/

250 https://web.archive.org/web/20210616234442/https:/trenchantobserver.com/2021/05/20/fascism-in-america-is-here-now-in-the-republican-party/

251 https://www.washingtonpost.com/opinions/2021/05/20/trump-republicans-violent-threats-election-2024/

252 https://www.washingtonpost.com/powerpost/senate-democrats-learned-of-managers-witness-decision-only-minutes-in-advance/2021/02/13/8e3e821e-6e2d-11eb-ba56-d7e2c8defa31_story.html

253 https://web.archive.org/web/20211203133415/https:/trenchantobserver.com/2021/01/26/unity-fascists-never/

254 https://www.state.gov/wp-content/uploads/2020/02/Agreement-For-Bringing-Peace-to-Afghanistan-02.29.20.pdf

255 https://www.washingtonpost.com/world/afghans-are-rooting-for-zalmay-khalilzad-a-former-us-envoy-to-end-up-in-trump-administration/2016/11/18/61731f16-adb0-11e6-8f19-21a1c65d2043_story.html

256 https://www.nytimes.com/2009/10/14/world/14biden.html

257 https://www.washingtonpost.com/politics/2020/02/18/biden-afghanistan-military-power/

258 https://www.lemonde.fr/international/article/2021/03/17/joe-biden-inflige-un-camouflet-aux-europeens-sur-le-dossier-afghan_6073450_3210.html

259 https://www.nytimes.com/2021/03/26/us/politics/biden-afghanistan-intelligence.html?searchResultPosition=1

260 https://web.archive.org/web/20210728093115/https:/trenchantobserver.com/2021/07/05/the-afghan-government-could-fall-quickly/

261 https://web.archive.org/web/20210616222555/https:/trenchantobserver.com/2021/05/28/the-u-s-doesnt-need-investigations-or-commissions-it-needs-prosecutions/

262 https://www.bostonglobe.com/2021/01/04/opinion/trumps-crime-spree-must-not-escape-investigation/

263 https://www.washingtonpost.com/opinions/2021/08/05/heres-roadmap-justice-department-follow-investigating-trump

264 https://www.politico.com/news/magazine/2021/07/06/department-of-justice-january-6-capitol-riots-investigations-498253

265 https://web.archive.org/web/20210118210337/https:/trenchantobserver.com/2021/01/18/trumps-future/

266 https://www.washingtonpost.com/opinions/2021/08/05/heres-roadmap-justice-department-follow-investigating-trump/

267 https://www.bostonglobe.com/2021/08/20/opinion/merrick-garland-must-investigate-donald-trumps-attempted-coup-not-retribution-deterrence/

268 https://www.wsj.com/articles/liz-cheney-confronts-a-house-of-cowards-11620342680

269 https://web.archive.org/web/20210507044329/https:/trenchantobserver.com/2021/05/06/liz-cheney-and-the-republican-gleichschaltung/

270 https://www.theatlantic.com/ideas/archive/2021/05/liz-cheney-trump-fraud/618820/

271 https://en.wikipedia.org/wiki/July_1932_German_federal_election

272 https://www.washingtonpost.com/politics/stefanik-cheney-trump/2021/05/06/eee70eb8-ae94-11eb-acd3-24b44a57093a_story.html

273 https://www.nytimes.com/2021/05/06/us/politics/liz-cheney-elise-stefanik.
html?action=click&module=Spotlight&pgtype=Homepage

274 https://web.archive.org/web/20210616232550/https:/trenchantobserver.
com/2021/06/06/29251/

275 https://www.cfr.org/blog/2020-election-numbers

276 https://www.nytimes.com/2021/01/07/us/politics/republicans-against-certification.html

277 https://www.vox.com/2021/1/6/22218058/republicans-objections-election-results

278 https://www.telegraph.co.uk/news/2021/08/28/
joe-biden-deaf-dumb-blind-chaos-us-has-unleashed/

279 https://www.lemonde.fr/international/article/2021/05/28/vingt-ans-apres-leur-intervention-
en-afghanistan-les-americains-s-en-vont-sur-un-sentiment-d-echec_6081907_3210.html

280 https://web.archive.org/web/20210918162908/https:/trenchantobserver.com/2021/08/31/
joe-biden-s-foreign-policy-judgment-you-cant-fill-a-bucket-with-a-hole-in-it/

281 https://www.wsj.com/articles/afghanistan-withdrawal-fiasco-biden-mcchrystal-
gates-holbrooke-obama-military-taliban-11630612285?mod=followpeggyn
oonan

282 https://web.archive.org/web/20210922205302/https:/trenchantobserver.com/2021/09/15/
afghanistan-faces-famine-economic-collapse-as-international-community-poses-conditions-
for-aid/

283 https://www.nytimes.com/2021/09/10/opinion/trump-republicans-coup.html

284 https://web.archive.org/web/20211203105921/https:/trenchantobserver.
com/2021/10/31/30574/

285 https://www.washingtonpost.com/opinions/2021/09/23/robert-kagan-constitutional-crisis/

286 https://www.tcm.com/tcmdb/title/27532/ship-of-fools#overview

287 https://www.famous-trials.com/
dreyfus/2613-j-accuse-by-emile-zola-texts-in-english-and-french

288 https://web.archive.org/web/20210801134555/https://trenchantobserver.com/2021/06/21/
impunity-the-biggrest-and-most-important-story-no-one-will-cover/

289 https://web.archive.org/web/20210616225237/https://trenchantobserver.com/

290 https://www.washingtonpost.com/opinions/2021/05/20/
trump-republicans-violent-threats-election-2024/

291 https://web.archive.org/web/20210117100231/https://trenchantobserver.com/2021/01/14/
three-immediate-steps-stop-threats-assassination-acts-political-terror/

292 https://www.cnn.com/2021/08/20/opinions/trump-conduct-needs-federal-investigation-ayer-eisen/index.html

293 https://web.archive.org/web/20210918180016/https:/trenchantobserver.com/2021/08/05/the-indictment-of-trump-the-democratic-wall-of-silence-begins-to-break/

294 Originally drafted in September and December 2021. Revised and updated in April and August 2024.

295 Shelby County v. Holder, 570 U.S. 529 (2013).

296 United States Supreme Court, Trump v. U.S. (July 1, 2024), Syllabus. https://www.supremecourt.gov/opinions/23pdf/23-939_e2pg.pdf

297 *See* Devlin Barrett and Perry Stein, "Trump's Classified Documents Case Dismissed by Judge Aileen Cannon; Special Counsel Jack Smith Says He Will Appeal the Judge's Ruling That He Was Improperly Appointed," *Washington Post*, July 15, 2024 (updated at 5:44 p.m. EDT). https://www.washingtonpost.com/national-security/2024/07/15/trump-classified-trial-dismisssed-cannon/
For an updated analysis of the status of the cases against Trump, see David A. Graham, "The Cases Against Trump: A Guide; Thirty-four felony convictions. Charges of fraud, election subversion, and obstruction. One place to keep track of the presidential candidate's legal troubles," *The Atlantic*, September 13, 2024 (2:18 p.m. ET). https://www.theatlantic.com/ideas/archive/2024/09/donald-trump-legal-cases-charges/675531/

298 Laurence H. Tribe and Dennis Aftergut, "Attorney General Merrick Garland Should Appoint a Special Counsel to Investigate Trump," *Washington Post*, March 9, 2022 (2:08 p.m. EST).

299 Merrick Garland, "Merrick Garland: It Is Time for Congress to Act Again to Protect the Right to Vote," *Washington Post*, August 5, 2021 at 6:09 p.m. EDT. https://www.washingtonpost.com/opinions/2021/08/05/merrick-garland-voting-rights-act-anniversary-congress/

300 See James Rowles, *Trenchant Observations 2022-present*. https://jamesrowles.substack.com/

Acknowledgements

So many people have contributed to the development of my values, my sensibility, and my writing and analytical abilities, all of which made this book possible, that to thank them all would turn this Acknowledgments section into an autobiography. I cannot thank them all by name, but I want to express a special note of gratitude to those named below.

First of all, I want to thank Molly Faraji, my companion, whose love and support have benefitted my writing and the writing of this book in more ways than I can count.

I owe a particular debt of gratitude to the team or world-class professionals who helped me turn a promising manuscript into a beautiful book.

Michael Grossman, my book designer, not only produced a great cover and interior design, but also responded quickly and proactively to all my questions, comments, and suggestions. I cannot imagine a more talented and dedicated book designer. Melissa Prideaux, my copy editor, worked patiently and with great dedication and dispatch, despite the delays caused by me which resulted from an extremely ambitious production schedule given the timeliness of the book. Her copy-editing was superb, reflecting great resourcefulness and expertise. Eve Morey Christiansen not only produced a terrific index but also showed an impressive willingness to stand by but at-the-ready as we experienced repeated delays. Her index will be of extraordinary usefulness to readers who want to explore a particular topic or to locate material which they have already read.

It has been a great pleasure to work with three professionals who must be among the best in the world.

I owe a special debt of gratitude to Zaida Arguedas, my former wife, who accompanied and encouraged me in many ways, particularly during the writing of two books and numerous law review articles.

I also want to thank Edward M. Kovachy, Jr., my coach, who over the years manifested an unfailing appreciation of the quality of my writing and unshakable faith that this book would one day be published.

Special gratitude is due to Dr. Robert Louis Dodd, Stanford neurosurgeon *sans pareil* (without equal), without whose timely interventions this book might never have been written.

Michael Mauldin offered constant feedback and encouragement at the time each of these chapters was written. His comments, at times critical, helped me strengthen aspects of the articles that were weak or not fully developed. His steady encouragement spurred me on.

I also want to thank Joy Beeson, whose positive attitude after losing everything in the Paradise Fire (also known as the Camp Fire) in California in 2018 has been an inspiration, and whose encouraging comments on my columns, many of which make up this book, provided reassurance that I was writing something that was meaningful for my readers.

Mark Miller, whose artistic name is Octavious Sage and who is also known as Marcus Miller, provided such engaging intellectual interaction that we often lost track of time for hours in spirited conversation. His example as an author and an artist inspired me to reach for the highest goals. His painting, which adorns the cover, has captured in one visual image the heart of what this book is all about.

I also want to thank Gerard Lum, a friend and talented professional photographer, for his patience in our photo shoot and the author's final phtograph selected for the book.

Stanford Law School classmates Alan Alhadeff, Jerry Halligan, John Mitchell, Dick Morningstar, Mike Roster, and Fred Smith offered encouragement and support in many ways for what turned out to be a long-term but fruitful endeavor.

Special thanks are due to Bill Wilby, lifelong friend who has followed the zigs and zags of my career over the years, providing encouragement and support which helped make this book possible.

Cynthia Travis and Larry Litt, fellow members of the Harvard Club of San Francisco Writer's Group, offered valuable feedback on different drafts and encouragement as this book was being written.

Also, I want to thank Russell Gonzaga and Rosie Llamado, constant participants in my Tracy Writer's Group, who provided valuable feedback on various writing exercises and encouragement of my writing.

Finally, I wish to acknowledge the enormous debt of gratitude I owe to three former mentors, who unfortunately are no longer with us today. Gordon A. Craig – perhaps the leading American historian of Germany for many years, was a model of what a great historian can be. Taking his courses and under his direction of my Senior Honors Thesis in History at Stanford, I learned much about the tragic history of Germany in the twentieth century and the phenomenon of pure evil in the form of Adolf Hitler and the Nazis during the Third Reich.

Professor John Henry Merryman of Stanford Law School was an inspirational teacher and mentor, who imbued in me a deep appreciation of the Civil Law Tradition which emerged from Rome, as well as as a deep interest in international development. His creative approach reshaped the study of Comparative Law in the United States, an approach which I myself used when I taught Comparative Law in law school settings. I also had the opportunity to work with him as a member of the Stanford Studies in Law and Development Project (SLADE) which he led (along with Professor Lawrence M. Friedman. Above all, he was a kind and understanding teacher who elicited excellence from me and from his other students.

At Harvard Law School I had the good fortune to persuade Abram Chayes to supervise my dissertation for the degree of Doctor of Juridical Science in International Law (S.J.D.). Abe, who I considered to be the greatest international lawyer of his generation, was a magnificent mentor and fantastic human being who showed deep compassion and understanding when I faced some of the hard vicissitudes of life. His approach to international law and his example continue to shape my understanding of international law not simply as a set of norms in books but rather as a vital instrument which can be used by individuals, officials, and governments to avoid and halt wars, defend the human rights of discrete human beings, and solve the many international challenges which the world faces. Abe was the State Department Legal Adviser in October 1962 during the Cuban Missile Crisis which using international law he helped to defuse. He also led the drafting of arms control agreements which helped safeguard international peace and security for a generation. I will be forever grateful for his friendship and example.

About The Author

James P. Rowles is an author and international affairs columnist, and former law professor and international lawyer. He holds the advanced doctoral degree of Doctor of Juridical Science) in International Law (S.J.D.) from Harvard University, where he has taught human rights courses as a Lecturer on Law. He was also a Visiting Scholar at Harvard's Center for International Affairs (CFIA) and the recipient of a Harvard MacArthur Fellowship in International Peace and Security. Working in the field of international development, he served as Associate Director of International Programs at the Center for Criminal Justice (CCJ) at Harvard Law School,where he played a leading role in the development and implementation of a program of cooperation with the Guatemalan Judiciary during a hopeful period of civilian rule.

He has also taught international and comparative law courses at other universities, including Brandeis, the University of Pittsburgh, and the University of Kansas.

In addition, Dr. Rowles has worked as an international lawyer at a leading national law firm in Boston and at major global corporations on matters in Latin America, Europe, the Middle East, and Asia.

As an international development practitioner, he has worked on judicial reform, human rights, and access to justice projects in Latin America, Africa, the Middle East, Afghanistan, and Russia.

Early in his career, he was a senior staff attorney at the Inter-American Commission on Human Rights (IACHR) of the Organization of American States (OAS), in Washington, D.C. Dr. Rowles also was a recipient of the Rómulo Gallegos Fellowship in International Human Rights awarded by the Commission.

He received an A.B. in History from Stanford University, where he graduated "With Great Distinction" (*summa cum laude*). At Stanford, he won the James Birdsall Weter prize for the best senior honors thesis in history, which dealt with Germans' reexamination of their past after World War II.

He also received a J.D. (Juris Doctor, or Doctor of Law) from Stanford Law School, where his major concentration was in the areas of international and foreign and comparative law.

After graduating from law school, Dr. Rowles was a Stanford Postgraduate Fellow in Law and Development, working in Costa Rica as a Visiting Professor at the University of Costa Rica Faculty of Law, where he focused on law and development issues. In Costa Rica, he also worked as a member of the Costa Rican team of Stanford's Studies in Law and Development (SLADE) project, a six-nation study of law and social change in Costa Rica, Colombia, Peru, Chile, Spain, and Italy.

Upon returning to Stanford, he continued work on the SLADE project, wrote a thesis based on his research in Costa Rica, and obtained a Master of the Science of Law (J.S.M.=Ll.M.) in Comparative Law and Development.

Dr. Rowles has published two books and numerous articles on international and comparative law subjects. Since 2009, he has been the author of *The Trenchant Observer: International Law, Politics, and Security*, a blog which chronicles international political developments, with particular attention to the international legal aspects of these developments. *See* Preface regarding the availability on the Wayback Machine of the *Internet Archive* of articles from the blog, which has been hacked, probably by a state actor. Since 2022, he has been the author of *Trenchant Observations*, a Substack newsletter (https://jamesrowles.substack.com/).

He lives near San Francisco.

Index

Q

Qatar, Saudi Arabian blockade and
boycott of, 102–3, 134
The Question of German Guilt
(Jaspers), vii, 109–10, 183
Quijano, Elaine, 20–21

R

racism
Jews and anti-Semitism, 96–97
Ku Klux Klan, 4, 18
Minneapolis protests and,
194–95, 202–5
Muslim refugees, ban of, 53
Trump and, 4, 18, 47, 97, 195
Trump's support of Marine Le
Pen's policies as, 73–74
of Trump supporters, 47
White supremacists and extremists,
4, 18, 47, 96–98, 194, 207
Rasmussen Daily Tracking Poll, 150,
152, 154, 162, 177, 398
Reagan, Ronald, 36
Reid, Harry, 53
Reinoehl, Michael, 228–33,
238–39, 247, 266, 298
Republicans
blocking Electoral College vote and,
xix, 303–4, 309, 311–14, 337–38
cancer on the American body
politic, 335–39
Liz Cheney's refusal to endorse
voter fraud lie, 364–69, 378
contingent election, Trump's attempt
at using, 259–61, 270

Republicans (*cont.*)
corruption of, 280, 282
criticism of Trump, 3, 4
fascism and, 242, 281–82, 347–48
impeachment trials of Trump and,
xx, 157–58, 175–76, 181,
215, 217, 242, 336, 361, 366
indictment of Trump and
co-conspirators, argument
for, 395–404
January 6, 2021 capitol insurrection
and, xix, 303–4, 309, 336–37
Kavanaugh, confirmation
process for, 129–32
Michigan, voter fraud in, 280–83
oaths of office and impeachment trial
of Trump, 331–34, 337–39, 361
political violence, accomplices to, 248
retention of power, Trump's
strategies for, 221
Trump and obstruction of justice, 119
Trumpism as political cult,
84, 330, 368–70, 380
Trump's investigation into
opponents and, 117
2016 Congressional wins, 34
2020 election, vote count
delays by, 251–57
2020 election, voter fraud lies about,
xix, 336, 350–51, 376–79, 396
voter suppression attempts,
219, 371, 407–9
The Revolt of the Masses (Ortega
y Gasset), xxiii–xxiv
Rhinoceros (Ionesco), 84–85, 242
Richardson, Elliot, 376

S